FROM
Biba's
Italian
Kitchen

BIBA CAGGIANO

Hearst Books
NEW YORK

ALSO BY BIBA CAGGIANO

Trattoria Cooking
Modern Italian Cooking
Northern Italian Cooking

Copyright © 1995 by Biba Caggiano

Photography by Susan Mantle
Styling by Bunny Martin

It is the policy of William Morrow and Company, Inc., and its imprints and affiliates,
recognizing the importance of preserving what has been written, to print the books
we publish on acid-free paper, and we exert our best efforts to that end.

Library of Congress Cataloging-in-Publication Data

Caggiano, Biba.
From Biba's Italian kitchen / Biba Caggiano.
p.   cm.
Includes index.
ISBN 0-688-13865-9
1. Cookery, Italian.   I. Title.
TX723.C247   1995
641.5945—dc20   94-40010
CIP

Printed in the United States of America

First Edition

1 2 3 4 5 6 7 8 9 10

BOOK DESIGN BY ALISON LEW / VERTIGO DESIGN

To my daughters,

Carla and Paola, who have enriched my life to the fullest

Con tanto amore

Acknowledgments

I want to thank the following people who have helped me with this book in many different ways.

To Vincent Caggiano, my husband, for his constant support and for his companionship along the trail as I researched and collected recipes.

To Renzo Cattabiani of the Consorzio of the Parmigiano-Reggiano and dear friend, who for many years has generously shared his time and food expertise.

My "kids" in the kitchen, Don Brown and John Eichhorn, chef and sous-chef of Biba Restaurant, for their help and constant support and encouragement.

Pam Barton, Tony Sanguinetti, T. K. Kodsuntie, and Clancy Ball for testing and retesting recipes and the food preparation, which allowed me to get into the kitchen and start cooking.

To my friends Susan Mantle and Bunny Martin for their splendid work. Their talent made my food shine.

To Maureen and Eric Lasher, my agents, for their friendship; for believing in me and helping me make great career choices.

To Ann Bramson, my editor at William Morrow, who made this book happen quickly and who trusted my instincts and my expertise.

Then of course there is Italy for which I have so much to thank: great beauty, a glorious culinary heritage and passionate cooks, open markets and wondrous specialty stores, remarkable restaurants, trattorie, and osterie, and "slow food," which preserves Italy's great culinary traditions. Without Italy, this book would not be possible.

Contents

Introduction

I was born and raised in Bologna, Italy, a food lover's paradise where great eating is as essential to life—as it is in most of Italy—as breathing. With its particular heritage of outstanding food, this city gave me an early appreciation of excellent cooking. Most women in Bologna are superb cooks. My mother and grandmother were among the best.

Like millions of other Italians, I was raised in the kitchen, always the heart and soul of the Italian home. Watching my mother cook filled me with a love of food and cooking. When I was twelve she taught me the art of making pasta. My mother was a simple, instinctive cook who relied on her senses and on the skills transmitted to her by *her* mother to prepare wonderful food.

While the daily meals in our home were simply prepared, the Sunday meals were celebrations. By 10 o'clock on Sunday morning our whole apartment was engulfed with the aroma of meat broth slowly simmering on the stove. My mother, who had been up cooking for hours, would prepare golden homemade tagliatelle or tiny tortellini to be cooked in that delicate broth and served as our first course. The mixed meats from the broth would be served as a second course, accompanied by the classic salsa verde, and by a flavorful peperonata. It was during these ritual dinners, through the preparation and sharing of good food, that we felt nurtured and connected.

In 1960, when I married and moved to New York with my American-born husband, Vincent, I brought my country's and my family's food customs with me. In New York I discovered that my husband's family carried out those same traditions. Every Sunday my mother-in-law would prepare splendid meals from her native region of Campania. A testament to the Italian way of life.

In 1968 we left New York for Sacramento, California, where my husband joined a group of physicians, and I became a full-time mother to our two daughters, Carla and Paola. Since I could not find in Sacramento the food that was familiar to me, I began to do a great deal of cooking. Aided by my palate, I learned how to duplicate the dishes from home. I knew how a certain dish was supposed to taste, how it was supposed to look and smell. I also realized I had a considerable memory bank of tangible flavors, aromas, tastes, and textures. I found that when I cooked the food of my region and served it to my family and friends, I was also sharing the traditions and culture of my land, which gave me great pleasure. Here I was, thousand of miles away from Bologna, and yet able to serve a lasagne verdi alla Bolognese that tasted and looked just like my mother's. It was a terrific feeling!

To further perfect my Italian cooking, I combined my trips to Italy to visit family and friends with study tours throughout many regions, learning all I could about my country's diverse culinary traditions.

As my time in the kitchen increased, my reputation as a cook began to surface and before I realized it, I was giving cooking classes in Sacramento, and up and down California. I taught the uncomplicated, straightforward cooking of *la buona cucina casalinga*, good, uncontrived, regional Italian home cooking, prepared simply, and with an abundance of fresh ingredients.

In each and every class I tried to emphasize the importance of understanding Italian ingredients and the benefits of using them properly. I urged my students to taste absolutely everything; to touch, to smell, and to remember the look, as well as the taste, of a dish, so that down the road they too would be able to cook as Italians do, guided only by their palate and their senses, without the rigidity of a recipe.

If you have watched me cook on The Learning Channel, you know that I love nononsense food, real food; food that is rooted in tradition, simple to prepare, beautiful to look at, and very good to eat. I also believe in flexibility. Within a certain framework, you should be able to express a bit of your own personality through the way you cook and serve food.

I have assembled here dishes that fit all of these criteria, dishes that are strongly rooted in tradition, lightened and revitalized to fit our contemporary lifestyle. You'll find the dishes I love in the pages of this book. It is the food I serve at my restaurant, Biba, in Sacramento and that I prepare for my family and my friends at home. It *is* the food of home: *la buona cucina casalinga*. I hope you will try these wonderful recipes and share them with all the people in your life.

Tips and Techniques

There are certain ingredients basic to a well-stocked Italian pantry that will give that special Italian flavor to your dishes.

BREAD

Italians never discard bread unless it is stale. With bread that is a day or so old you can grill it to make crostini; use it in a soup; soak it in milk and add it to a stuffing; grill it, cube it, and add it to a salad; and you can always use it to make bread crumbs.

To make bread crumbs: Use bread that is two or three days old, cut it into pieces, and chop it very fine in a food processor. Spread the bread on a platter and let it stand overnight to dry further. Store the dried bread in a plastic bag or a jar.

PARMIGIANO-REGGIANO

- Parmigiano-Reggiano is a low-fat cow's milk cheese that has a high protein content. This cheese is produced from the best possible milk and is completely free of additives.

- In buying Parmigiano, look for the words "Parmigiano-Reggiano" etched on the rind of the cheese. By law, this cheese is aged a minimum of 1 year.

- Good Parmigiano should have a pale yellowish color, with a moist, crumbly consistency. Buy a nice chunk and store it in the refrigerator.

- To keep Parmigiano from drying out, wrap it in plastic wrap, then wrap it again in foil, and store it on the bottom shelf of the refrigerator.

- If kept for a few months, Parmigiano tends to dry out a bit. In that case, wet a kitchen towel lightly and wrap it around the cheese, then wrap the towel with plastic wrap and refrigerate cheese for several hours. After that, remove the towel, wrap the cheese in fresh plastic wrap, and refrigerate again.

- For utmost freshness, grate Parmigiano as needed.

- In Italy, Parmigiano is always grated, never shredded.

- Parmigiano and fresh fruit go hand in hand. Make sure to serve Parmigiano at room temperature.

GARLIC

- Even though garlic is available all year round, it is at its best in the spring. Fresh garlic has moist cloves and a sweet taste. As it gets older, garlic shrivels and becomes sharp tasting.

- Choose a nice, compact, heavy head of garlic. Do not use a garlic press, for it will reduce the garlic to a soggy mess.

- Chop the garlic as needed. Or place the chopped garlic in a small bowl and cover completely with olive oil. Refrigerate and use within a few days.

- For just a hint of garlic in a sauce, cook the whole garlic clove in oil until it is lightly golden, then discard it.

- When sautéing garlic, watch it carefully, for it will color in no time at all. If the garlic is too dark, it will taste unpleasantly bitter.

EXTRA-VIRGIN OLIVE OIL

- Extra-virgin olive oil is produced without chemical means, by mechanically stone-crushing and cold-pressing hand-picked olives. It is the first pressing of the oil and has the lowest level of acidity, less than 1 percent.

- Italy has a wide range of extra-virgin olive oils, each with its own aroma, flavor, and color. Regardless of which oil you choose, the overall characteristic should be freshness. The oil should be light and should linger pleasantly on the palate.

- The traditional Italian salad is dressed simply with salt, extra-virgin olive oil, and vinegar. How much of each? Well, there is an old Italian proverb that says, "Be judicious with the salt, prodigal with the olive oil, stingy with the vinegar, and patient in tossing the salad."

- Olive oil can be kept for a few months, provided that you store it in a tightly closed bottle in the coolest, darkest part of your pantry. Olive oil does not need to be refrigerated.

TOMATOES

For a great tomato sauce, select plum tomatoes; they are meaty and plump and are less watery than regular tomatoes. Drop them into boiling water for 30 to 40 seconds until the skin begins to split. Then drain and peel them. Dice, chop, or puree them, and use in your favorite sauce.

HERBS IN THE ITALIAN KITCHEN

Fresh herbs are widely used in good Italian home cooking. Keep in mind, however, that they should be used in moderation.

- Parsley (*prezzemolo*) is the fundamental herb of Italian cooking. Italian parsley has flat, broad leaves and a sweet, fragrant flavor that enhances innumerable dishes.

- Basil (*basilico*) is one of the most popular herbs. Fresh basil is at its best when it is uncooked. It shines in salads and when sprinkled over pasta. In using basil, it is best if you tear the leaves with your hands so they won't discolor. Use a knife only if the basil needs to be chopped or cut into thin strips. Even though basil can be frozen or preserved in oil, this is one of those herbs that I do not use unless it is fresh.

- Bay leaf (*alloro*) is used in marinades, pasta sauces, and stews, and as a component of grilled meat or fish skewers. Use dry bay leaves in moderation.

- Rosemary (*rosmarino*) is a wonderful aromatic herb that is used extensively in Italian cooking with grilled or roasted meats and fowl, and with stews and soups. Dried rosemary used in moderation is quite acceptable.

- Sage (*salvia*) is a very popular herb, especially in northern Italy, where it is paired with game, savory breads, potatoes, and marinades. Use dried sage judiciously because it can be quite assertive.

- To keep fresh herbs looking fresh for a few days, sprinkle them with water, place them in a container half full of water, as you would for flowers, cover the top of the leaves with plastic wrap or a large plastic bag, and store them in the refrigerator.

WINE AS A FLAVORING AGENT

In Italian cooking many sauces for meat and fowl are produced by adding a bit of wine to the pan juices and by cooking and reducing them together until they are thick and glazy, and the flavors are thoroughly blended. Therefore, the quality of wine used to produce a sauce is important. If you use a low-quality wine to make your sauce, the overall flavor of the dish will suffer. But if you think of wine as an important ingredient that is going to affect the flavor of your dish, then perhaps you won't mind using good wine. Choose the wine you want to serve with the dish you are preparing, then use some of it in cooking.

- Marsala is an aromatic wine from Sicily that is customarily served at the end of a meal as a dessert wine. However, Marsala is also wonderful for cooking, and can be paired extremely well with veal, pork, or fowl.

- Always use dry Marsala for cooking and sweet Marsala for desserts. Look for imported Marsalas, such as Florio and Pellegrino, which have a richness of color and taste that is in a class of its own.

From Biba's Italian Kitchen

GRILLED MUSHROOM AND PANCETTA SKEWERS

SCALLOPS WITH ANCHOVIES AND TOMATOES

SAUTÉED SHRIMP, BEANS, AND MUSHROOMS
WITH CHILE PEPPER

BRUSCHETTA WITH ROASTED PEPPERS

BRUSCHETTA WITH FRESH TOMATOES AND GARLIC

SAVORY EGGPLANT "POLPETTE"

FRIED EGGPLANT AND MOZZARELLA "SANDWICH"

SOFT POLENTA WITH MUSHROOM RAGÙ

SPECK WITH FRESH TOMATOES AND MOZZARELLA

SMALL ARTICHOKES WITH SUN-DRIED TOMATOES AND OLIVE OIL

MOZZARELLA AND ROASTED RED PEPPER SALAD

CANNELLINI BEAN AND GRILLED SHRIMP SALAD

RUSTIC PIE WITH RADICCHIO AND ONION

ARTICHOKE TART

SWISS CHARD TART

POTATO AND SMOKED HAM CAKE

BAKED SWISS CHARD FRITTATA

FRITTATA WITH PASTA

POTATO AND ONION FRITTATA

FRITTATA WITH TOMATO

Antipasti, Savory Pies and Tarts, and Frittate

ANTIPASTO IS THE opening act to a meal. An antipasto can be as simple as a few slices of prosciutto and figs, or as rustic as Bruschetta with Roasted Peppers (page 8). It can be as elegant as Sautéed Shrimp, Beans, and Mushrooms (page 7), or as hearty as Soft Polenta with Mushroom Ragù (page 13). An antipasto should be served in portions just large enough to tease the appetite.

ANTIPASTI OFTEN PLAY multiple roles. For example, many vegetable preparations can be served as an antipasto or a side dish. Many other appetizers can also be served as entrées, especially now that the modern way of eating has become less structured.

FOUND ALL OVER Italy, savory pies and tarts change according to local traditions and the inventiveness of the cook. They can be rustic or elegant, filled with cheeses, vegetables, even sausage and ham. These splendid dishes are not reserved for special occasions but are served in caffès and pizzerie, trattorie and open-air markets, as well as at home. Enjoy them as appetizers, between meals, or for lunch or a light supper.

FRITTATE ARE FLAT egg "cakes" or open-faced omelets. Eggs and a variety of other ingredients are cooked together and eaten for breakfast, brunch, lunch, or dinner, or placed between two slices of bread for a great-tasting sandwich. Frittate make delicious appetizers: Cut them into squares or wedges, arrange them on a serving platter, and serve with an *aperitivo*.

Grilled Mushroom and Pancetta Skewers

SPIEDINI DI FUNGHI ALLA GRIGLIA

I TRY TO *go to Italy in the spring and fall because this is when porcini mushrooms are in season. These fabulous wild mushrooms, which grow under chestnut trees, have a meaty texture and a unique fragrance. The best way to prepare fresh porcini is simply to grill them, brush with good extra-virgin olive oil, and season with salt and pepper.*

SINCE FRESH PORCINI *mushrooms are not easily available in this country, you can substitute meaty, flavorful portobello, shiitake, or crimini mushrooms for them. Thread the mushrooms onto skewers with some pancetta and fresh sage, then brush with olive oil and vinegar, season generously and grill. Serve them as an appetizer, a side dish, or an entrée.*

SERVES 4

2–3 ounces pancetta, cut into ⅛-inch slices
⅓ cup, plus 1 tablespoon, extra-virgin olive oil
⅓ cup red wine vinegar
1 pound medium-size assorted mushrooms, such as shiitake, portobello, and crimini (see Note)

16 fresh sage leaves
Salt and freshly ground black pepper
2 tablespoons chopped fresh flat-leaf Italian parsley or regular parsley

CUT the pancetta into 2-inch pieces. Heat 1 tablespoon of the oil in a medium skillet over medium-high heat. Add the pancetta and stir for 1 to 2 minutes until pancetta turns lightly golden. Transfer pancetta to paper towels to drain.

PREHEAT the grill or the broiler well ahead of time so it will be nice and hot when you are ready to use it.

IN a small bowl combine the remaining oil and the vinegar. Wipe the mushroom caps with a damp towel. Thread the mushrooms, pancetta, and sage leaves alternately onto the skewers, brush them with the oil and vinegar, and season with salt and pepper.

IF using the broiler, put the skewers on a baking sheet and place under the broiler, 4 to 5 inches from the heat source. Broil, turning the skewers over, until mushrooms are golden on all sides, 6 to 7 minutes. If using a grill, place the skewers over the hot grill and turn them until golden on all sides, 6 to 7 minutes. Brush them a few times with oil and vinegar as they cook.

PLACE skewers on a large platter, brush them one more time with the oil-vinegar mixture, sprinkle with some parsley, and serve alone, or with a few slices of grilled or fried polenta (see page 131).

Note: If shiitake, portobello, and crimini mushrooms are not available in your area, you can use white cultivated mushrooms. The flavor will be different, but the dish will still taste very good.

Scallops with Anchovies and Tomatoes

CAPPE SANTE CON ACCIUGHE E POMODORI

THIS TYPE OF *dish offers the cook great flexibility. For example, you can use shrimp or large prawns instead of scallops. The tomatoes can just be seeded and diced without blanching and peeling. The amount of garlic and anchovies can be increased or decreased to suit your palate, and the dish can be served as an appetizer or as an entrée. The final bonus is that you can put everything together in less than 10 minutes. Serve this antipasto followed by a fresh mixed green or spinach salad.*

SERVES 4 AS AN APPETIZER OR 2 AS AN ENTRÉE

4 ripe, juicy tomatoes, about
    ½ pound
⅓ cup extra-virgin olive oil
1 pound sea scallops, thoroughly
    washed and dried
2 garlic cloves, minced
2 anchovy fillets, chopped

½ cup dry white wine
Salt to taste
Chopped fresh red chile pepper or
    dried red pepper flakes to taste
1 tablespoon chopped fresh flat-
    leaf Italian parsley or regular
    parsley

In winter I like to serve this tasty dish over grilled or fried polenta or grilled or toasted Italian bread.

BRING a medium-size saucepan of water to a boil. Cut a cross at the root end of the tomatoes and drop them into the boiling water. Cook until the skin of the tomatoes begins to split, 1 to 2 minutes. Transfer the tomatoes to a bowl of iced water. Peel, seed, and dice the tomatoes, and place them in a bowl with all their juices.

HEAT the oil in a large skillet over medium heat. Add the scallops and cook until scallops are lightly golden, about 2 minutes. Add the garlic and anchovies, stir once or twice, then add the wine. Stir for a minute or so until wine is almost all reduced. Add the tomatoes, and season with salt and chile pepper. Cook, stirring, until the juices of the tomatoes have thickened, 2 to 3 minutes. Taste and adjust the seasoning, and serve at once.

Sautéed Shrimp, Beans, and Mushrooms with Chile Pepper

GAMBERI, CANNELLINI, E FUNGHI CON
PEPERONCINO IN PADELLA

YEARS AGO AT *a fashionable restaurant on Lake Garda, I was served an appetizer of large shrimp, porcini mushrooms, and white beans. Even though the combination of ingredients was a bit unusual, I eagerly tried the dish. It was so good that I almost canceled my entrée to order one more portion!*

SINCE FRESH PORCINI *mushrooms are seldom available in this country, I use a combination of mushrooms as shown below. Select fresh herbs whenever possible because their clean, aromatic taste will greatly enrich this antipasto. Serve it as an appetizer or as an entrée.*

SERVES 4 AS AN APPETIZER OR 2 AS AN ENTRÉE

½ cup dried cannellini beans, cooked as instructed on page 18

⅓ cup extra-virgin olive oil

¾ pound medium-size shrimp, shelled and deveined

½ pound mushrooms, such as white cultivated, shiitake, crimini, or chanterelles, wiped clean and thinly sliced

1 garlic clove, finely minced

5–6 fresh sage leaves, chopped, or 1–2 dried sage leaves, finely crumbled

1 small sprig fresh rosemary, chopped, or 1 teaspoon dried rosemary, chopped

Salt to taste

Chopped fresh red chile pepper or dried red pepper flakes to taste

½ cup dry white wine

Additional oil, if needed

COOK the beans and set aside until ready to use.

HEAT 3 tablespoons of the oil in a large skillet over medium-high heat. Add the shrimp and cook until golden on all sides, about 2 minutes. With a slotted spoon transfer shrimp to a plate.

continued

PUT the skillet back on high heat and add remaining oil. When the oil is very hot, add the mushrooms. Cook, stirring, until mushrooms have a nice golden color, 2 to 3 minutes.

REDUCE the heat to medium, and add the garlic and herbs to the skillet. Stir quickly once or twice. Add the beans and the cooked shrimp. Season with salt and chile pepper. Add the wine and cook until it is almost all reduced, about 2 minutes. Taste and adjust the seasoning, and serve at once.

Bruschetta with Roasted Peppers

BRUSCHETTA AI PEPERONI ARROSTO

I LOVE TO *serve this rustic appetizer in the garden, perhaps while the steaks are cooking on the barbecue and guests are enjoying a nice glass of wine.*

SERVES 4

2 medium red bell peppers, roasted
   and peeled as instructed on
   page 86
2 garlic cloves, minced
2 anchovy fillets, chopped
¼ cup extra-virgin olive oil

1 tablespoon chopped fresh flat-
   leaf Italian parsley or regular
   parsley
Salt and freshly ground black
   pepper to taste
4 slices crusty Italian bread, cut
   ½ inch thick

CUT the bell peppers into ½-inch strips and place in a deep bowl.

IN a small bowl combine the garlic and the anchovies with the olive oil, and mix to blend. Pour oil mixture over the peppers. Add the parsley, season with salt and several grindings of pepper, and toss everything well. Taste and adjust the seasoning, and set aside until ready to use. The dish can be prepared up to this point several hours ahead. Keep it tightly covered in the refrigerator. Bring the peppers back to room temperature before serving.

BRUSH the bread slices lightly with olive oil and place on a hot grill or under a broiler until golden on both sides. Top with peppers and serve.

Bruschetta with Fresh Tomatoes and Garlic

BRUSCHETTA CON POMODORI E AGLIO

ORIGINALLY BRUSCHETTA WAS *simply a slice of grilled Italian bread lightly rubbed with garlic and drizzled with freshly pressed green olive oil. This delicious, humble Roman dish, a mainstay of peasants, has now been rediscovered and reinvented, and can be prepared with a variety of unusual ingredients. For me, however, the best-tasting bruschetta is one topped with fresh, ripe tomatoes. it should have just a hint of garlic, the sweet taste of basil, and the fragrance of great olive oil.*

SERVES 8

1½ pounds ripe, juicy tomatoes
8 slices crusty Italian bread, cut
   ½ inch thick
1 garlic clove, minced
1–2 tablespoons capers, rinsed and
   pat-dried

¼ cup loosely packed fresh
   oregano leaves or 10–12 fresh
   basil leaves, shredded
Salt and freshly ground black
   pepper to taste
⅓ cup extra-virgin olive oil

BRING a medium-size saucepan of water to a boil. Cut a cross at the root end of the tomatoes and drop them into the boiling water. Cook until the skin of the tomatoes begins to split, 1 to 2 minutes. Transfer the tomatoes to a bowl of iced water. Peel and seed the tomatoes, then roughly chop them. Place the tomatoes in a strainer and put strainer over a bowl for 20 to 30 minutes, to allow tomatoes to release all juices.

If fresh oregano or basil is unavailable, substitute 1 to 2 tablespoons chopped fresh parsley.

BRUSH the bread lightly with olive oil and place over a hot grill or under a broiler until golden on both sides.

PUT the tomatoes, garlic, capers, oregano or basil in a medium-size bowl. Season with salt and several grindings of pepper. Add the oil and mix everything well. Spoon the tomato mixture over each bread slice, arrange on a large platter, and serve.

Savory Eggplant "Polpette"

POLPETTE DI MELANZANE

WHEN I WAS *growing up in Bologna, my mother would prepare savory meatballs, polpette di carne, at least once a week. Sometimes they were fried and piled high on a platter. Other times she would cook them with a sauce that contained vegetables or large chunks of potatoes. It was good, wholesome food that fed a family fairly inexpensively.*

DURING ONE OF *my trips to Sicily, while I was exploring Vucciria, the incredible open-air food market of Palermo, I bought some eggplant "polpette" from a vendor who was making and frying them while you waited. They were incredibly good.*

IF YOU PLAN *to use the polpette as an antipasto for a casual, sit-down dinner, serve them along with some grilled vegetables or with Cauliflower and Green Olive Salad (page 209).*

MAKES APPROXIMATELY 15 POLPETTE, SERVES 4 TO 6

1 medium-size eggplant, trimmed, peeled, and cut into ½-inch rounds
Salt
1 large egg yolk
1 garlic clove, minced
10–12 fresh basil leaves, chopped, or 2 tablespoons chopped fresh parsley

½ cup freshly grated Parmigiano-Reggiano cheese
1½ cups plain dried bread crumbs, spread over a sheet of aluminum foil
Olive oil for frying

PUT the eggplant slices on a large baking sheet, sprinkle with salt, and let stand about 1 hour. The salt will draw out the bitter eggplant juices. Pat slices dry with paper towels.

BRING a medium-size saucepan of water to a boil over medium heat. Add the eggplant slices and cook 3 to 4 minutes, or until eggplant is tender. Drain and place slices on paper towels to drain and to cool.

These polpette are great to serve with drinks at an informal gathering. Pile them on a platter and let your guests help themselves.

In Sicily the cheese used for the polpette is pecorino, which is made from sheep's milk. The pecorino cheese available in the United States is usually Pecorino Romano. Since this cheese is too sharp and pungent, I have substituted Parmigiano-Reggiano.

CHOP the eggplant very fine with a large knife or in a food processor, and place in a medium-size bowl. (If you are using a food processor, make sure not to puree the eggplant.)

IN a small bowl mix the egg yolk with the garlic and add to the eggplant together with the basil or parsley, the Parmigiano, and 2 to 3 tablespoons of bread crumbs. Season with salt and pepper, and mix everything well with a wooden spoon or with your hands. Cover the bowl and refrigerate for about 1 hour to allow mixture to firm up.

TAKE about 1 scant tablespoon of the eggplant mixture between the palms of your hands and roll into a ball. Repeat with the remaining mixture. When all the polpette have been shaped, coat them with the bread crumbs. They can be fried immediately, or they can be placed on a platter and refrigerated, uncovered, for a few hours.

HEAT 1 inch of oil in a medium-size skillet over medium heat. When the oil is hot, lower a few polpette at a time into the oil with a slotted spoon. Cook until they are lightly golden on both sides, 1 to 2 minutes. Remove them with the slotted spoon and transfer to paper towels to drain. Serve hot or at room temperature.

Fried Eggplant and Mozzarella "Sandwich"

MELANZANE E MOZZARELLA IN CARROZZA

SOUTHERN ITALIANS LOVE *eggplant and use it in many interesting preparations. At Corsi, one of my favorite little trattorie in Rome, I had a simply wonderful appetizer of deep-fried eggplant and mozzarella. It came to the table piping hot, with a golden-crisp crust, oozing with soft, melted cheese. I could have made a whole meal out of it!*

SERVES 8

1 large eggplant, about 1 pound, peeled and sliced into ¼-inch rounds
½ pound whole-milk mozzarella, cut into ⅛-inch slices
4 anchovy fillets, cut into small pieces, optional

2 large eggs, lightly beaten in a small bowl with a pinch of salt
2 cups plain dried bread crumbs, spread over a sheet of aluminum foil
Olive oil for frying
Salt

The eggplant sandwiches can be prepared until just before frying them, several hours ahead. Refrigerate the sandwiches, uncovered, then bring them back to room temperature before frying. Keep in mind that because of the shape of the eggplant, some of the sandwiches will be smaller than others.

PLACE the eggplant slices on a large platter, sprinkle with salt, and let stand for about 30 minutes to allow the salt to draw out the bitter eggplant juices. Pat the slices dry with paper towels.

PUT 1 or 2 slices of mozzarella over a slice of eggplant. Add a few pieces of anchovy, if using, and top with another slice of eggplant to form a "sandwich." Repeat until all the eggplant slices are used up.

DIP the sandwiches into the beaten eggs and coat with the bread crumbs, pressing the crumbs in with the palms of your hands.

HEAT 1 inch of oil in a medium-size skillet over medium-high heat. When the oil is hot, fry the eggplant sandwiches, a few at a time, until they are golden and crisp on both sides, 2 to 3 minutes. Remove with a slotted spoon and transfer to paper towels to drain. Serve piping hot.

Soft Polenta with Mushroom Ragù

POLENTA CON RAGÙ DI FUNGHI

THIS IS THE *type of dish that used to be standard fare in many northern Italian homes. A large batch of soft polenta, topped with a sauce made from a variety of vegetables or meats, would feed a large family fairly inexpensively. Today, polenta is not made at home as often as it used to be, but Italians still love it and seek it out in restaurants and trattorie.*

SERVES 6 TO 8 AS AN APPETIZER OR 4 AS AN ENTRÉE

FOR THE POLENTA

5 cups water
1 tablespoon salt
1 cup coarsely ground cornmeal
    mixed with ½ cup finely
    ground cornmeal
2 tablespoons unsalted butter
⅓ cup freshly grated Parmigiano-
    Reggiano cheese

FOR THE MUSHROOM RAGÙ

1 ounce dried porcini mushrooms,
    soaked in 2 cups lukewarm
    water for 20 minutes
⅓ cup olive oil, plus 2 tablespoons

½ pound white cultivated
    mushrooms, wiped clean and
    thinly sliced
2 ounces sliced pancetta, diced
1 garlic clove, minced
2 tablespoons chopped fresh flat-
    leaf Italian parsley or regular
    parsley
2 cups canned imported Italian
    plum tomatoes, with their
    juice, put through a food mill
    to remove the seeds
Salt and freshly ground black
    pepper to taste
½ cup freshly grated Parmigiano-
    Reggiano cheese

The polenta can be cooked an hour or so ahead. Just before serving, bring the water in the bottom part of the double boiler back

PREPARE the polenta as instructed in Polenta Cooked in a Double Boiler (page 131), using the proportions given in this recipe.

DRAIN the porcini mushrooms and reserve the soaking water. Rinse the mushrooms well under cold running water. Strain the soaking water through a few layers of paper towels over a small bowl to get rid of the sandy deposits, and set aside.

continued

to a gentle simmer and reheat the polenta. Then stir in the butter and the Parmigiano. If the polenta is a bit too thick, mix in some water, milk, or cream.

The mushroom sauce can be prepared several hours or a day ahead. Keep it tightly covered in the refrigerator and reheat it gently just before serving. This sauce is great served over pappardelle, penne, or rigatoni, so you might want to make a double batch.

HEAT ⅓ cup of the oil in a large skillet over high heat. When the oil is very hot, add the sliced mushrooms without crowding the skillet, and cook until they are lightly golden, about 2 minutes. With a slotted spoon transfer mushrooms to paper towels and pat dry with more paper towels.

HEAT the remaining 2 tablespoons of oil in a small saucepan over medium heat. Add the pancetta and cook, stirring, until it is lightly golden, 2 to 3 minutes. Add the garlic and the parsley, and stir once or twice. Add the mushrooms and the porcini. Stir for a minute or two, then add 1 cup of the reserved porcini soaking water and the tomatoes. Season with salt and pepper, and bring the sauce to a boil. Reduce the heat to low and simmer, uncovered, for 15 minutes, or until the sauce has a medium-thick consistency. Taste and adjust the seasoning, and set aside until ready to use.

JUST before serving, add the butter and the Parmigiano to the polenta, and mix until well combined. Spoon the soft polenta onto serving dishes, top with some mushroom ragù, sprinkle with some more Parmigiano, and serve.

Speck with Fresh Tomatoes and Mozzarella

SPECK CON POMODORI E MOZZARELLA

THE SMOKY, PEPPERY *taste of speck (smoked Italian ham) marries very well with ripe tomatoes and delicate, creamy mozzarella. While prosciutto can be used instead of speck, I urge you to go the extra mile to find good whole-milk mozzarella. Look for it at your local Italian market or at a specialty food store.*

SERVES 4

½ pound thinly sliced speck (see
    Note) or prosciutto
2 ripe, juicy tomatoes
One 4-ounce ball whole-milk
    mozzarella
6 pitted green olives, quartered

8–10 fresh basil leaves, shredded
Salt to taste
¼ cup extra-virgin olive oil
Freshly ground black pepper to
    taste

ARRANGE the slices of speck on serving dishes.

IN a small bowl combine the tomatoes, mozzarella, olives, and basil. Season lightly with salt. Add the olive oil and mix everything well. Spoon this mixture loosely over the speck, season with a few grindings of pepper, and serve.

Note: Speck is a smoked ham that is a specialty of the Trentino–Alto Adige region in northeastern Italy. It is available at many Italian markets or specialty food shops.

Small Artichokes with Sun-dried Tomatoes and Olive Oil

CARCIOFINI ALL'OLIO

EVERY TIME I *visit Tamburini in Bologna or Peck in Milano, two of Italy's greatest food stores, I buy large quantities of pickled carciofini (artichoke hearts), pickled onions, and small, strong green peppers, because these vegetables go perfectly with good prosciutto or salame and fresh mozzarella.*

THIS RECIPE USES *cooked small baby artichokes and plenty of good extra-virgin olive oil and tosses them with a touch of garlic and some sun-dried tomatoes. At my restaurant in Sacramento, I serve this appetizer as part of an antipasto misto or as a salad.*

SERVES 4

3 pounds baby artichokes
Juice of 1 lemon
Salt
1 garlic clove, minced
1–2 tablespoons minced sun-dried
   tomatoes
⅓–½ cup extra-virgin olive oil

Freshly ground black pepper to
   taste
1 tablespoon chopped fresh flat-
   leaf Italian parsley or regular
   parsley
4 slices grilled or toasted Italian
   bread, optional

REMOVE the green leaves of the artichokes by snapping them off at the base. Stop when the leaves closer to the base are pale yellow and the tips of the artichokes are green. Slice off the green top. Cut the stem off at the base and, with a small knife, trim off the remaining green part at the base. Place artichokes in a bowl of cold water with the lemon juice to prevent discoloring.

BRING a medium-size saucepan of water to a boil over medium heat. Add 1 tablespoon of salt and the artichokes. Cook, uncovered, 7 to 10 minutes, depending on size. Prick the bottom of one artichoke with a toothpick or a thin knife. If the toothpick goes in without resistance, the artichokes are cooked.

DRAIN artichokes and cool under cold running water. Pat dry with paper towels, slice into wedges, and place in a large salad bowl. Cover and refrigerate until ready to use. (The dish can be prepared up to this point several hours or a day ahead.)

IN a small bowl combine the garlic, sun-dried tomatoes, and olive oil. Season artichokes with salt and several grindings of pepper. Stir in the parsley and the oil mixture. Toss everything well, taste and adjust the seasoning, and serve alone or with a slice of toasted or grilled bread.

Mozzarella and Roasted Red Pepper Salad

INSALATA DI MOZZARELLA PEPERONI ARROSTITI

THIS COLORFUL AND *tasty salad takes its inspiration from the well-known mozzarella and tomato salad. In winter, when tomatoes are less than satisfactory, I roast the peppers, pair them with slices of fresh whole-milk mozzarella, and drizzle on dressing of olive oil and anchovies. This makes a lovely appetizer or a light luncheon dish.*

SERVES 4

4 large red bell peppers, roasted as instructed on page 86
1 pound fresh whole-milk mozzarella
Salt to taste
2 anchovy fillets, chopped
1 garlic clove, minced
1 tablespoon chopped fresh flat-leaf Italian parsley or regular parsley
¼ cup extra-virgin olive oil

ROAST the peppers and cut into 2-inch slices.

CUT the mozzarella into ¼-inch slices and arrange, alternate with the sliced peppers, on individual serving dishes. Season lightly with salt.

IN a small bowl combine the anchovies, garlic, and parsley with the olive oil, and drizzle the dressing over the peppers and mozzarella. Serve at room temperature.

Cannellini Bean and Grilled Shrimp Salad

INSALATA DI CANNELLINI E GAMBERI ALLA GRIGLIA

WHEN I MAKE *bean soup, I generally cook more beans than I need. Later I use them in a vegetable dish or turn them into a delicious salad.*

SERVES 4

FOR THE BEAN SALAD

1 cup dried cannellini beans or white kidney beans, picked over and soaked overnight in cold water to cover

12 medium-size shrimp, shelled, about 10 ounces

Oil for brushing

½ cup plain dried bread crumbs, mixed with 1 tablespoon chopped parsley

1 red bell pepper, roasted and peeled as instructed on page 86, cut into thin strips

½ small red onion, peeled and thinly sliced

2 tablespoons minced chives or chopped flat-leaf Italian parsley

Salt and freshly ground black pepper to taste

FOR THE MUSTARD DRESSING

2 teaspoons Dijon mustard

¼ cup red wine vinegar

⅓–½ cup extra-virgin olive oil

The beans can be cooked up to 2 to 3 days ahead. Just leave them in their cooking liquid and when cooled, refrigerate them, tightly covered, in their own liquid.

PREPARE THE BEANS: Discard any beans that come to the surface of the water. Drain and rinse the beans under cold running water and put them in a large pot. Cover the beans with cold water and bring to a gentle boil, uncovered, over medium heat. Cook 30 to 40 minutes, or until beans are tender. Stir a few times during cooking. Drain the beans, place them in a large salad bowl, and set aside to cool.

PREHEAT the grill well ahead of time. Thread the shrimp onto the skewers, brush them lightly with oil, and sprinkle with the bread crumb–parsley mixture. Place the skewers on the hot grill and cook 2 to 3 min-

The shrimp can be grilled several hours ahead. If you do not have a grill, simply sauté the shrimp in a few tablespoons of olive oil until they are golden and proceed with the recipe.

utes on each side. Remove the skewers from the grill, and as soon as the shrimp are cool enough to handle, remove them from the skewers and set aside until ready to use.

ADD the cooled shrimp to the beans together with the bell pepper, onion, and chives. Season generously with salt and several grindings of pepper.

PREPARE THE DRESSING: With a fork or a small whisk, beat the mustard into the vinegar until well blended. Add the oil slowly, beating constantly until the ingredients are thoroughly blended. Pour the dressing over the salad and mix well. Taste and adjust the seasoning, and serve.

Rustic Pie with Radicchio and Onion

TORTA RUSTICA AL RADICCHIO E CIPOLLA

THIS COUNTRY-STYLE *vegetable pie traditionally is prepared with a basic pizza dough. Simple and tasty ingredients, onion, radicchio, olives, and capers make up the filling. However, the season of the year and the mood of the cook can dictate the choice of filling.*

SERVES 8

1 recipe Basic Pizza Dough (see pages 215–216)

FOR THE FILLING
3–4 tablespoons extra-virgin olive oil
1 large yellow onion, about 1 pound
3 medium heads radicchio, about 1½ pounds, thinly sliced

10–12 pitted black olives, cut into fourths
2 tablespoons capers, rinsed
2 garlic cloves, peeled and crushed
Salt and pepper to taste
½ cup freshly grated Parmigiano-Reggiano cheese

1 large egg, lightly beaten

PREPARE the pizza dough and let it rise.

PREHEAT the oven to 400°.

continued

PREPARE THE FILLING: Heat the oil in a large skillet over medium heat. Add the onion and cook, stirring, until it is lightly golden, 4 to 5 minutes. Add the radicchio, olives, capers, and the crushed garlic. Season with salt and pepper, and cover the skillet. Reduce the heat to medium low and cook until radicchio is soft, 10 to 12 minutes.

TRANSFER the radicchio mixture to a bowl to cool. Stir the Parmigiano into the cooled radicchio and mix well. Taste and adjust the seasoning.

OIL a 10-inch springform cake pan. Divide the dough and form into 2 balls, one slightly larger than the other. On a lightly floured surface roll out the larger ball of dough into a 12-inch circle and place in the oiled cake pan, fitting the dough against the sides of the pan. Let the excess dough drape over the sides of the pan. Pour the radicchio mixture into the pan and level the top with a spatula.

ROLL out the remaining dough and place over the filling, letting the excess dough drape over the pan. There should be no more than ½ inch of dough hanging over the sides of the pan. If necessary, trim the dough a bit. Pinch the edges of the top and bottom dough together to seal. Brush the top crust with the beaten egg and prick it with a fork in several places.

BAKE until the crust is golden, 20 to 25 minutes. Cool the pie completely to room temperature before removing it from the pan.

Artichoke Tart

TORTA DI CARCIOFI

VEGETABLE PIES AND *tarts have been made in Italy for centuries. Some are simple and rustic, others are more complex and elegant, but they all have one thing in common: a good crust. Whether made with flour, oil, and water, or enriched with butter and eggs, a good crust gives character and taste to the tart. When I make this basic pie dough, I often double the recipe and freeze half the batch.*

SERVES 6 TO 8

FOR THE PIE DOUGH

1⅓ cups unbleached all-purpose flour

3 ounces unsalted butter, at room temperature for hand mixing, or cold and in small pieces for the food processor

Pinch salt

1 large egg

3–4 tablespoons chilled dry white wine

2 cups uncooked beans or rice for weighting the pastry shell

1 large egg white, lightly beaten, to brush over the pastry

FOR THE FILLING

¼ cup extra-virgin olive oil

½ cup thinly sliced yellow onion

2 pounds baby artichokes, cleaned and cooked as instructed on page 16

2 garlic cloves, minced

1 tablespoon minced sun-dried tomatoes

4 large eggs

½ cup freshly grated Parmigiano-Reggiano cheese

2 tablespoons chopped fresh flat-leaf Italian parsley or regular parsley

Salt and freshly ground black pepper to taste

PREPARE THE PIE DOUGH: In a medium-size bowl, or in a food processor fitted with the metal blade, mix the flour and the butter until crumbly. Add the salt, egg, and wine, and mix into a soft dough. Shape the dough into a ball, wrap it in plastic wrap, and refrigerate for 1 hour.

continued

PREHEAT the oven to 375°. On a lightly floured surface roll out the dough to a 12-inch circle. Put the dough into a 10-inch tart pan with a removable bottom. Trim the edges of the dough by gently rolling the rolling pin over the top of the pan. Prick the bottom of the shell in several places with a fork, and line it with aluminum foil. Fill the foil with uncooked beans or rice, and bake for 15 minutes. Remove the foil and the beans or rice, brush the dough with the beaten egg white, and bake 8 to 10 minutes longer, or until the pastry is lightly golden. Cool the shell in the tart pan.

PREPARE THE FILLING: Heat the oil in a large skillet over medium heat. Add the onion and cook, stirring, until it is lightly golden and soft, 4 to 5 minutes. Add the artichokes, garlic, and sun-dried tomatoes, and stir for 1 to 2 minutes. With a slotted spoon transfer artichoke mixture to a bowl and cool.

BEAT the eggs in a large bowl. Add the Parmigiano and parsley, and season with salt and pepper. Add the beaten eggs to the artichokes, and mix until thoroughly combined. Fill the pastry shell evenly with the mixture, and level the top with a spatula. Bake until the top is lightly golden and firm to the touch, 15 to 20 minutes.

COOL for 10 to 15 minutes, then transfer tart to a serving dish. Serve warm or at room temperature.

Swiss Chard Tart

TORTA DI BIETE

THIS TART CAN *be served as an appetizer or as a main dish for a light luncheon. Perfect to take along on camping trips or picnics. You can change the filling to fit the season and your mood.*

SERVES 6 TO 8

1 recipe Basic Pie Dough
   (see page 229)
1½ pounds Swiss chard
Salt
1 tablespoon unsalted butter
2 tablespoons olive oil
½ cup finely minced yellow onion

2 garlic cloves, minced
4 anchovy fillets, chopped
Freshly ground black pepper
½ pound ricotta
2 large eggs, lightly beaten
½ cup freshly grated Parmigiano-
   Reggiano cheese

PREPARE THE PIE DOUGH: Follow the instructions on page 229. Roll out and pre-bake the pie shell as indicated.

PREPARE THE FILLING: Remove the Swiss chard leaves from the stems and reserve the stems for another use. Wash the leaves thoroughly under cold running water. Put the leaves in a large pot with 2 cups water and 1 teaspoon salt. Cook, uncovered, over medium heat until the leaves are tender, 5 to 6 minutes. Drain chard, squeeze out any excess water, and chop it fine.

HEAT the butter and the oil in a large skillet over medium heat. Add the onion and cook, stirring, until it is lightly golden and soft, 4 to 5 minutes. Add the garlic and the anchovies, and stir for about 1 minute. Add the Swiss chard to the skillet, season lightly with salt and pepper, and cook, stirring, for 2 to 3 minutes. Transfer chard to a large bowl and cool.

PREHEAT the oven to 375°.

continued

ADD ricotta, eggs, and Parmigiano to the cooled chard, and mix until thoroughly combined. Fill the pastry shell evenly with the filling, and level the top with a spatula.

BAKE until the top of the tart is lightly golden and firm to the touch, 15 to 20 minutes. Cool it, then remove tart from the baking pan and place on a large serving dish. Serve warm or at room temperature.

Potato and Smoked Ham Cake

TORTINO DI PATATE E SPECK

IN THIS APPETIZING *preparation, slices of cooked potatoes are layered with soft onions, smoked Italian ham (speck), and mozzarella, then the tortino, "small cake," is baked until it turns a beautiful golden brown. Serve it as a side dish with roasted meats, or all by itself.*

SERVES 10 TO 12

8 large boiling potatoes, about
    4 pounds
5 tablespoons unsalted butter
2 large yellow onions, about
    1 pound, thinly sliced
Butter for the baking pan
2–3 tablespoons fine plain dried
    bread crumbs

½ pound speck (smoked Italian
    ham), cut into thin slices
    (see Note, page 15)
½ pound mozzarella, cut into thin
    slices (see Note)
¼ cup freshly grated Parmigiano-
    Reggiano cheese
1 cup milk

PUT the potatoes in a large pot and cover with water. Bring the water to a boil and cook, uncovered, over medium heat until potatoes are tender but still a bit firm to the touch. Drain potatoes and set aside to cool. Peel potatoes and cut them into ¼-inch rounds.

HEAT 3 tablespoons of the butter in a large skillet over medium heat. Add the onions and cook until they are lightly golden and soft, 4 to 5 minutes. Set aside.

PREHEAT the oven to 400°. Butter a 10-inch springform cake pan and coat it with bread crumbs.

LINE the bottom of the pan with the potato slices, slightly overlapping each other. Cover the potatoes with a layer of sautéed onions. Top the onions with a layer of speck, and top speck with slices of mozzarella. Repeat with one more layer of potatoes, onion, speck, and mozzarella. Arrange the remaining potatoes over the top and sprinkle the Parmigiano over the potatoes. Pour in the milk and dot with the remaining butter.

BAKE until the top of the cake has a nice golden-brown color, 30 to 35 minutes. Cool for 10 to 15 minutes, then transfer the cake to a serving dish. Serve warm or at room temperature.

Note: Select the best possible mozzarella at your Italian market or specialty food store. Do not use the rubbery, tasteless supermarket mozzarella. If soft, freshly made mozzarella is unavailable, substitute Italian fontina cheese.

Baked Swiss Chard Frittata

FRITTATA VERDE AL FORNO

SERVES 3 TO 4 AS AN ENTRÉE OR 6 TO 8 AS AN APPETIZER

1 pound Swiss chard
Salt
2 tablespoons extra-virgin olive oil
1 cup minced yellow onion
1 garlic clove, minced

6 large eggs, beaten in a medium
   bowl
½ cup freshly grated Parmigiano-
   Reggiano cheese

REMOVE the Swiss chard leaves from the stems and reserve the stems for another use. Wash the leaves thoroughly under cold running water. Put the leaves in a pot with 1 cup water and 1 teaspoon salt. Cook, over medium heat, until leaves are tender, 5 to 6 minutes. Drain and squeeze as much water as possible out of the leaves. Chop the leaves very fine.

For a filling and tasty sandwich, place a large piece of frittata between 2 slices of bread, layer with ripe tomato slices seasoned with salt, pepper, and oil, and some sliced sweet onion.

PREHEAT the oven to 350°. Butter an 8-inch or 10-inch round baking dish.

HEAT the oil in a medium-size skillet. Add the onion and cook, stirring, until it is lightly golden and soft, 4 to 5 minutes. Add the garlic and the Swiss chard, and cook 2 to 3 minutes. Transfer mixture to a bowl to cool.

STIR the cooled mixture into the beaten eggs, season with salt, and mix in the Parmigiano. Place the eggs into the prepared baking dish and bake until the top of the frittata has a nice golden color, 15 to 20 minutes. Cool the frittata a bit, then invert it onto a large, flat plate and serve warm or at room temperature.

Frittata with Pasta

FRITTATA DI PASTA

ALMOST ANY TYPE *of leftover pasta can be added to a frittata. However, factory-made pasta, especially spaghetti or linguine, works best. You can choose from Pasta with Roasted Red Bell Pepper (page 86) or Spaghettini with Fresh and Sun-dried Tomatoes and Goat Cheese (page 89). Another suggestion: Cook some spaghetti, toss it with hot oil, garlic, and chile pepper. Have the pasta the first night, then use the leftovers the next day to make a splendid frittata.*

SERVES 2 AS AN ENTRÉE OR 4 AS AN APPETIZER

2 cups cooked pasta of your choice

4 large eggs, beaten in a medium bowl

Salt to taste

⅓ cup freshly grated Parmigiano-Reggiano cheese

2 tablespoons extra-virgin olive oil

ADD the cooked pasta to the beaten eggs. Season with salt and stir in the Parmigiano.

HEAT the oil in an 8-inch or 10-inch nonstick skillet over medium heat. When the oil is very hot, add the egg mixture. Cook until the bottom of the frittata is golden and the top begins to solidify, 4 to 5 minutes.

PLACE a large, flat plate over the skillet and turn the frittata onto the plate. (This step is much easier than it sounds.) Slide the frittata back into the skillet to cook the other side. Cook until the bottom is lightly browned, 2 to 3 minutes. Slide the frittata onto a serving dish, and serve warm or at room temperature.

Note: If you are apprehensive about turning the frittata onto a plate, here are some alternate cooking methods:

- Once the bottom of the frittata is cooked, place the skillet under a broiler for a few seconds until the top of the frittata begins to brown lightly.
- A frittata can also be cooked completely in the oven. Assemble the egg mixture and place into a buttered baking dish. Bake in a preheated 350° oven until the top of the frittata has a nice golden color, 10 to 15 minutes.

Potato and Onion Frittata

FRITTATA DI PATATE E CIPOLLE

LEFTOVER BOILED OR *roasted potatoes can be cut into pieces and used in a frittata.
Pair them with onion, salame, tomatoes, or other vegetables of your choice.*

SERVES 2 AS AN ENTRÉE OR 4 AS AN APPETIZER

1 cup peeled, diced boiling
    potatoes
2–3 tablespoons extra-virgin
    olive oil
1 medium yellow onion, peeled
    and thinly sliced
2 ounces pancetta or prosciutto,
    diced

4 large eggs, beaten in a medium
    bowl
Salt to taste
⅓ cup freshly grated Parmigiano-
    Reggiano cheese

BRING a small saucepan of water to a boil and add the potatoes. Cook until potatoes are tender but still firm to the bite. Drain and set aside.

HEAT 2 tablespoons of the oil in an 8-inch or 10-inch nonstick skillet over medium heat. Add the onion and cook, stirring, for 2 to 3 minutes. Add the pancetta and the potatoes. Cook until the pancetta, potatoes, and onion are lightly golden. With a slotted spoon, scoop up the mixture and place in a bowl to cool. Stir the cooled mixture into the eggs, season with salt, and stir in the Parmigiano.

PUT the skillet back on medium heat and add the remaining olive oil, if needed. When the oil is very hot, add the egg mixture. Cook until the bottom of the frittata is golden and the top begins to solidify, 4 to 5 minutes.

PLACE a large, flat plate over the skillet and turn the frittata onto the plate. Slide the frittata back into the skillet to cook the other side. Cook until the bottom is lightly browned, 2 to 3 minutes. Slide the frittata onto a serving dish, and serve warm or at room temperature.

Frittata with Tomato

FRITTATA DI POMODORO

A FRITTATA CAN *be prepared in a short amount of time. Therefore, it is perfect for summer menus, versatile, delicious, and eye-pleasing. Summer frittate can be gloriously colorful when made with fresh, ripe red tomatoes, fragrant green basil, and the golden frittata itself. In this recipe the frittata is cooked a slightly different way than usual. It is browned on one side only and the top is allowed to settle and cook without being turned onto a plate.*

SERVES 2 AS AN ENTRÉE OR 4 AS AN APPETIZER

2–3 tablespoons extra-virgin olive oil

½ cup minced red onion

4 large eggs, beaten in a medium bowl

Salt to taste

⅓ cup freshly grated Parmigiano-Reggiano cheese

1–2 tablespoons chopped fresh flat-leaf Italian parsley or regular parsley

1 large tomato, cut into 6 round slices

HEAT 2 tablespoons of the oil in an 8-inch or 10-inch nonstick skillet over medium heat. Add the onion and cook, stirring, until it is lightly golden and soft, 4 to 5 minutes. With a slotted spoon, transfer the onion to a bowl to cool. Stir the cooled onion into the eggs, season with salt, and stir in the parsley and the Parmigiano.

PUT the skillet back on medium heat and add the remaining oil, if needed. When the oil is very hot, add the egg mixture. As soon as the bottom of the frittata begins to solidify and the top is still runny, 1 to 2 minutes, arrange the tomatoes on the eggs and season them lightly with salt. Reduce the heat to low and cover the skillet. Cook until the top of the frittata has become firm, 3 to 5 minutes.

SLIDE the frittata onto a serving dish and serve warm or at room temperature.

Soups

IN ITALY SOUPS are often eaten as a first course instead of pasta, risotto, or gnocchi. While the latter are generally preferred for lunch, soups come into their own at dinnertime.

A SOUP CAN tell you its origin almost instantly. There are the rice soups of the Veneto and the thick bean and bread soups of Tuscany. There are the hearty soups of the mountain areas and the fish soups of the seacoasts and the islands. Each area, city, and town of Italy has its own unique variety. When I was growing up in Bologna, the Sunday meal was always soup. Rich, aromatic clear broth, cooked for hours, would get the addition of homemade thin tagliolini, and the incredible aroma would engulf the house.

I BELIEVE THAT soup is the perfect food for the nineties. The ingredients take only minutes to assemble, then the soup cooks all by itself, needing only an occasional stir. A soup enriched with vegetables, beans, or pasta often needs only a fresh green salad or some cheese to transform it into a meal.

BECAUSE OF MY cooking show on The Learning Channel, I have had the opportunity to demonstrate a lot of this type of food. The letters I receive are warm, friendly, and appreciative of the show. One woman wrote me that she began making soups after watching the show, and became proficient at preparing them. One day after a particularly good soup quickly disappeared after being brought to the table, her husband and children "got up and gave her a standing ovation"! What a joy to be able to reach the people we love in this manner.

Basic Meat Broth

BRODO DI CARNE

A GOOD HOMEMADE *broth is an essential base for many Italian soups as well as risottos, braised meat dishes, and sauces. Make a good supply of this meat broth and freeze it in several containers. It will come in handy when you need to prepare soup on the spur of the moment.*

MAKES APPROXIMATELY 4 TO 5 QUARTS

4 pounds bones and meat scraps
    from beef, chicken, and veal
A few fresh parsley sprigs
2 carrots, cut into chunks
2 stalks celery, cut into chunks

1 small yellow onion, peeled and
    quartered
2 ripe tomatoes, quartered
Salt to taste

PUT all the ingredients except the salt in a large stockpot and cover by 2 to 3 inches with cold water. Set the cover askew on the pot and bring the liquid to a gentle boil over medium heat. Reduce the heat to low and skim the scum that comes to the surface of the water with a slotted spoon or a skimmer.

SIMMER 2½ to 3 hours. Season with salt during the last few minutes of cooking.

IF you are planning to use the broth right away, strain it through a strainer into another pot. If you plan to use it the next day or to freeze it, strain the broth into a large bowl and allow to cool, then refrigerate it overnight. The next day remove the fat that has solidified on the surface. The broth is now fat free, ready to use or to freeze. It will keep 3 to 4 days in the refrigerator, about 1 month frozen.

Homemade Chicken Broth

BRODO DI GALLINA

MANY COOKS MAKE *chicken broth from chicken scraps, bones, and vegetables only (see Note). I like to add a large, plump chicken so that the chicken can be eaten as a second course.*

MAKES 5 TO 6 QUARTS

3 pounds bones and meat scraps
    from chicken and veal
3–3½ pounds whole chicken
A few fresh parsley sprigs
2 carrots, cut into chunks

2 celery stalks, cut into chunks
1 small yellow onion, peeled and
    quartered
2 ripe tomatoes, quartered
Salt to taste

PUT all the ingredients except the salt in a large stockpot and cover by 2 to 3 inches with cold water. Set the cover askew on the pot and bring the liquid to a gentle boil over medium heat. Reduce the heat to low, and skim the scum that comes to the surface of the water with a slotted spoon or a skimmer. Simmer 1½ hours.

REMOVE the chicken from the pot and set it aside. Simmer the broth 1 hour longer. Add salt to taste during the last few minutes of cooking.

IF you are planning to use the broth right away, strain it into another pot. If you plan to use it the next day or to freeze it, strain the broth into a large bowl and allow it to cool, then refrigerate it overnight. The next day remove all the fat that has solidified on the surface. The broth is now fat free, ready to use or to freeze. It will keep 3 to 4 days in the refrigerator, about 1 month in the freezer.

Note: If you find you have no time to prepare meat broth or chicken broth from scratch, do what many hurried housewives do: Make an instant broth with bouillon cubes. Keep in mind, however, that bouillon cubes can be quite salty and while convenient, cannot match the light flavor of homemade broth.

Chick-pea, Mushroom, and Swiss Chard Soup

ZUPPA DI CECI, FUNGHI, E BIETE

THIS IS A *traditional, sturdy Ligurian soup that combines chick-peas, dried porcini mushrooms, and Swiss chard. The chick-peas need to be soaked overnight and cooked over moderate heat for about 1 hour. The dried porcini mushrooms add a unique woodsy taste. In a pinch you can substitute canned chick-peas for the dried ones.*

SERVES 4 TO 6

1 cup dried chick-peas (garbanzos), picked over and soaked overnight in cold water to cover geneorusly

1 ounce dried porcini mushrooms, soaked in 2 cups lukewarm water for 20 minutes

½ pound Swiss chard

⅓ cup extra-virgin olive oil

1 cup minced yellow onion

2 garlic cloves, minced

2 cups canned imported Italian plum tomatoes, with their juices, put through a food mill to remove the seeds

Salt and freshly ground black pepper to taste

DRAIN and rinse the chick-peas under cold running water. Put them in a large pot and cover with 4 to 5 cups of cold water. Cover the pot partially and bring the water to a gentle boil over medium heat. Reduce the heat to low and simmer gently, stirring occasionally, until the chick-peas are tender, 40 to 50 minutes.

WHILE the chick-peas are cooking, prepare the soup base. Strain the porcini mushrooms and reserve the soaking liquid. Rinse the mushrooms well under cold running water and chop them roughly. Line a strainer with two paper towels and strain the mushroom liquid into a bowl to get rid of the sandy deposits. Set aside.

REMOVE the leaves from the Swiss chard and reserve the stems for another use. Wash the leaves thoroughly under cold running water and chop them roughly.

HEAT the oil in a medium-size saucepan over medium heat. Add the onion and garlic and cook, stirring, until onion is lightly golden, 4 to 5 minutes. Add porcini mushrooms and Swiss chard, and cook, stirring, for a minute or two. Add tomatoes and 1 cup of the strained reserved porcini liquid. Season with salt and pepper, and bring to a gentle boil. Reduce the heat to low and simmer 15 to 20 minutes. Stir a few times during cooking.

STIR the tomato sauce into the pot with the chick-peas and cook 4 to 5 minutes longer. Taste and adjust the seasoning, and serve hot.

Emma's Great Bean Soup

LA ZUPPA DI FAGIOLI DELL'EMMA

MY SISTER-IN-LAW *Emma, who lives in Bologna, is a marvelous regional cook. The food she serves is simple, the ingredients are fresh, and the preparation is short. This is one of the dishes she makes for me when I visit her and my brother. It is one of the best and easiest bean soups I have ever had.*

SERVE 6 TO 8

1 pound dried cannelli beans or white kidney beans, picked over and soaked overnight in cold water to cover generously
2 quarts chicken broth, preferably homemade (see page 33), or 1 quart canned chicken broth and 1 quart water
1 large boiling potato, peeled and cut into chunks
¼ cup extra-virgin olive oil

2 garlic cloves, minced
2 tablespoons chopped fresh flat-leaf Italian parsley or regular parsley
2 cups canned imported Italian plum tomatoes, with their juice, put through a food mill to remove the seeds
Salt and freshly ground black pepper to taste
Olive oil to taste

continued

Most soups taste better several hours after being made. Also, bean, lentil, and vegetable soups become thicker and denser upon standing. If the soup is not thick enough for your taste, simmer it, uncovered, until it reaches the preferred consistency.

For a heartier soup, add some pastina, or toast some bread slices in the oven, place them in the bowls, and top with the soup.

DISCARD any beans that have floated to the surface of the water. Drain and rinse the beans under cold running water, put them in a large pot, and add the broth and the potato. Cover the pot partially and bring the broth to a gentle boil over medium heat. Reduce the heat to low and simmer gently, stirring occasionally, until the beans are tender, 45 minutes to 1 hour.

WHILE the beans are cooking, prepare the soup base. Heat the oil in a medium-size saucepan over medium heat. Add the garlic and the parsley and cook, stirring, until garlic begins to color, about 1 minute. Add the tomatoes and bring to a gentle boil. Season with salt and pepper, and reduce the heat to medium low. Simmer until sauce has a medium-thick consistency, 20 to 25 minutes.

PUREE the beans, potato, and all the broth in a food processor until smooth, and return puree to the pot. (You might have to puree the soup in batches.) Add the tomato sauce to the beans and cook, over medium heat, 4 to 5 minutes longer. Serve hot or at room temperature and drizzle a few drops of olive oil over each serving.

Leek and Potato Soup

PASSATO DI PORRI E PATATE

THIS IS A *type of thick soup that Italians call* passati. *A passato (the word means "to go through") is generally made of vegetables or legumes, which after being cooked are put through a food mill to achieve a denser consistency. In Montecatini, in Tuscany, I once ate a passato of white beans with small pasta in it that was so delicious and thick that it could have been eaten with a fork.*

IN THE SMALL *town of Gradiscutta in the Friuli region, I had a passato of leeks and potatoes that filled me up after only one bowl. This great soup will nourish and satisfy you.*

SERVES 6 TO 8

1 pound leeks
2 tablespoons unsalted butter
2 tablespoons olive oil
¼ pound sliced speck (see Note, page 15) or prosciutto, cut into thin, short strips
1 pound boiling potatoes, peeled and roughly diced

2 quarts chicken broth, preferably homemade (see page 33), or 1 quart canned chicken broth and 1 quart water
Salt to taste
¼ cup heavy cream
2 tablespoons minced chives or parsley

CUT off the roots of the leeks and remove one third of the green stalks. Cut leeks in half lengthwise and slice them. Place leeks in a colander and wash them well under cold running water, making sure to remove all the dirt.

HEAT the butter and oil in a large pot over medium heat. When the butter foams, add the leeks and cook, stirring, until they begin to soften, 6 to 7 minutes. Add the speck and the potatoes, and stir for a minute or two. Add the broth and season with salt. Cover the pot partially and bring the broth to a gentle boil. Cook 30 to 40 minutes or until leeks and potatoes are tender.

IN a food processor, puree the soup in a few batches, until smooth. Press the pureed soup through a fine sieve back into the pot. Add cream and cook 5 minutes longer. Taste and adjust the seasoning. Just before serving, sprinkle chives or parsley on top. Serve hot.

Cabbage and Bread Soup

ZUPPA DI CAVOLO E PANE

THIS WONDERFUL TUSCAN *peasant soup was originally made with water, not broth. This version uses meat broth, and grated Parmigiano is sprinkled on at the time of serving. Allow the soup to settle for 15 to 20 minutes before serving.*

SERVES 8 TO 10

⅓ cup extra-virgin olive oil

1 cup minced yellow onion

½ cup minced carrot

½ cup minced celery stalk

2 tablespoons chopped fresh flat-leaf Italian parlsey or regular parsley

¼ pound pancetta, finely diced

1 small head Savoy cabbage, 2½ to 3 pounds, sliced into thin strips and diced

1 cup canned imported Italian plum tomatoes, with their juice, put through a food mill to remove the seeds

2 quarts meat broth, preferably homemade (see page 32), or 1 quart canned meat broth and 1 quart water

Salt

6–8 small slices of toasted or grilled crusty Italian bread, cut into rough pieces

½ cup freshly grated Parmigiano-Reggiano cheese

This soup becomes even denser because of the addition of bread, which should be thick-crusted Italian or French-style bread. If the soup is too thick for your taste, simply add a bit more broth or omit the bread.

HEAT the oil in a medium-size saucepan over medium heat. Add the onion, carrot, celery, and parsley and cook, stirring, until vegetables are soft and lightly colored, 5 to 6 minutes. Add the pancetta and cook until it is lightly golden, 2 to 3 minutes.

ADD the cabbage and stir for a minute or two until cabbage is well blended with the savory base. Add the tomatoes and the broth, and season with salt. Bring the soup to a gentle boil over medium heat, then reduce the heat to low and cover the pot partially. Simmer, stirring several times, until the cabbage is tender, about 1 hour.

ADD the bread to the soup and simmer 4 to 5 minutes longer. Stir the soup vigorously with a wooden spoon to break down the bread a bit. Let the soup rest 10 to 15 minutes. Sprinkle on some Parmigiano and serve.

Biba's Vegetable Soup

IL MIO MINESTRONE

A GOOD MINESTRONE *takes advantage of seasonal bounty. Winter vegetables will make the minestrone hearty and filling. Spring vegetables create a light and delicate soup. In summer minestrone is generally served at room temperature to bring out the individual flavors of the vegetables.*

WHEN FRESH ASPARAGUS, *tender peas, and young zucchini come to the market, I prepare this soup because my customers love it. The minestrone becomes better, thicker, and more flavorful as it sits.*

SERVES 6 TO 8

¼ cup extra-virgin olive oil
2 garlic cloves, minced
½ cup minced red onion
2 tablespoons chopped fresh flat-leaf Italian or regular parsley
1 large boiling potato, peeled and roughly diced
½ pound white cultivated mushrooms, wiped clean and thinly sliced
½ pound small string beans, roughly diced
½ pound thin asparagus, tough ends removed, roughly diced

1 cup shelled fresh or frozen peas
½ pound small zucchini, roughly diced
½ pound fresh, firm plum tomatoes, seeded and roughly diced
2 quarts chicken broth, preferably homemade (see page 33), or 1 quart canned chicken broth and 1 quart water
Salt and freshly ground black pepper to taste
⅓ cup freshly grated Parmigiano-Reggiano cheese

HEAT the oil in a large pot over medium heat. Add garlic, onion, and parsley. Cook, stirring, until onion begins to color, 4 to 5 minutes.

continued

ADD all the vegetables to the savory onion base and stir for a minute or two. (If using frozen peas, add to minestrone during the last 10 minutes of cooking.) Add the broth and bring it to a gentle boil. Season with salt and just a bit of pepper, and cover the pot partially. Simmer, stirring occasionally, until the vegetables are tender, 30 to 40 minutes. Taste and adjust seasoning, and serve sprinkled with Parmigiano.

Artichoke Soup

PASSATO DI CARCIOFI

I LOVE ARTICHOKES *and try to use them in as many preparations as possible. This creamy soup, which is served regularly at my restaurant in Sacramento, is made with baby artichokes because they are much easier to prepare than the large ones.*

THE SMALL ARTICHOKES *are cleaned and quartered, and are quickly sautéed in butter with sun-dried tomatoes. Then they are covered with good, homemade broth and finish cooking gently for about 40 minutes. The addition of potato gives the soup thickness and smoothness. While in the classic cooking of Italy there are no "cream of vegetable soups," modern Italian cooks do not worry about such restrictions.*

SERVES 6

4 pounds baby artichokes
Juice of 1 lemon
3 tablespoons unsalted butter
2 tablespoons minced sun-dried
   tomatoes
1 garlic clove, minced
1 large boiling potato, peeled and
   roughly diced

2 quarts chicken broth, preferably
   homemade (see page 33), or
   1 quart canned chicken broth
   and 1 quart water
Salt to taste
⅓ cup heavy cream
½ cup freshly grated Parmigiano-
   Reggiano cheese

REMOVE the green leaves of the artichokes by snapping them off at the base. Stop when the leaves closer to the base are pale yellow and the tips of the arti-

If you like, you can take a few slices of white bread and brown them in butter. Then cut the bread into small cubes and add to the soup at the time of serving. Or, toast ¼-inch slices of Italian or French bread in the oven, then place them at the bottom of the soup bowls, sprinkle with Parmigiano, and top with the soup.

chokes are green. Slice off the green top. Cut the stem off at the base and, with a small knife, trim off the remaining green part at the base. Cut the artichokes into small wedges and place them in a bowl of cold water with the lemon juice to prevent discoloring.

HEAT the butter in a medium-size pot over medium heat. Drain the artichokes and add to the pot. Add the sun-dried tomatoes and the garlic, and stir for about 1 minute. Add the diced potato and cook, stirring, 2 to 3 minutes. Add the broth and season with salt. Cover the pot partially and bring the broth to a gentle boil. Cook 30 to 40 minutes, or until artichokes and potato are tender.

IN a food processor puree the soup in a few batches until smooth. Press the pureed soup through a fine sieve back into the pot. Add the cream and ¼ cup of the Parmigiano, and bring the soup to a gentle simmer. Cook 5 to 6 minutes longer. Taste, adjust the seasoning, and serve with additional Parmigiano, if desired.

Potato Soup

ZUPPA DI PATATE

TUSCANY PROBABLY HAS *a greater variety of soups than any other Italian region. Since Tuscan food is wholesome and basically straightforward, the soups reflect the same philosophy. This potato soup, which is made with water not broth, is delicious and substantial, and it is put together quickly with a minimum amount of fuss. In pureeing the vegetables, make sure to pulse the machine on and off so that the soup retains some texture. These soups are called* passati.

SERVES 6 TO 8

3 pounds boiling potatoes, peeled and cut into medium chunks

1 celery stalk, cut into pieces

1 medium carrot, cut into pieces

1 small yellow onion, peeled and cut into chunks

¼ cup extra-virgin olive oil

2 garlic cloves, minced

2 tablespoons chopped fresh flat-leaf Italian parsley or regular parsley

1 pound fresh, ripe plum tomatoes, seeded and diced

Salt and freshly ground black pepper to taste

Eight ¼-inch slices of toasted or grilled Italian bread

½ cup freshly grated Parmigiano-Reggiano cheese

PUT potatoes, celery, carrot, and onion into a large pot and cover with cold water. (You will need approximately 2 quarts of water.) Bring the water to a boil over medium heat, cover the pot partially, and reduce the heat a bit. Simmer, stirring occasionally, until the vegetables are tender, 30 to 40 minutes.

HEAT the oil in a small saucepan over medium heat. Add the garlic and parsley and cook, stirring, about 1 minute. Add tomatoes, and season with salt and a bit of pepper. Cook 4 to 5 minutes, stirring tomatoes a few times. Add tomatoes to the pot with the soup and mix well. In a food processor puree the soup in a few batches, pulsing the machine on and off, and return to the pot. On low heat simmer the soup 5 more minutes. Taste and adjust the seasoning. Just before serving, place a slice of grilled bread into each serving bowl, ladle the soup over the bread, and serve with a generous sprinkling of Parmigiano.

Lentil and Rice Soup

ZUPPA DI LENTICCHIE E RISO

NOT TOO LONG ago, homemakers all over Italy used to prepare great batches of appetizing soups as a matter of course. There was something wonderfully reassuring about the gentle bubbling of soup as it cooks. The tantalizing aroma pervaded not only the kitchen, but the whole house. Making soups from scratch is not a major enterprise. It is in fact quite simple. All you need are some basic ingredients, a bit of good broth (or water), and 15 to 20 minutes of time.

SERVES 4 TO 6

⅓ cup extra-virgin olive oil
½ cup minced yellow onion
¼ pound pancetta, finely chopped
2 tablespoons chopped fresh flat-leaf Italian parsley or regular parsley
½ pound (1½ cups) brown or green lentils, washed in several changes of cold water
2 cups chopped canned imported Italian plum tomatoes, with their juice

1½ quarts meat broth, preferably homemade (see page 32), or 3 cups canned meat broth and 3 cups water
Salt and freshly ground black pepper to taste
½ cup imported Italian Arborio rice or short-grain California pearl rice
½ cup freshly grated Parmigiano-Reggiano cheese
2 garlic cloves, minced

HEAT the oil in a medium-size saucepan over medium heat. Add the onion, garlic, pancetta, and parsley and cook, stirring, until the onion and pancetta are lightly golden, 4 to 5 minutes. Add the lentils and stir once or twice. Add the tomatoes and cook a minute or two. Add the broth and bring to a gentle boil. Season with salt and pepper. Cover the pot partially and cook over low heat until lentils are tender, 40 to 50 minutes. Stir a few times during cooking.

BRING a small saucepan of water to a boil and add the rice. Cook, uncovered, until rice is tender but still firm to the bite, about 15 minutes. Drain the rice and add it to the soup. Let the soup rest for 20 minutes or so before serving. Serve hot or at room temperature with a generous sprinkling of freshly grated Parmigiano.

Barley and Mushroom Soup

ZUPPA DI ORZO E FUNGHI

I LOVE THESE kinds of soups. Thick, sturdy, and loaded with taste and character. In the small town of Tricesimo, just outside Udine, there is a trattoria called Al Grop that serves the traditional food of the area. This is one of the delicious dishes I enjoyed there.

SERVES 8

2 ounces dried porcini mushrooms, soaked in 2 cups lukewarm water for 20 minutes
½ cup extra-virgin olive oil
1 cup minced yellow onion
1 garlic clove, minced
2 tablespoons chopped fresh flat-leaf Italian parsley or regular parsley

½ pound pearl barley, rinsed under cold running water
2 medium boiling potatoes, peeled and cut into small dice
2½ quarts cold water
Salt and freshly ground black pepper to taste

DRAIN the porcini mushrooms and reserve the soaking water. Rinse the mushrooms well under cold running water. Strain the soaking water through a few layers of paper towels over a small bowl to get rid of the sandy deposits, and set aside.

This soup tastes better and becomes thicker if it is allowed to sit for a few hours before reheating and serving.

HEAT the oil in a large pot over medium heat. Add the onion, garlic, and parsley and cook, stirring, until the onion is pale yellow and soft, 4 to 5 minutes. Add the porcini mushrooms, the barley, and the potato, and stir for a minute or two until they are well blended with the savory base.

ADD the cold water and the reserved porcini soaking liquid. Season with salt and pepper. Bring mixture to a boil over medium heat, then reduce the heat to medium low and cover the pot partially. Simmer, stirring several times, until the barley is tender, 1 to 1½ hours. Add a bit more water if the soup becomes too thick. Taste and adjust the seasoning, and serve hot.

Rice and Spinach Soup

MY FATHER LOVED *soups, and invariably they were his regular evening meals. He was a thin man, not prone to overeating, even though he enjoyed a few glasses of wine. Of all the soups my mother would prepare for him, this one made of rice and spinach was one of his favorites. He loved it because it was light and nourishing, enriched with eggs and Parmigiano. I had almost forgotten about this lovely soup and, after I tried it, a lot of loving memories of my father came rushing back.*

SERVES 6 TO 8

1 pound fresh spinach, stems and bruised leaves discarded

Pinch salt

2 tablespoons unsalted butter

2 quarts chicken broth, preferably homemade (see page 33), or 1 quart canned chicken broth and 1 quart water

¾ cup rice, preferably imported Italian Arborio

3 large eggs

Salt to taste

Pinch freshly grated nutmeg

⅓ cup freshly grated Parmigiano-Reggiano cheese

WASH the spinach thoroughly under cold running water. Bring 2 cups of water to a boil over medium heat. Add salt and the spinach and cook, uncovered, until tender, 5 to 6 minutes. Stir a few times during cooking. Drain the spinach and squeeze out any excess water. Chop the spinach with a large knife or in a food processor, pulsing the machine on and off. Do not puree the spinach.

HEAT the butter in a medium-size skillet over medium heat. When the butter begins to foam, add the spinach and mix quickly. Place spinach in a medium bowl until ready to use.

BRING the broth to a boil in a medium-size pot over medium heat. Add the rice and cook until tender but still firm to the bite, about 15 minutes.

BEAT the eggs in a medium-size bowl. Season with salt, nutmeg, and the Parmigiano. Stir the eggs into the spinach. Stir the egg-spinach mixture into the hot soup and bring the soup to a gentle simmer. Cook 2 to 3 minutes longer, stirring quickly with a wooden spoon. Taste and adjust the seasoning, and serve hot.

SPAGHETTI WITH BROCCOLI, SCALLOPS, AND CHILE PEPPER ·
SPAGHETTI WITH CLAMS IN PARCHMENT · SPAGHETTINI WITH
SWORDFISH AND FRESH TOMATOES · FETTUCCINE WITH
SCALLOPS, PORCINI MUSHROOMS, AND CREAM · SEAFOOD
CANNELLONI · RAVIOLI WITH SHRIMP FILLING · RAVIOLI WITH
ARTICHOKES · TORTELLI WITH POTATOES · TORTELLONI WITH
GORGONZOLA SAUCE · TORTELLONI WITH ASPARAGUS SAUCE ·
SWISS CHARD PANSOTTI WITH WALNUT PESTO · CANNELLONI
WITH MIXED MUSHROOMS · PAPPARDELLE WITH LAMB AND
BELL PEPPER SAUCE · PAPPARDELLE WITH CABBAGE, SPECK,
AND TOMATOES · TAGLIOLINI ALLA BOSCHETTI · TAGLIATELLE
WITH FRESH TOMATOES AND GARLIC · SPINACH TAGLIATELLE
WITH PROSCIUTTO AND TOMATOES · BOW TIES WITH
PROSCIUTTO, PEAS, AND FRESH TOMATOES · BUCKWHEAT
NOODLES WITH SWISS CHARD · SHELLS WITH SHRIMP AND
ARTICHOKES · PASTA WITH ROASTED RED BELL PEPPERS ·
PASTA WITH BROCCOLI RABE · SPAGHETTINI WITH FRESH
AND SUN-DRIED TOMATOES AND GOAT CHEESE · SPAGHETTI
WITH OLIVE PASTE, SUN-DRIED TOMATOES, AND CAPERS ·
PENNE WITH BAKED STUFFED TOMATOES · PENNETTE WITH
SPECK, PEAS, AND CREAM · RIGATONI WITH SAUSAGE
AND PORCINI MUSHROOMS

Pasta

Homemade Pasta

THE ITALIAN TRADITION of homemade pasta is unsurpassed. For me, pasta is as essential as water. There is no other food on earth that is as satisfying and soothing as a large plate of perfectly cooked, perfectly sauced pasta. Every Italian region takes pride in its own special pasta. However, the consensus is that the homemade pasta of Emilia-Romagna is in a class by itself. For centuries the agricultural riches of this region have provided first-rate ingredients: superlative soft wheat and eggs for the pasta itself, sweet butter, cream, prosciutto, and great cheeses for the sauces.

MY MOTHER TAUGHT me to make pasta at a very early age. I must have been eleven or twelve years old when she put me in front of the large wooden board used only for pasta making, piled flour on the board, placed eggs on the flour, and said, "Today you are going to learn how to make pasta." It was not until later that I realized that at that moment she was passing an important tradition on to me.

LEARNING TO MAKE fresh pasta is not difficult, provided you are willing to set aside a little time to master the various steps. I have tried to explain the procedures to the best of my ability.

INCLUDED ARE TWO alternate methods of making pasta: pasta made with a food processor and with an electric mixer. Both methods work quite well and will save you a lot of time.

IF YOU ARE a beginner, read the instructions carefully and make your first batch on a day when you are free from distractions. Do not worry if your first attempts are less than satisfactory. The most you will lose are a few eggs and some flour. Keep in mind that "practice makes perfect"!

USEFUL EQUIPMENT FOR PASTA MAKING

- a large wooden board or a Formica board for pasta made by hand
- a fork to mix the flour with the eggs
- a dough scraper to clean sticky dough from the board
- a hand-cranked pasta machine to roll out the pasta dough
- a fluted pastry wheel to cut the pasta into the desired shapes

INGREDIENTS FOR THE DOUGH

- unbleached all-purpose flour and eggs (see individual recipes for the proportions)

MAKING THE DOUGH BY HAND

Heap the flour on a wooden or Formica board or other surface. With your fingers, make a hollow, round well in the center of the flour. Break the eggs into the well. Beat the eggs briefly with a fork, then begin to draw some of the flour from the inside of the well, over the eggs. Add the flour a little at a time, always mixing with the fork. When you reach the point where a soft paste begins to stick to the fork, switch to a dough scraper.

With the dough scraper, push all the remaining flour to one side of the board while you scrape off the bits and pieces attached to the board. Add to the paste some of the flour you have pushed aside and begin kneading the dough, gently at first. As you keep incorporating more flour, your kneading will become more energetic. Do not add the flour too hastily because you might not need to use all of it. The moment you have a soft, manageable dough, clean the board again of sticky pieces and wash your hands. Knead the dough more energetically now, pushing the dough with the palms of your hands away from you and folding half of the dough over toward you. Keep turning the dough as you knead it. Push, fold over, and turn. Knead the dough about 8 minutes, adding a bit more flour if it sticks to the board and to your hands.

Push a finger into the center of the dough. If it comes out barely moist, the dough is ready to be rolled out. If the dough is sticky, knead it a little longer, adding a bit more flour. At the end of the kneading time, the dough should be compact, pliable, and smooth. Keep in mind that a well-kneaded dough is vital to good pasta. So do not skimp on the kneading. The dough is now ready to be rolled out. If you need to hold the dough for a while, keep it wrapped in plastic wrap.

MAKING THE DOUGH IN A FOOD PROCESSOR

Break the eggs into a food processor fitted with the metal blade, and process briefly to mix the eggs. Add the flour. Turn the machine on and off until the dough is all gathered *loosely* around the blade. At this point the dough should be moist and slightly sticky. If the dough is too dry, beat an extra egg in a small bowl and add half of it to the dough. If the dough is too wet, add a bit more flour.

Put the dough on a wooden board or work surface. Dust your hands with flour and knead the dough for a few minutes by hand, adding some more flour if the dough is too sticky. Dough kneaded by food processor is not as elastic as dough kneaded by hand. However, it should still be smooth, pliable, and satisfactory. The dough is now ready to be rolled out. If you need to hold the dough for a while, keep it wrapped in plastic wrap.

MAKING THE DOUGH WITH AN ELECTRIC MIXER

Break the eggs into the bowl of an electric mixer fitted with a dough hook, and beat briefly at low speed. Add the flour, a little at a time, beating well after each addition. When all the flour has been added, increase the speed and let the mixer knead the dough for 5 to 6 minutes. Check the consistency of the dough. If it is too moist, work in a bit more flour. If it is too dry, work in half a beaten egg. Remove the dough from the bowl and knead it for a few minutes by hand. The dough is now ready to be rolled out. If you need to hold it for a while, keep it wrapped in plastic wrap.

ROLLING OUT THE PASTA BY MACHINE

Set the rollers of the pasta machine at their widest opening. Cut off one small piece of dough, about the size of a large egg, and flatten it with the palm of your hand. Keep the rest of the dough wrapped in plastic wrap. Dust the flattened piece of dough lightly with flour, and run it once through the machine. Fold the dough in half, pressing it down with your fingertips. Run it through the machine again. Repeat this step 4 to 5 times, rotating the dough and dusting it with flour until it is smooth and not sticky. During these steps the dough will acquire a firmer consistency, since at this point the machine is doing the kneading for you. (Do not skimp on this step or as you thin the pasta, it will probably stick to the rollers.) Now that the dough is smooth and firm, it is ready to be stretched into a long, thin sheet of pasta.

Change the rollers to the next thinnest setting and run the dough through *once without folding it any more*. Keep changing the setting and working the pasta sheet through the rollers once each time until it reaches the desired thinness.

CUTTING RIBBON PASTA

If you are planning to make ribbon pasta, like noodles or angel hair, place the sheet of dough on a lightly floured tablecloth and let it dry for 8 to 10 minutes before cutting it. Roll out remaining dough in the same manner. When the sheets of pasta are no longer sticky, put them through the cutting blades of the pasta machine, according to the desired width of noodles. Arrange the noodles in soft bundles on a board or a tablecloth. They can be cooked immediately or they can be allowed to dry and cooked later on.

PAPPARDELLE - Roll out the dough into thin sheets and with a fluted pastry wheel or a sharp knife, cut the sheets into ¾-inch-wide noodles, or pappardelle.

PIZZOCCHERI - Roll out the dough into thick 6- to 7-inch long sheets. (Do not roll out the sheets past setting number 3 on the pasta machine.) Let the sheets dry for 12 to 15 minutes, then put them through the widest cutter of the pasta machine.

FETTUCCINE - Roll out the dough into thin sheets and let them dry for 8 to 10 minutes. Put the sheets through the widest cutter of the pasta machine.

TAGLIATELLE - Roll out the dough into thin sheets and let them dry for 8 to 10 minutes. Put the sheets through the widest cutter of the pasta machine.

TAGLIOLINI - Roll out the dough into thin sheets and let them dry for 8 to 10 minutes. Put the sheets through the thinner cutter of the pasta machine.

BOW TIES - Roll out the dough into thin sheets. Cut the sheets into rectangles 1½ inches wide and 2 inches long. Pinch the two long sides of each rectangle together in the center to make bow ties.

FOR STUFFED PASTA

If you plan to make stuffed pasta, *each* sheet of dough should be stuffed and sealed immediately *before* another sheet of dough is rolled out. The stuffed pasta can be cooked immediately or it can be placed on a lightly floured platter and refrigerated, uncovered, for several hours.

RAVIOLI - Roll out one thin sheet of dough at a time and trim it so that it has straight edges and is 6 inches wide. Place large tablespoons of the filling 3 inches apart on the sheet of dough. Fold the sheet in half over the filling, cut between the filling, and press the edges to seal. Repeat with remaining dough.

TORTELLI - Roll out and stuff the dough as for ravioli.

TORTELLONI - Roll out one thin sheet of dough at a time, and cut it into 3-inch squares. Place 1 heaping teaspoon in the center of each square and fold in half to form a triangle. Press the edges firmly to seal. Bend each tortellone around your finger, pressing one pointed end slightly over the other. Repeat with remaining dough.

PANSOTTI - Roll out one thin sheet of dough at a time, and cut it into 3-inch squares. Place the 1 heaping teaspoon of filling in the center of each square and fold in half to form a triangle. Press the edges firmly to seal.

CANNELLONI - Roll out one thin sheet of dough at a time and cut it into 3 × 4-inch rectangles. Drop the rectangles in boiling water and cook 30 to 35 *seconds*. Scoop up the pasta with a large strainer and place in a large bowl of cold water. Remove the pasta, spread it on kitchen towels, and pat dry. Spread a thin layer of filling in the center of each rectangle. Fold the pasta loosely over the filling to make cannelloni.

COLORED PASTA

Traditionally, colored pasta in Italy is made with spinach and with tomato paste.

For spinach pasta, add 2 tablespoons cooked, finely chopped, fresh or frozen spinach, thoroughly squeezed of moisture, to the eggs. Mix the spinach with the eggs, then add the flour and proceed to make the dough by hand or by machine.

For tomato pasta, mix ½ teaspoon tomato paste into the eggs, then add the flour and proceed to make the dough by hand or by machine.

Factory-made Pasta

While homemade pasta is made with soft flour and eggs, good factory-made pasta uses durum wheat flour (semolina) and water, nothing else. Durum wheat flour has a high gluten content, which gives spaghetti, maccheroni, penne, etc., a firmer texture and sturdier consistency. The pasta is called "factory made" because it is produced with large, industrial-strength machines that knead the hard dough and turn it into hundreds of different shapes. The pasta is then dried in special "humidifier" rooms at a controlled temperature. To my mind, Italian factory-made pasta belongs in a class by itself.

Factory-made pasta has always been more popular in southern Italy. However, today since the majority of Italian women work outside the home, the consumption of factory-made pasta has increased all over the country, even in the north. Penne, spaghetti, rigatoni, orecchiette, linguine, these are what I reach for when I want to put a good, wholesome plate of pasta on the table fast. The sauces in this chapter are not only delicious, they are wonderfully quick to make and I hope they will inspire you to cook, serve, and enjoy one of the best foods in the world: Pasta!

TIPS ON COOKING PASTA

- Always use a large pot with plenty of water. For 1 pound of fresh or dried pasta you will need approximately 4 to 5 quarts of water.

- When the water boils add the salt and the pasta all at once. Cover the pot and bring the water back to a boil, then remove the lid.

- Stir the pasta a few times as it cooks. If there is plenty of water in the pot, the pasta will *not* stick together.

- The cooking time of fresh pasta will depend on the size, type, and shape. Fresh homemade noodles will cook faster than fresh homemade stuffed pasta, since stuffed pasta has double thickness.

- The cooking time of factory-made pasta depends on the shape, thickness, and brand. To be safe, read the cooking instructions on the package, but *taste* the pasta for doneness often during the cooking.

- Perfectly cooked pasta should be tender but still firm to the bite. To an Italian, there is no greater sin than overcooked pasta.

- Once pasta is cooked, drain it, transfer it to a warm bowl, and toss it immediately with the sauce. (This can be done in a large, warm bowl or in the skillet where the sauce is kept simmering.)

- *Never* rinse pasta *unless* you are making lasagne or cannelloni. These are the only instances when pasta is quickly precooked, rinsed to stop the cooking, and dried before being stuffed and baked.

Spaghetti with Broccoli, Scallops, and Chile Pepper

SPAGHETTI CON BROCCOLI, CAPPE SANTE, E PEPERONCINO

THIS IS A *quickly prepared, delicious, and healthy pasta dish that follows a classic theme, and combines the best that land and sea have to offer.*

SERVES 4 TO 6

2 bunches broccoli
Salt
¼–⅓ cup extra-virgin olive oil
1 pound sea scallops, the smallest you can find, cut in half horizontally

2 garlic cloves, minced
1 cup dry white wine
Chopped fresh red chile pepper or dried red pepper flakes to taste
1 pound spaghetti

WASH the broccoli and remove and discard the tough parts of the stalks. Separate the florets from the stalks. Peel the stalks and cut them into small, thin rounds. Bring a medium-size saucepan of water to a boil, and add 1 teaspoon of salt, the broccoli florets, and the sliced stalks. Cook, uncovered, until they are barely tender to the touch, 3 to 4 minutes. Drain and set aside.

HEAT the oil in a large skillet over medium-high heat. Add the scallops and cook until they are lightly golden on all sides, 1 to 2 minutes. Add the garlic and stir quickly a few times. (The skillet is very hot, and the garlic will change color almost immediately.) Add the wine and cook, stirring, until wine is reduced by half, 2 to 3 minutes. Add the broccoli, and season with salt and chile pepper. Turn the heat off under the skillet.

MEANWHILE, bring a large pot of water to a boil. Add 1 tablespoon of salt and the spaghetti. Cook, uncovered, over high heat until pasta is tender but still firm to the bite.

DRAIN pasta and add it to the skillet with the sauce. Mix everything quickly over low heat until the pasta and sauce are well combined. Taste and adjust the seasoning, and serve at once.

Spaghetti with Clams in Parchment

SPAGHETTI CON LE VONGOLE AL CARTOCCIO

IMAGINE YOURSELF SITTING *at a little trattoria overlooking the vast blue waters of the Adriatic, and all around you are sounds of tinkling glasses and happy laughter. Then the waiter brings a large, puffed-up bundle to your table, and begins to open it on a cart nearby. Suddenly a wonderful aroma overwhelms your senses. The aromatic steam escapes the parchment-wrapped bundle and when you take the first bite of the pasta, you will wonder why you waited so long to try this dish.*

SERVES 4 TO 6

2½ pounds clams, the smallest
    you can find
¼–⅓ cup extra-virgin olive oil
3 garlic cloves, minced
2 anchovy fillets, chopped
Chopped fresh red chile pepper or
    dried red pepper flakes to taste
1½ pounds fresh, ripe plum
    tomatoes, seeded and diced

½ cup dry white wine
Salt to taste
1 pound spaghetti
2 tablespoons finely chopped flat-
    leaf Italian parsley or regular
    parsley
Parchment paper

SOAK the clams in cold water for 20 minutes to purge them of sand. Wash and scrub them well under cold running water. Discard any clams that stay open when handled. Put the clams in a large saucepan with 1 cup of water. Cover the pan and cook over high heat until the clams open. Remove them to a bowl with a slotted spoon as they open. Toss out any clams that do not open. Bring the cooking liquid back to a boil and cook until it is reduced by half, 2 to 3 minutes. Line a strainer with paper towels and strain the thickened liquid into a small bowl to remove any sandy deposits. Set aside.

REMOVE the clam meat from half of the shells, and leave the other clams in their shells.

HEAT the oil in a large skillet over high heat. Add the garlic, anchovies, and chile pepper, and stir once or twice. Add the tomatoes and cook until they begin to soften, 2 to 3 minutes. Add the wine and the reserved clam liquid. Season with salt and cook, stirring, until liquid reduces by half, 2 to 3 minutes. (Do not reduce the liquid too much or the completed dish will be dry.) Add all the clams and the parsley, and mix quickly to combine, then turn off the heat under the skillet.

PREHEAT the oven to 400°. Bring a large pot of water to a boil. Add 1 tablespoon of salt and the spaghetti. Cook, uncovered, over high heat until the pasta is cooked only halfway through. Drain the pasta, add it to the skillet with the sauce, and mix everything well off the heat. Taste and adjust the seasoning.

Unwrap the parchment cautiously because the hot steam will blast out when you open it.

PLACE 2 large sheets of parchment paper on a large baking sheet and brush each sheet lightly with oil. Divide the pasta between the 2 parchment sheets, placing it slightly off center. Fold the parchment over the pasta and fold the edges to make a border and seal the edges. Make sure not to wrap the bundles too tightly. There should be plenty of empty space around the pasta so the bundles can puff up as they cook. Bake for 7 to 8 minutes. Unwrap the parchment sheets and place spaghetti and every little bit of sauce into serving dishes. Serve at once.

Spaghettini with Swordfish and Fresh Tomatoes

SPAGHETTINI COL PESCE SPADA E POMODORI

A PLEASANT LITTLE *trattoria called Benso in Bologna once served me this good, simple, and straightforward dish. The pasta was tagliatelle, tossed with fresh tomatoes and tender morsels of swordfish. If you do not have time to make your own tagliatelle, you can prepare this lovely dish with good imported thin dried spaghetti and have it on the table in less than 15 minutes.*

SERVES 4 TO 6

¼–⅓ cup extra-virgin olive oil

One ½-inch-thick swordfish steak, about 10–12 ounces, cut into small cubes

4 medium, ripe plum tomatoes, about 1 pound, seeded and diced

2 garlic cloves, minced

1–2 tablespoons sun-dried tomatoes, minced

1 cup dry white wine

1 tablespoon unsalted butter

Salt and freshly ground black pepper to taste

1 pound spaghettini (thin spaghetti)

1–2 tablespoons chopped fresh flat-leaf Italian parsley or regular parsley

HEAT the oil in a large skillet over medium-high heat. Add the swordfish and cook, stirring, until lightly golden, 2 to 3 minutes. Add the fresh tomatoes, garlic, and sun-dried tomatoes, and stir about 1 minute. Add the wine and cook until it is reduced by half, 2 to 3 minutes. Stir in the butter, and season with salt and several grindings of pepper.

MEANWHILE, bring a large pot of water to a boil. Add 1 tablespoon of salt and the spaghettini. Cook, uncovered, over high heat until the pasta is tender but still a bit firm to the bite.

DRAIN the pasta and add to the skillet with the sauce. Add the parsley, and mix everything quickly over low heat until the pasta and sauce are well combined. Taste and adjust the seasoning, and serve at once.

Fettuccine with Scallops, Porcini Mushrooms, and Cream

FETTUCCINE MARE E MONTI

TWO GREAT INGREDIENTS, *one from the sea and the other from the mountains, combine to make a delicious and unusual topping for pasta. I love the sauce served over delicate fettuccine, but it is also extremely good over commercially made penne or bow tie pasta.*

SERVES 4 TO 6

FOR THE FETTUCCINE
2 cups unbleached all-purpose flour
3 extra-large eggs

FOR THE SAUCE
1 ounce porcini mushrooms, soaked in 2 cups lukewarm water for 20 minutes
2 tablespoons unsalted butter
1–2 tablespoons olive oil

¾ pound sea scallops, the smallest you can find, cut in half horizontally
1 garlic clove, minced
½ cup dry white wine
½ cup heavy cream
Salt to taste
1–2 tablespoons chopped fresh flat-leaf Italian parsley or regular parsley

PREPARE the pasta dough as instructed on pages 48–49, using the flour and eggs in this recipe.

ROLL out the dough and cut into fettuccine as instructed on page 50.

continued

Keep in mind that homemade ribbon pasta soaks up the sauce rather quickly. For this reason, it's a good idea to have on hand some additional broth, cream, or porcini mushroom soaking liquid. The tossing of the pasta and sauce over low heat should be done quickly, to prevent the sauce from drying out. If it does dry out, simply add a bit more of one or all of the liquids mentioned and stir into the fettuccine.

PREPARE THE SAUCE: Strain the porcini mushrooms and reserve the soaking water. Rinse the mushrooms well under cold running water and chop them roughly. Line a strainer with two paper towels and strain the mushroom water into a bowl to get rid of the sandy deposits. Set aside.

HEAT the butter and the oil in a large skillet over medium heat. When the butter begins to foam, add the scallops and sauté until they are lightly golden, about 2 minutes. Add the garlic and the porcini mushrooms, and stir for about 1 minute. Add ½ cup of the reserved mushroom water, the wine, and the cream, and season with salt. Cook, stirring, until the liquid is reduced by half and has a medium-thick consistency, 2 to 3 minutes. Turn the heat off under the skillet.

MEANWHILE, bring a large pot of water to a boil. Add 1 tablespoon of salt and the fettuccine. Cook, uncovered, over high heat until the pasta is tender but still a bit firm to the bite. Drain the pasta and place it in the skillet with the sauce. Stir in the parsley and toss everything quickly over low heat until the pasta and the sauce are well combined. Taste and adjust the seasoning, and serve.

Seafood Cannelloni

CANNELLONI DI PESCE

I CAN HEAR *you say, "My goodness, look at all the steps in this recipe!" Let me reassure you that cannelloni is perhaps one of the easiest of all stuffed pasta dishes to make. Here's how I do it:*

I MAKE THE *filling a day ahead. Then I make the pasta and stuff the cannelloni early in the day I plan to serve them. A few hours before dinner I make the sauce and, at the last moment, I bake the cannelloni. I hope you will make this dish because it is truly wonderful.*

SERVES 4

FOR THE FILLING

1 cup dry white wine
Juice of 1 lemon
1 pound assorted fish fillets, such as halibut, sea bass, salmon, or sole
2 tablespoons unsalted butter
½ cup finely minced yellow onion
½ cup heavy cream
⅓ cup freshly grated Parmigiano-Reggiano cheese
1–2 tablespoons chopped fresh flat-leaf Italian parsley or regular parsley
Salt to taste
Pinch white pepper

FOR THE CANNELLONI

1¼ cups unbleached all-purpose flour
2 extra-large eggs

FOR THE SAUCE

2 tablespoons unsalted butter
3 cups canned imported Italian plum tomatoes, with their juice, put through a food mill to remove the seeds
¼ cup heavy cream
Salt to taste

⅓ cup freshly grated Parmigiano-Reggiano cheese
1–2 tablespoons unsalted butter

PREPARE THE FILLING: Fill a medium-size saucepan halfway with cold water. Add the wine and the lemon juice, and bring to a boil over medium heat.

continued

Add all the fish, turn the heat down, and simmer, uncovered, 5 to 6 minutes. Remove the fish with a large slotted spoon and drain on paper towels. With a large knife, chop the fish very fine and place into a medium-size bowl.

HEAT the butter in a medium-size skillet over medium heat. When the butter begins to foam, add the onion and cook until onion is pale yellow and soft, 7 to 8 minutes. Stir in the cream, the parsley, and the fish. Season lightly with salt and mix just enough to combine. Return mixture to the bowl and stir in the Parmigiano. Cool before using. (The filling can be prepared several hours or a day ahead and refrigerated.)

PREPARE the pasta dough as instructed on pages 48–49, using the flour and eggs in this recipe.

ROLL out the dough and prepare cannelloni as instructed on page 51.

BUTTER a 9 × 13-inch baking dish generously and arrange the cannelloni all in one row in the dish. Cover with plastic wrap and set aside or refrigerate until ready to use.

PREPARE THE SAUCE: Heat the butter in a medium-size skillet over medium heat. When the butter begins to foam, add the tomatoes and the cream, and season with salt. Simmer, uncovered, until the sauce has a medium-thick consistency, 8 to 10 minutes.

PREHEAT the oven to 450°. If cannelloni have been refrigerated, bring them back to room temperature. Spoon some tomato-cream sauce over the cannelloni and sprinkle with Parmigiano. Dot with butter and bake until cannelloni are lightly golden, about 10 minutes. Serve hot.

Ravioli with Shrimp Filling

RAVIOLI CON GAMBERI

I OFTEN SERVE *this pasta dish at my restaurant in Sacramento. It is both delicious and impressive-looking. For dinner parties at home, I prepare the filling the day before and make the ravioli early on the day of the gathering. Before the guests arrive, I prepare the sauce, so that at the last moment all that has to be done is to cook the ravioli, toss them with the sauce, and bring them to the table. Scallops or lobster can be substituted for the shrimp filling.*

SERVES 4 TO 6

FOR THE FILLING

3 tablespoons extra-virgin olive oil
1 pound medium-size shrimp,
    shelled and deveined
1 garlic clove, minced
½ cup dry white wine
½ cup heavy cream
½ cup freshly grated Parmigiano-
    Reggiano cheese
¼ cup chopped fresh flat-leaf
    Italian parsley or regular
    parsley
Salt and white pepper to taste

FOR THE RAVIOLI

2 cups unbleached all-purpose
    flour
3 extra-large eggs

FOR THE SAUCE

2 tablespoons unsalted butter
2 tablespoons extra-virgin olive oil
1 garlic clove, minced
½ pound firm, ripe tomatoes,
    seeded and diced
2 tablespoons diced sun-dried
    tomatoes
¼ cup chicken broth
Salt and freshly ground black
    pepper to taste

PREPARE THE FILLING: Heat the oil in a large skillet over medium-high heat. Add the shrimp without crowding the skillet, and cook until they are lightly golden on all sides, about 2 minutes. With a slotted spoon transfer shrimp to a dish. Add the garlic to the skillet and stir once or twice. Add the wine and stir to scrape up any bits on the bottom of the skillet. When the wine is reduced by half, about 2 minutes, add the cream. Cook until the cream has a thick consistency. At this point there should be about ⅓ to ½ cup of thick sauce left in the skillet.

PUT the shrimp in the bowl of a food processor and turn the machine on and off until shrimp are chopped very fine. Make sure not to puree them; they should retain some consistency. Transfer shrimp to a medium-size bowl and stir in the reduced cream. Add the Parmigiano and the parsley, and season with salt and a bit of white pepper. Mix everything well, and taste and adjust the seasoning. Cover the bowl and refrigerate for a few hours to firm up the filling. (The filling can be prepared several hours or a day ahead.)

PREPARE the pasta dough as instructed on pages 48–49, using the flour and eggs in this recipe.

ROLL out the dough and prepare the ravioli as instructed on page 51.

PREPARE THE SAUCE: Heat 1 tablespoon of the butter and the olive oil in a large skillet over medium heat. When the butter foams, add the garlic, tomatoes, sun-dried tomatoes, and broth. Season with salt and pepper. Bring the sauce to a gentle simmer and cook, stirring a few times, until the tomatoes are soft and their juice has thickened, 3 to 4 minutes. Stir in the remaining tablespoon of butter and, as soon as it has melted, turn the heat off under the skillet.

WHILE the sauce is cooking, bring a large pot of water to a boil. Add 1 tablespoon of salt and the ravioli. Cook, uncovered, over high heat until ravioli are tender but still firm to the bite. Drain ravioli and place in the skillet with the sauce. Over low heat mix gently and quickly until the pasta and the sauce are well combined. Serve immediately.

Ravioli with Artichokes

RAVIOLI CON CARCIOFINI

ONE DAY AT my restaurant in Sacramento, I was sautéing artichoke hearts with oil, garlic, and sun-dried tomatoes to use as a side dish. When I tasted the artichokes, they were so good that I thought they would work well as a stuffing for pasta. After some experimenting, I knew I had done a good job when the ravioli sold out in no time at all.

SERVES 4 TO 6

FOR THE FILLING

2 pounds baby artichokes
Juice of 1 lemon
2 tablespoons extra-virgin olive oil
1 garlic clove, minced
2 tablespoons minced sun-dried tomatoes
¼ pound ricotta
¼ cup freshly grated Parmigiano-Reggiano cheese
2 tablespoons chopped fresh flat-leaf Italian parsley or regular parsley
Salt to taste

FOR THE RAVIOLI

2 cups unbleached all-purpose flour
3 extra-large eggs

FOR THE SAUCE

2 tablespoons olive oil
3 tablespoons unsalted butter
5 fresh, ripe plum tomatoes, about ¾ pound, seeded and diced
6–8 fresh basil leaves, cut into thin strips, or 1 tablespoon chopped fresh flat-leaf Italian parsley
Salt to taste
½ cup freshly grated Parmigiano-Reggiano cheese

There is no doubt that homemade pasta takes time. To simplify preparation make the filling a day ahead and keep it tightly wrapped in the refrigerator.

PREPARE THE FILLING: Remove the green leaves of the artichokes by snapping them off at the base. Stop when the leaves closer to the base are pale yellow and the tips of the artichokes are green. Slice off the green top. Cut the stem off at the base and, with a small knife, trim off the remaining green part at the base. Cut the artichokes into small wedges and place them in a bowl of cold water with the lemon juice to prevent discoloring.

continued

BRING a medium-size saucepan of water to a boil over medium heat. Add 1 teaspoon of salt and the artichokes, and cook gently until tender, 3 to 4 minutes. Drain artichokes, place in a bowl, and cool.

HEAT the oil in a large skillet over medium heat. Add the garlic, sun-dried tomatoes, and artichokes, and stir for a few minutes. Put the artichokes mixture in the bowl of a food processor and turn the machine on and off until artichokes are chopped very fine. Make sure they are not puree; they should retain a bit of granular consistency. Place the artichokes mixture in a medium bowl. Add the ricotta, Parmigiano, and parsley, and season with salt. Cover the bowl and refrigerate for a few hours to firm up the filling.

PREPARE the pasta dough as instructed on pages 48–49, using the flour and eggs in this recipe.

ROLL out the dough and prepare ravioli as instructed on page 51.

PREPARE THE SAUCE: Heat 2 tablespoons of the butter and the olive oil in a large skillet over medium heat. When the butter foams, add the tomatoes and the basil, and season with salt. Cook, stirring a few times, until the tomatoes are soft and their juice has thickened, 3 to 4 minutes. Stir in the remaining tablespoon of butter and turn the heat off under the skillet.

WHILE the sauce is cooking, bring a large pot of water to a boil. Add 1 tablespoon of salt and the ravioli. Cook, uncovered, over high heat until ravioli are tender but still a bit firm to the bite. Drain ravioli and place in the skillet with the sauce. Toss gently and quickly over low heat until the pasta and the sauce are well combined. If pasta seems dry, add a few tablespoons of the pasta cooking water. Serve with a sprinkling of Parmigiano.

Tortelli with Potatoes

TORTELLI DI PATATE

THERE IS NO *other Italian region that prepares as many stuffed pasta dishes as does Emilia-Romagna. Even the humble potato becomes a delicious filling. The possibilities are endless.*

SERVES 4 TO 6

FOR THE FILLING

2 large boiling potatoes, about
   1 pound
1–2 tablespoons unsalted butter
½ cup finely minced yellow onion
1 garlic clove, minced
½ pound ricotta
⅓ cup freshly grated Parmigiano-
   Reggiano cheese
1 medium egg, lightly beaten
½ teaspoon freshly grated nutmeg
Salt to taste

FOR THE TORTELLI

2 cups unbleached all-purpose flour
3 extra-large eggs

FOR THE SAUCE

1 tablespoon olive oil
2–3 tablespoons unsalted butter
3–4 ounces sliced pancetta or
   prosciutto, cut into small strips
Salt to taste
2 tablespoons finely chopped flat-
   leaf Italian parsley or regular
   parsley
⅓ cup freshly grated Parmigiano-
   Reggiano cheese

PREPARE THE FILLING: Put the potatoes in a medium-size saucepan and cover them generously with cold water; bring the water to a boil over medium heat and cook until tender, about 1 hour. Drain and cool potatoes, then peel and mash them with a potato masher or put them through a food mill. Place mashed potatoes in a bowl.

HEAT the butter in a small skillet over medium-low heat. Add the onion and cook, stirring, until onion is pale yellow and soft, 7 to 8 minutes. Add the garlic and cook less than 1 minute. Stir the onion into the potatoes. Add the ricotta,

Parmigiano, egg, and nutmeg, and season with salt. Mix well to combine. Cover the bowl and refrigerate until ready to use. (The filling can be prepared several hours or a day ahead.)

For perfect boiled potatoes, always boil potatoes with the skin on so they won't absorb too much water.

PREPARE the pasta dough as instructed on pages 48–49, using the flour and eggs in this recipe.

ROLL out the dough and prepare tortelli as instructed on page 51.

PREPARE THE SAUCE: Heat the oil and butter in a large skillet over medium heat. When the butter foams, add the pancetta and cook, stirring, until pancetta is lightly golden, 2 to 3 minutes.

Always start cooking potatoes in cold water and bring the water to a gentle boil. If potatoes are added to boiling water, the skin will burst.

MEANWHILE, bring a large pot of water to a boil. Add 1 tablespoon of salt and the tortelli. Cook, uncovered, over high heat until tortelli are tender but still firm to the bite. Drain the tortelli gently and place them in the skillet. Season lightly with salt, and sprinkle with parsley and Parmigiano. Mix gently over low heat to combine. (If pasta seems a bit dry, add a few tablespoons of the pasta cooking water.) Serve at once with more Parmigiano, if desired.

Tortelloni with Gorgonzola Sauce

TORTELLONI AL GORGONZOLA

TORTELLONI ARE LARGE, *plump, stuffed fresh pasta "pillows." The traditional filling consists of fresh ricotta, Parmigiano, nutmeg, and chopped fresh parsley, and the classic Bolognese sauce for tortelloni is called* burro e oro, *butter and tomatoes. Here, we depart from tradition by serving tortelloni in a creamy but not too heavy Gorgonzola sauce. Select young, mild Gorgonzola and use it with a light hand.*

SERVES 4 TO 6

FOR THE FILLING
1 pound ricotta
½ cup freshly grated Parmigiano-
    Reggiano cheese
½ teaspoon freshly grated nutmeg
1 medium egg, lightly beaten
¼ cup chopped fresh flat-leaf
    Italian or regular parsley
Salt to taste

FOR THE TORTELLONI
2 cups unbleached all-purpose flour
3 large eggs

FOR THE GORGONZOLA SAUCE
3–4 tablespoons unsalted butter
2–3 ounces mild Gorgonzola
    (see Note)
Salt to taste

To simplify this dish, prepare the filling a day ahead. You can make the tortelloni early on the day you plan to serve them and store them, uncovered, in the refrigerator. Then, at the last moment, cook the tortelloni and prepare the sauce.

PREPARE THE FILLING: Put all the filling ingredients in a medium-size bowl and mix well to combine. Taste and adjust the seasoning. Cover the bowl and refrigerate until ready to use. (The filling can be prepared several hours or a day ahead.)

PREPARE the pasta dough as instructed on pages 48–49, using the flour and eggs in this recipe.

ROLL out the dough and prepare tortelloni as instructed on page 51.

HEAT the butter in a large skillet over low heat. Add the Gorgonzola and stir gently until it is melted. Turn the heat off under the skillet.

BRING a large pot of water to a boil. Add 1 tablespoon of salt and the tortelloni. Cook, uncovered, over high heat until tortelloni are tender but still firm to the bite. Drain tortelloni and gently place them in the skillet. Season lightly with salt, add the parsley, and mix gently over low heat to combine. If pasta seems a bit dry, add a few tablespoons of pasta cooking water to the skillet and stir briefly. Serve at once.

Note: Tips for buying Gorgonzola:

- Look for a warm white color and a soft creamy texture. If the cheese is dry, crumbly, and yellow, it is not at its best.
- To store Gorgonzola, wrap it securely in plastic and use it within a week or two.
- If you are planning to serve Gorgonzola at the end of a meal with fruit, make sure to serve it at room temperature to enjoy its flavor fully.

Tortelloni with Asparagus Sauce

TORTELLONI CON SALSA DI ASPARAGI

GIANFRANCO BOLOGNESI IS *the owner of one of Italy's best restaurants, La Frasca, located in Castrocaro Terme, a small town in Emilia-Romagna. The last time I dined in this beautiful, romantic place, I was served a spinach tortelloni in a light asparagus sauce that was a masterpiece. If you don't mind spending a little extra time in the kitchen, prepare this dish for the special people in your life.*

SERVES 4 TO 6

FOR THE FILLING
1 pound ricotta
6 ounces cooked fresh or frozen chopped spinach, squeezed dry
½ cup freshly grated Parmigiano-Reggiano cheese
½ teaspoon freshly grated nutmeg (see Note)
1 large egg, lightly beaten
Salt to taste

FOR THE TORTELLONI
2 cups unbleached all-purpose flour
3 extra-large eggs

FOR THE ASPARAGUS SAUCE
¾ pound asparagus tips, approximately 4 pounds asparagus
1 cup heavy cream
½ cup chicken broth (see page 33) or clear vegetable broth
3 tablespoons unsalted butter
Salt to taste
½ cup freshly grated Parmigiano-Reggiano cheese

PREPARE THE FILLING: Put all the filling ingredients in a medium-size bowl and mix well to combine. Taste and adjust the seasoning. Cover the bowl and refrigerate until ready to use. (The filling can be prepared several hours or a day ahead.)

PREPARE the pasta dough as instructed on pages 48–49, using the flour and eggs in this recipe.

ROLL out the dough and prepare tortelloni as instructed on page 51.

PREPARE THE SAUCE: Bring a small saucepan of salted water to a boil. Add the asparagus tips and cook until tender but still firm to the bite, 1 to 2 minutes, depending on size. Drain asparagus tips and reserve about one third. Combine the remaining asparagus tips with the cream and the broth, and puree in a food processor to a smooth consistency.

HEAT the butter in a large skillet. Add the pureed asparagus and reserved asparagus tips. Season with salt. Simmer the sauce over very low heat for a few minutes, or until sauce has a medium-thick, creamy consistency. Keep sauce warm over very low heat while you cook the tortelloni.

BRING a large pot of water to a boil. Add 1 tablespoon of salt and the tortelloni. Cook, uncovered, over high heat until tortelloni are tender but still firm to the bite. Drain tortelloni gently and place them in the skillet. Add Parmigiano and mix over low heat to combine. Serve immediately with some more Parmigiano, if desired.

Note: Nutmeg is the dried nut encased in an apricot-like fruit of an evergreen tree native to Indonesia. When the fruit is ripe, it splits open to release the nut.

Nutmeg is used in many Italian dishes, especially in fillings for pasta. Buy nutmeg whole and grate it as needed. Use it with a bit of restraint because its taste can be overwhelming.

Swiss Chard Pansotti with Walnut Pesto

PANSOTTI DI BIETE CON PESTO DI NOCI

PANSOTTI, WHICH MEANS *"little bellies," are triangular stuffed pasta, a native of Liguria, the Italian Riviera. One of the typical Ligurian fillings for pansotti is made with ricotta and assorted wild greens. Since Ligurian wild greens are not available here, I substitute ricotta, Swiss chard, spinach, and Parmigiano-Reggiano cheese, and top the pansotti with a light, delicious walnut pesto.*

SERVES 4 TO 6

FOR THE FILLING
1 pound Swiss chard
1 pound fresh spinach
Salt
½ pound ricotta
1 large egg, lightly beaten
⅓–½ cup freshly grated
    Parmigiano-Reggiano cheese
Salt and white pepper to taste

FOR THE WALNUT PESTO
2 cups loosely packed fresh basil
    leaves
½–¾ cup extra-virgin olive oil
⅓ cup shelled, chopped walnuts
2 garlic cloves
Salt to taste
¼ cup freshly grated Parmigiano-
    Reggiano cheese

FOR THE PANSOTTI
2 cups unbleached all-purpose flour
3 extra-large eggs

PREPARE THE FILLING: Remove the leaves from the Swiss chard and the spinach. Wash the leaves thoroughly in several changes of cold water to remove all the gritty sand. Put Swiss chard and spinach in a large pot with 2 cups of water and a pinch of salt. Cover and cook over medium heat until tender. Drain and squeeze out any excess water. Chop the greens very fine by hand or with a food processor, but do not puree.

IN a large bowl combine Swiss chard and spinach with the ricotta, egg, and Parmigiano, and season with salt and just a touch of white pepper. Cover the

The worst thing you can do to pesto is to heat it. Pesto should always be served uncooked, at room temperature or chilled, to preserve its light, fragrant taste and color. It should be mixed with the pasta off the heat and served quickly. Refrigerate or freeze any leftover pesto.

bowl and refrigerate until ready to use. (The filling can be prepared several hours ahead.)

PREPARE the pasta dough as instructed on pages 48–49, using the flour and eggs in this recipe.

ROLL out the dough and prepare pansotti as instructed on page 51.

PREPARE THE PESTO: Put all the ingredients except the cheese in the bowl of the food processor and process until smooth. Pour the sauce into a small bowl and stir in the Parmigiano. Taste and adjust the seasoning. Set aside or refrigerate until ready to use. You will have about 1 cup pesto.

MEANWHILE, bring a large pot of water to a boil. Add 1 tablespoon of salt and the pansotti. Cook, uncovered, until pansotti are tender but still firm to the bite. Drain the pansotti gently and place in a large, heated bowl. Add about ⅓ cup of the pesto and mix thoroughly. Add more pesto if needed. Taste and adjust the seasoning, and serve.

Cannelloni with Mixed Mushrooms

CANNELLONI AI FUNGHI MISTI

I OFTEN PREPARE *this dish at my restaurant in Sacramento. Good, light, homemade pasta is essential to its success. For the filling I use a mixture of the mushrooms listed below. However, when these types of mushroom are not available or are too expensive, you can substitute white cultivated mushrooms and reconstituted dried porcini mushrooms. You can also use this delicious filling for ravioli or tortelli.*

SERVES 4

FOR THE FILLING

¼ cup extra-virgin olive oil

1 pound mixed mushrooms, such as cultivated white, chanterelle, shiitake, oyster, and porcini, wiped clean and thinly sliced

2 garlic cloves, minced

2 tablespoons chopped fresh flat-leaf Italian parsley or regular parsley

⅓ cup dry Marsala wine

5 ounces ricotta

½ cup freshly grated Parmigiano-Reggiano cheese

Salt to taste

FOR THE CANNELLONI

1¼ cups unbleached all-purpose flour

2 extra-large eggs

FOR THE SAUCE

2 tablespoons unsalted butter

3 cups canned imported Italian plum tomatoes, with their juice, put through a food mill to remove the seeds

Salt to taste

⅓ cup freshly grated Parmigiano-Reggiano cheese

1–2 tablespoons unsalted butter

PREPARE THE FILLING: Heat the oil in a large skillet over high heat. When the oil begins to smoke, add the mushrooms without crowding the skillet. (You might have to sauté the mushrooms in a few batches.) Cook, stirring, until the mushrooms are lightly golden, 1 to 2 minutes. Add the garlic and parsley, and stir quickly once or twice. Add the Marsala and cook, stirring, until the wine is all reduced. Place mushrooms in a bowl and let cool.

Cook mushrooms in a very hot skillet with very hot oil __without crowding__ them. This will allow the juices to evaporate quickly and the mushrooms to turn a perfect golden brown.

PUT the cooled mushrooms in a food processor and chop them into very small, fine pieces. Do not puree them. Return mushrooms to the bowl, mix in the ricotta and the Parmigiano, and season with salt. Chill the filling in the refrigerator for an hour or so before using. (The filling can also be prepared several hours or a day ahead and refrigerated.)

PREPARE the pasta dough as instructed on pages 48–49, using the flour and eggs in this recipe.

ROLL out the dough and prepare cannelloni as instructed on page 51.

BUTTER a 9 × 13-inch baking dish generously and arrange the cannelloni all in one row in the dish. Cover with plastic wrap and set aside or refrigerate until ready to use. (Cannelloni can be prepared up to this point a few hours or a day ahead.)

PREPARE THE SAUCE: Heat the butter in a medium-size skillet over medium heat. When the butter begins to foam, add the tomatoes and season with salt. Simmer, uncovered, until the sauce has a medium-thick consistency, 8 to 10 minutes.

PREHEAT the oven to 450°. If the cannelloni have been refrigerated, bring them back to room temperature. Spoon some tomato sauce over cannelloni, sprinkle with Parmigiano, and dot with butter. Bake until cannelloni are lightly golden, about 10 minutes. Serve hot.

Pappardelle with Lamb and Bell Pepper Sauce

PAPPARDELLE CON SUGO D'AGNELLO E PEPERONI

PASTA WITH LAMB *sauce is a much loved traditional dish of Abruzzo. In Italy this pasta dish is called* alla chitarra *because a sheet of homemade hard wheat pasta used to be cut by forcing it through the wires of a rectangular-shaped loom resembling a guitar.*

RED BELL PEPPERS, *cooked gently with the lamb and the tomatoes, impart their sweet, mellow taste to the sauce.*

 SERVES 4

FOR THE SAUCE

¼–⅓ cup extra-virgin olive oil
1 pound lamb shoulder, cut into
    small cubes
3 garlic cloves, minced
Chopped fresh red chile pepper or
    dried red pepper flakes to taste
2 tablespoons finely chopped fresh
    flat-leaf Italian parsley or
    regular parsley
1 cup dry white wine
2 cups canned imported Italian
    plum tomatoes, with their
    juice, roughly chopped

2 red bell peppers, seeded and cut
    into short, thin strips
Salt to taste
½–1 cup chicken broth

FOR THE PAPPARDELLE

2 cups unbleached all-purpose flour
3 extra-large eggs

1 tablespoon unsalted butter
2 tablespoons freshly grated
    pecorino Romano or ¼ cup
    freshly grated Parmigiano-
    Reggiano cheese

PREPARE THE SAUCE: Heat the oil in a large skillet or a wide-bottomed saucepan over high heat. Add the lamb and cook, stirring several times, until the lamb is lightly colored, 2 to 3 minutes. Add the garlic, chile pepper, and parsley, and stir for about 1 minute. Add the wine. Cook, stirring, until the wine is reduced by half, 3 to 4 minutes. Add the tomatoes and the bell peppers, season with salt, and stir for about a minute or two, then stir in ½ cup of the broth. Reduce the heat to low and cover the skillet. Cook 45 minutes to 1 hour, stirring a few times. At the end of cooking, the lamb should be meltingly tender and the sauce should be nice and thick. Set aside until ready to use.

PREPARE the pasta dough as instructed on pages 48–49, using the flour and the eggs in this recipe.

ROLL out the dough and prepare the pappardelle as instructed on page 50.

BRING a large pot of water to a boil. Add 1 tablespoon of salt and the pappardelle. Cook, uncovered, over high heat until the pasta is tender but still firm to the bite.

WHILE the pasta is cooking, warm up the meat sauce over medium heat, and stir in 1 tablespoon of butter. If the sauce looks dry, add the remaining broth and simmer it down for a few minutes.

DRAIN the pasta and place it in a large, heated serving bowl. Add half of the sauce and a sprinkling of pecorino Romano, and mix well. Add more sauce if needed. Taste and adjust the seasoning, and serve.

Pappardelle with Cabbage, Speck, and Tomatoes

PAPPARDELLE CON CAVOLO, SPECK, E POMODORI

TO ME, CABBAGE *and smoked ham go together in a rustically perfect combination. In the Friuli area of Friuli–Venezia Giulia, a rugged mountainous region where the food is unfussy, basic but tasty, these humble ingredients often receive a star treatment. The tomatoes add a splash of color and flavor.*

SERVES 4

FOR THE PAPPARDELLE
2 cups unbleached all-purpose flour
3 extra-large eggs

FOR THE SAUCE
2 tablespoons extra-virgin olive oil
¼ pound speck (see Note, page 15), cut into thick slices and diced
½ pound Savoy cabbage, cut into strips and diced

1 cup chicken broth, preferably homemade (see page 33)
2 medium fresh, ripe tomatoes, seeded and diced
Salt and freshly ground black pepper to taste
2 tablespoons unsalted butter
1 tablespoon chopped fresh flat-leaf Italian or regular parsley

At the end of the cooking, the sauce should have a thick yet juicy consistency. Adding butter at the last moment lends body and smoothness to the dish. It is a good idea to have a bit of extra broth on hand to add to the pasta if it seems a bit dry.

PREPARE the pasta dough as instructed on pages 48–49, using the flour and eggs in this recipe.

ROLL out the dough and prepare the pappardelle as instructed on page 50.

HEAT the oil in a large skillet over medium heat. Add the speck and stir a few times. Add the cabbage and cook, stirring, for a few minutes. Add the broth, cover the skillet, and turn the heat to low. Simmer until cabbage is tender and the liquid in the skillet is reduced by half, 8 to 10 minutes. (If the liquid is completely reduced, add a bit more broth.) Raise the heat to high, add the tomatoes, and season with salt and pepper. Cook, uncovered, stirring a few times, until the tomatoes are soft. Add the butter and cook over medium heat until the juices in the skillet have thickened. Turn the heat off under the skillet.

MEANWHILE, bring a large pot of water to a boil. Add 1 tablespoon of salt and the pappardelle. Cook, uncovered, over high heat until the pasta is tender but still a bit firm to the bite. Drain the pasta and place in the skillet with the sauce. Mix everything quickly over low heat until the pasta and the sauce are well combined. Taste and adjust the seasoning, and serve at once.

Tagliolini alla Boschetti

SOME OF THE *best food my husband and I had during our last trip to Italy was at Ristorante Boschetti, in the small town of Tricesimo, just outside Udine. This is one of the dishes they served. Freshly made tagliolini were tossed in a delicious sauce of thinly sliced smoked ham, fresh, ripe tomatoes, garlic, and red pepper flakes. According to the restaurant owner, the sauce was his adaptation of the classic Amatriciana sauce of Rome. You can substitute commercial spaghettini or penne if you do not have time to make your own tagliolini.*

SERVES 4

FOR THE TAGLIOLINI
2 cups unbleached all-purpose flour
3 extra-large eggs

FOR THE SAUCE
2 pounds fresh, ripe tomatoes
3–4 tablespoons extra-virgin
    olive oil

1 garlic clove, minced
2–3 ounces speck (see Note,
    page 15) or prosciutto, cut
    into thick slices and diced
Salt to taste
Chopped fresh red chile pepper or
    dried red pepper flakes to taste
1 tablespoon unsalted butter

PREPARE the pasta dough as instructed on pages 48–49, using the flour and eggs in this recipe.

continued

ROLL out the dough and prepare the tagliolini as instructed on page 50.

BRING a large pot of water to a boil. Cut a cross at the root end of the tomatoes and drop them into the boiling water. Cook until the skin of the tomatoes begins to split, 1 to 2 minutes. Transfer the tomatoes to a bowl of iced water. Peel, seed, and dice the tomatoes, and place them in a bowl with all their juice.

HEAT the oil in a large skillet over medium heat. Add the garlic and the speck, and stir once or twice. Add the tomatoes and season with salt and chile pepper. Cook, stirring a few times, until the tomatoes are soft and their juice has thickened, 4 to 6 minutes. Stir in the butter and turn the heat off under the skillet.

MEANWHILE, bring a large pot of water to a boil. Add 1 tablespoon of salt and the tagliolini. Cook, uncovered, over high heat until the pasta is tender but still firm to the bite. Drain the pasta and place in the skillet with the sauce. Mix everything quickly over low heat until the pasta and sauce are well combined. Taste and adjust the seasoning, and serve at once.

Tagliatelle with Fresh Tomatoes and Garlic

TAGLIATELLE ALLA ROMAGNOLA

GOOD HOMEMADE NOODLES, *ripe, fragrant, fresh tomatoes, a bit of garlic, and high-quality extra-virgin olive oil are all you need to make this dish, a specialty of the Emilia-Romagna region. Because the sauce is light and fresh tasting, you do not need to add grated cheese. Good dried penne or bow ties work just as well as tagliatelle, if you do not have time to make your own pasta.*

SERVES 4 TO 6

FOR THE TAGLIATELLE

2 cups unbleached all-purpose
 flour
3 extra-large eggs

FOR THE SAUCE

4 tablespoons extra-virgin olive oil
2 garlic cloves, finely minced

2 tablespoons chopped fresh flat-
 leaf Italian or regular parsley
2 pounds fresh, ripe tomatoes,
 seeded and diced
⅓ cup chicken broth, if needed
Salt and freshly ground black
 pepper to taste

PREPARE the pasta dough as instructed on pages 48–49, using the flour and eggs in this recipe.

ROLL out the dough and prepare the tagliatelle as instructed on page 50.

PREPARE THE SAUCE: Heat the oil in a large skillet over medium heat. Add the garlic and parsley, and stir a few times. Add the tomatoes, and season with salt and pepper. Reduce the heat to medium low and cook, uncovered, stirring occasionally for 10 to 15 minutes.

PUT the sauce through a food mill or puree it in a food processor. Return sauce to the skillet and keep it warm over very low heat while you cook the pasta. If sauce is too thick, stir in some chicken broth.

BRING a large pot of water to a boil. Add 1 tablespoon of salt and the tagliatelle. Cook, uncovered, over high heat until the pasta is tender but still firm to the bite.

DRAIN the pasta and place it in a large, heated serving bowl. Add the sauce and mix well. Taste and adjust the seasoning, and serve.

Spinach Tagliatelle with Prosciutto and Tomatoes

TAGLIATELLE VERDI AL PROSCIUTTO E POMODORI

SPINACH TAGLIATELLE ARE *the classic egg noodles of Emilia-Romagna, and this dish incorporates some of the best ingredients of the region: prosciutto from the hills of Langhirano outside Parma, Parmigiano-Reggiano cheese produced in a defined area in Emilia; and, of course, good homemade pasta.*

IF YOU DON'T *want to make your own pasta, select dried egg noodles or spinach noodles imported from Italy, such as Fini, Del Verde, or De Cecco. All are excellent brands and easily available in Italian specialty stores.*

SERVES 4 TO 6

FOR THE SPINACH TAGLIATELLE
2 cups unbleached all-purpose flour
3 extra-large eggs
2 tablespoons cooked, finely chopped fresh or frozen spinach, squeezed of all moisture

FOR THE SAUCE
2 tablespoons unsalted butter
2 tablespoons olive oil
½ cup minced yellow onion
⅓ cup minced carrot
⅓ cup minced celery
¼ pound prosciutto, cut into a ⅛-inch slice and then cut into thin strips
3 cups canned imported Italian plum tomatoes, with their juice, put through a food mill to remove the seeds
¼ cup heavy cream
Salt and freshly ground black pepper to taste
½ cup freshly grated Parmigiano-Reggiano cheese

PREPARE the spinach dough as instructed on pages 48–49, using the flour and the eggs in this recipe.

ROLL out the dough and cut it into tagliatelle as instructed on page 50.

Do not add all the sauce to the pasta at once, for you might not need it all. I generally mix the pasta with about half the sauce, then add more as needed. Any leftover sauce can be refrigerated or frozen.

PREPARE THE SAUCE: Heat the butter and oil in a medium-size saucepan over medium heat. Add the onion, carrot, and celery and cook, stirring, until vegetables are lightly golden and soft, 5 to 6 minutes. Add the prosciutto and cook 1 to 2 minutes, stirring a few times. Add the tomatoes and the cream and season with salt and just a touch of pepper. Reduce the heat to medium low and simmer, uncovered, until sauce has a medium-thick consistency, 10 to 15 minutes.

BRING a large pot of water to a boil. Add 1 tablespoon of salt and the tagliatelle. Cook, uncovered, over high heat until the pasta is tender but still firm to the bite.

DRAIN the pasta and place it in a large, heated serving bowl. Add the sauce and about ¼ cup of the Parmigiano, and mix well. Serve at once with additional Parmigiano.

Bow Ties with Prosciutto, Peas, and Fresh Tomatoes

STRICCHETTI CON PROSCIUTTO, PISELLI, E POMODORI

IN EMILIA-ROMAGNA *bow ties are called* stricchetti. *In other parts of Italy they are called* farfalle. *This is another of the many shapes of handmade pasta, and it is perhaps one of the easiest to prepare. For this dish I have chosen a very pretty, easy sauce: onion sautéed in sweet butter, tasty prosciutto, sweet peas, and ripe tomatoes.*

IF YOU DON'T *have time to make your own bow ties, buy a pound of good imported factory-made bow ties, fettuccine, or penne.*

SERVES 4

FOR THE BOW TIES
2 cups unbleached all-purpose flour
3 extra-large eggs

FOR THE SAUCE
1 cup shelled fresh or frozen peas, thawed
3–4 tablespoons unsalted butter

½ cup finely minced yellow onion
¼ pound sliced prosciutto, cut into short, thin strips
1 cup dry white wine
1 pound fresh, ripe tomatoes, seeded and diced
Salt and freshly ground black pepper to taste

PREPARE the pasta dough as instructed on pages 48–49, using the flour and eggs in this recipe.

ROLL out the dough and prepare bow ties as instructed on page 50.

IF you are using fresh peas, bring a small saucepan of water to a boil over medium heat. Add the peas to the water with a pinch of salt. Cook, uncovered, until tender, 5 to 10 minutes, depending on size. Drain peas and set aside until ready to use.

HEAT the butter in a large skillet over medium heat. Add the onion and cook, stirring, until onion is lightly golden, 4 to 5 minutes. Add the prosciutto and cook about 1 minute. Add the wine and cook, stirring, until wine is reduced by half, 2 to 3 minutes. Add tomatoes, season with salt and pepper, and cook 2 to 3 minutes. Stir in the peas and turn the heat off under the skillet.

BRING a large pot of water to a boil. Add 1 tablespoon of salt and the bow ties. Cook, uncovered, over high heat until the pasta is tender but still firm to the bite. Drain the pasta and place in the skillet with the sauce. Mix everything quickly over low heat until the pasta and the sauce are well combined. Taste and adjust the seasoning, and serve at once.

Buckwheat Noodles with Swiss Chard

PIZZOCCHERI CON BIETE

PIZZOCCHERI ARE SHORT, *thick noodles, made with eggs and a combination of plain and buckwheat flours. They are a specialty of the Valtellina in northern Lombardy on the Swiss border.*

IN THE VALTELLINA *pizzoccheri are generally paired with a sauce of cabbage, potatoes, sage, and soft local cheese. However, there are variations to this classic combination. In this version the pizzoccheri noodles are boiled together with Swiss chard leaves, then tossed with melted butter, garlic, sage, and fontina cheese. A tasty, satisfying dish especially suited for cold winter days.*

SERVES 4

FOR THE PIZZOCCHERI
¾ cup buckwheat flour,
    mixed with ¾ cup unbleached
    all-purpose flour
3 large eggs
1–2 tablespoons milk

FOR THE SAUCE
1 pound Swiss chard
4 tablespoons unsalted butter

½ cup diced yellow onion
3 garlic cloves, minced
Salt and freshly ground black
    pepper to taste
¼ pound fontina cheese, cut into
    small pieces
⅓ cup freshly grated Parmigiano-
    Reggiano cheese

PREPARE the pizzoccheri pasta dough following instructions on pages 48–49, using the flours and proportions in this recipe.

continued

ROLL out the dough a bit thicker than for tagliatelle or fettuccine (see page 50). Let the sheets of dough dry a few minutes until they are no longer sticky, then cut the sheets into short noodles.

PREPARE THE SAUCE: Remove the Swiss chard leaves from the stems and reserve the stems for another use. Wash the leaves thoroughly in several changes of cold water. Cut the chard leaves into thin strips.

HEAT 3 tablespoons of the butter in a large skillet over medium-low heat. When the butter begins to foam, add the onion and garlic and cook, stirring, until onion is pale yellow and soft, 4 to 5 minutes. Turn the heat off under the skillet.

BRING a large pot of water to a boil. Add 1 tablespoon of salt, the pizzoccheri, and the Swiss chard. Cook, uncovered, over high heat until pizzoccheri are tender but still firm to the bite. Scoop out 1 cup of the pasta cooking water and reserve it. Drain the pasta and the Swiss chard, and place in the skillet with the remaining tablespoon of butter. Season with salt and generously with pepper. Add the fontina cheese and the Parmigiano, and mix well over low heat until the fontina begins to melt, less than 1 minute. If the pasta seems a bit dry, stir in some of the reserved pasta cooking water. Serve at once.

Mozzarella and Roasted Red Bell Pepper Salad, *page 17.*

ABOVE: Emma's Great Bean Soup (*top*), *page 35*. Rice and Spinach Soup (*bottom*), *page 45*.
RIGHT: Calzoni with Onions, Olives, and Tomatoes (*top*), *page 218*. Four Seasons Pizza
(*center*), *page 221*. Small Fried Calzoni (*left*), *page 219*.

LEFT: Swiss Chard Pansotti with Walnut Pesto, *page 70*.
BELOW: Ricotta-Carrot Gnocchetti with Peas and Pancetta (*top*), *page 126*.
Tortelli with Potatoes (*bottom*), *page 65*.

ABOVE: Penne with Baked Stuffed Tomatoes, *page 92.*
RIGHT: String Beans with Sun-dried Tomatoes (*top*), *page 205.*
Potato, Onion, and Tomato Gratin (*bottom*), *page 191.*

LEFT: Risotto with Scallops, Porcini Mushrooms, and Saffron, *page 103*.
ABOVE: Shells with Shrimp and Artichokes, *page 85*.

ABOVE: Veal Shanks with Fresh Tomatoes and Peas, *page 174.*
RIGHT: Pancetta-Wrapped Pork Roast with Roasted Potatoes, *page 166.*

LEFT: Roasted Rabbit with Artichokes and Peas, *page 161.*
BELOW: Swiss Chard Salad (*top*), *page 210.* Roasted Pepper Salad (*center*), *page 208.*
   Cauliflower and Green Olive Salad (*bottom*), *page 209.*

Deep-Fried Sweet Pastry Balls (*top*), *page 238*. Apple, Fig, and Date Roll (*center*), *page 231*. Baked Pears (*bottom*), *page 251*.

Shells with Shrimp and Artichokes

CONCHIGLIE CON GAMBERI E CARCIOFI

IN SOUTHERN ITALY *there are many dishes that combine pasta with vegetables and seafood. This is one of my very favorites because it is not only delicious but simple to prepare. Blanched broccoli or cauliflower florets can be used instead of artichokes.*

WHEN A SAUCE *is made only of oil or butter, and perhaps some vegetables, ham, or fish, Italian cooks add a bit of starchy pasta water to the skillet, which, in cooking down, gives body to the sauce and moistens the pasta.*

SERVES 4 TO 6

2 pounds baby artichokes
Juice of 1 lemon
Salt
¼–⅓ cup extra-virgin olive oil
1 pound medium-size shrimp, shelled and deveined
2 tablespoons diced sun-dried tomatoes, packed in oil

2 garlic cloves, minced
2 tablespoons plain dried bread crumbs
Chopped fresh red chile pepper or dried red pepper flakes to taste
1 pound shells or penne
2 tablespoons finely chopped flat-leaf Italian or regular parsley

REMOVE the green leaves of the artichokes by snapping them off at the base. Stop when the leaves closer to the base are pale yellow and the tips of the artichokes are light green. Slice off the green top and discard. Cut the stem off at the base and, with a small knife, trim off the remaining green part at the base of the artichokes. Place the artichokes in a bowl of cold water with the lemon juice to prevent discoloring.

BRING a medium-size saucepan of water to a boil over medium heat. Add 1 teaspoon of salt and the artichokes, and cook gently 7 to 8 minutes, depending on size, or until artichokes are tender. Prick the bottom of one artichoke with a thin knife. It should go in without resistance. Drain artichokes and cool under cold running water. Pat dry with paper towels and slice them into halves or small wedges. (The artichokes can be cooked a day or so ahead of time. Keep them tightly wrapped in the refrigerator until ready to use.)

continued

HEAT the oil in a large skillet over medium heat. Add the shrimp and cook until they are golden on both sides, 1 to 2 minutes. Add the sun-dried tomatoes and garlic, and stir once or twice. Add the bread crumbs and stir quickly until crumbs begin to color, less than 1 minute. Add artichokes, season with salt and chile pepper, stir a few times, and turn the heat off under the skillet.

MEANWHILE, bring a large pot of water to a boil. Add 1 tablespoon of salt and the pasta. Cook, uncovered, over high heat until the pasta is tender but still firm to the bite. Drain the pasta and add to the skillet with the sauce. Add about ⅓ cup of the pasta cooking water and the parsley, and mix everything quickly over low heat until the pasta and sauce are well combined. Taste and adjust the seasoning, and serve at once.

Pasta with Roasted Red Bell Peppers

PASTA CON PEPERONI ARROSTO

ONE OF THE *joys and fun of cooking is the freedom to be creative. When I come back from a trip to Italy, filled with the memories of great meals, I am so inspired that I go right to the kitchen of my restaurant and start cooking, trying to recapture the flavors, aromas, and colors of the dishes that impressed me. This dish is one of the results of these experimentations.*

SERVES 4 TO 6

1 large red bell pepper, 10–12
   ounces
4 medium tomatoes, 10–12 ounces
3–4 tablespoons extra-virgin
   olive oil
2 large whole garlic cloves, peeled
¼ cup finely minced yellow onion

1 cup chicken broth
1 tablespoon unsalted butter
Salt and freshly ground black
   pepper to taste
1 pound penne or shells

TO roast the pepper, place it over a gas burner with the flame turned high or run it under a broiler. When the skin of the pepper is charred on one side, turn it with a long fork to char on the other sides. The skin of the pepper should be charred and blistered all over. Place the pepper in a plastic bag and secure it tightly. Leave the pepper in the bag to cool and to soften. Peel the pepper and discard the seeds. (This step can be done quickly under cold running water.) Cut the pepper into ¼-inch thin strips and cut the strips into small dice. Set aside.

TO peel the tomatoes, bring a medium saucepan of water to a boil. Cut a cross at the root end of the tomatoes and drop them into the water. Cook until the skin begins to split, 1 to 2 minutes. Transfer the tomatoes to a bowl of iced water. Peel, seed, and dice the tomatoes. Set aside.

HEAT the oil in a large skillet over medium heat. Add the garlic and cook until garlic is golden brown on all sides. Discard the garlic. Add the onion to the skillet and cook gently until the onion is pale yellow and soft, 3 to 4 minutes. Add the tomatoes and the pepper. Reduce the heat a bit and cook, stirring occasionally, until peppers and tomatoes are soft, 6 to 8 minutes. Add the broth and cook until it is reduced approximately by half, 3 to 4 minutes. Add the butter and stir a few times. Season with salt and pepper, and turn the heat off under the skillet.

MEANWHILE, bring a large pot of water to a boil. Add 1 tablespoon of salt and the pasta. Cook, uncovered, over high heat until the pasta is tender but still firm to the bite. Drain the pasta and place in the skillet with the sauce. Mix everything quickly over low heat until the pasta and the sauce are well combined. Taste and adjust the seasoning, and serve.

Pasta with Broccoli Rabe

PASTA CON CIME DI RAPE

CIME DI RAPE, *broccoli rape, broccoletti, or rapini, as it is variously called in Italy, is a green leafy vegetable with a slightly bitter, nutty taste. It resembles broccoli in its early stages of growth. Broccoli rabe is used in many parts of southern Italy, especially in rustic, savory pasta dishes. What is special about this recipe is that the vegetables and the pasta are boiled together, then quickly tossed with the hot oil-garlic-anchovy sauce.*

BROCCOLI RABE IS *available in this country all year round, with its peak from late fall to early spring. Broccoli or cauliflower, previously blanched, can be substituted.*

SERVES 4 TO 6

2 bunches broccoli rabe, about 1½ pounds (see Note)
Salt
1 pound orecchiette or shells
¼–⅓ cup extra-virgin olive oil
3 garlic cloves, minced
4 anchovy fillets, chopped

Chopped fresh red chile pepper or dried red pepper flakes to taste
2 tablespoons plain dried bread crumbs
2 tablespoons chopped fresh flat-leaf Italian parsley or regular parsley

WITH a paring knife, remove the stem ends of the broccoli rabe and peel the stalks. Discard any stalks that are too large and woody, and any leaves that are wilted. Wash the broccoli rabe well under cold running water.

BRING a large pot of water to a boil. Add 1 tablespoon of salt, the pasta, and the broccoli rabe. Cook, uncovered, over high heat until the pasta is tender but still firm to the bite.

WHILE the pasta is cooking, heat the oil in a large skillet over medium heat. Add the garlic, anchovies, and chile pepper, and stir until the garlic begins to color, less than a minute. Add the bread crumbs and stir quickly once or twice. (If the skillet is very hot, the bread crumbs will change color almost immediately.)

DRAIN the pasta and place it in the skillet. Stir in the parsley and season with salt. Mix everything quickly over low heat until the pasta and sauce are well combined. Taste and adjust the seasoning, and serve at once.

Note: This is a humble preparation, which employs basic everyday ingredients. It is also one of the healthiest, quickest, and tastiest pasta dishes to prepare. If you like chile pepper, you can use it with abandon. If you cannot find broccoli rabe in the market and don't feel like substituting cauliflower or broccoli, simply omit the vegetable. You will then have a very close version of the classic *aglio e olio* (garlic and oil) sauce, beloved of every Roman.

Spaghettini with Fresh and Sun-dried Tomatoes and Goat Cheese

SPAGHETTINI CON POMODORI E CAPRINO

EVERY AREA OF *Italy, and almost every Italian, has its own version of tomato sauce. A good tomato sauce can be made with olive oil or butter, fresh, ripe tomatoes or good canned plum tomatoes, which are a staple in a well-stocked Italian kitchen. You can also add vegetables or garlic or sun-dried tomatoes, or simply a handful of fresh herbs. The sauce is generally cooked quickly so that it retains its fresh, clear tomato taste. This is a wonderful-tasting uncomplicated sauce to be used on the spur of the moment.*

SERVES 4 TO 6

¼ cup extra-virgin olive oil

2 medium, ripe plum tomatoes, about 5–6 ounces, seeded and diced

2 garlic cloves, minced

1–2 tablespoons diced sun-dried tomatoes, packed in oil

3 cups canned imported Italian plum tomatoes, with their juice, put through a food mill to remove the seeds

Salt and freshly ground black pepper to taste

8–10 fresh basil leaves, shredded, or 2 tablespoons chopped fresh flat-leaf Italian parsley or regular parsley

1 pound spaghettini (thin spaghetti)

2–3 ounces goat cheese, crumbled

HEAT the oil in a large skillet over medium heat. Add the diced fresh tomatoes and cook, stirring, 1 to 2 minutes. Add the garlic and sun-dried tomatoes, and cook less than 1 minute. Add the canned tomatoes and season with salt and pepper. Cook 5 to 6 minutes, stirring the sauce a few times. Stir the basil or parsley into the sauce during the last minute of cooking.

MEANWHILE, bring a large pot of water to a boil. Add 1 tablespoon of salt and the spaghettini. Cook, uncovered, over high heat until the pasta is tender but still firm to the bite.

DRAIN the pasta and add to the skillet with the sauce. Mix everything quickly over low heat until the pasta and sauce are well combined. Taste and adjust the seasoning. Place the pasta into individual pasta bowls, sprinkle with goat cheese, and serve at once.

Spaghetti with Olive Paste, Sun-dried Tomatoes, and Capers

SPAGHETTI CON PESTO DI OLIVE

A UNIQUE ITALIAN *way of snacking at midnight is to whip up a* spaghettata, *a plate of spaghetti cooked impromptu late at night, generally when friends gather together at someone's house after going to the movies or the theater. The rule for a* spaghettata *is that the sauce must be prepared in the same time it takes the spaghetti to cook. So the sauce must be immensely appetizing and quick to assemble. This is one of my favorites.*

WHILE THE SPAGHETTI *cooks, garlic is sautéed lightly in oil with olive paste, sun-dried tomatoes, and capers. Then the pasta is tossed into the sauce and seasoned generously with salt and plenty of black pepper. What a great midnight snack!*

SERVES 4 TO 6

⅓ cup extra-virgin olive oil
3 garlic cloves, minced
1 tablespoon olive paste (see Note)
1 tablespoon chopped sun-dried
    tomatoes, packed in oil
1 tablespoon capers, rinsed

Salt
1 pound spaghetti
Freshly ground black pepper
1–2 tablespoons chopped fresh flat-
    leaf Italian parsley or regular
    parsley

HEAT the oil in a large skillet over medium heat. Add the garlic and stir once or twice. Add the olive paste, sun-dried tomatoes, and capers, and stir briefly. Turn the heat off under the skillet or the garlic will burn.

MEANWHILE, bring a large pot of water to a boil. Add 1 tablespoon of salt and the spaghetti. Cook, uncovered, over high heat until the pasta is tender but still firm to the bite. Drain the pasta and place it in the skillet with the sauce. Season with salt and several grindings of pepper, and add the parsley. Mix everything quickly over low heat until the pasta and the sauce are well combined. Taste and adjust the seasoning, and serve at once.

Note: I always keep a small jar of Italian olive paste in my refrigerator, for, with the addition of some garlic, I can whip up a delicious pasta dish on the spur of the moment. In selecting olive paste, look for a brand imported from Italy, such as Ardoino. The thick olive paste is mixed with extra-virgin olive oil. As you use the paste, add just enough fresh oil to the jar to cover the paste, and keep it tightly sealed in the refrigerator.

Penne with Baked Stuffed Tomatoes

PENNE CON POMODORI AL FORNO

THERE ARE MANY *versions of baked stuffed tomatoes in Italy, mostly served to accompany meat or fish. My mother used to prepare baked tomatoes that were so filling and tasty that often they were all I wanted to eat. I even used to put them between two slices of bread. One day I decided to dice the tomatoes, sauté them quickly in a bit of oil, and toss them with some pasta. What a beautiful dish, especially when fresh, ripe tomatoes are at their peak.*

SERVES 4 TO 6

FOR THE STUFFED TOMATOES

6 large, firm, ripe tomatoes, halved and seeded

3 garlic cloves, minced

¼ cup finely chopped flat-leaf Italian or regular parsley

2 tablespoons capers, drained and rinsed

3–4 flat anchovy fillets, packed in oil, finely minced

2 tablespoons diced sun-dried tomatoes, packed in oil

⅓ cup plain dried bread crumbs

⅓ cup freshly grated Parmigiano-Reggiano cheese

¼–⅓ cup extra-virgin olive oil

Salt and freshly ground black pepper to taste

Additional oil for the baking dish

FOR THE PASTA

1 pound penne rigate (grooved penne)

2 tablespoons extra-virgin olive oil

1 tablespoon chopped fresh flat-leaf Italian or regular parsley

PREHEAT the oven to 350°. Place tomatoes, cut side down, on paper towels to drain off excess juice.

IN a small bowl combine garlic, parsley, capers, anchovies, sun-dried tomatoes, bread crumbs, and cheese with olive oil. Season with salt and pepper.

DRIZZLE a little additional oil in the bottom of a baking dish. Season the tomato cavities lightly with salt, and place some of the filling into the tomato cavities. Place tomatoes in the baking dish and bake until the tops are lightly browned and the tomatoes are soft and a bit shriveled, about 20 minutes. Remove from oven and set aside until ready to use. (The tomatoes can be baked a day ahead.

Just put the tomatoes and all the juice in a bowl, wrap in plastic wrap, and refrigerate until needed.)

BRING a large pot of water to a boil. Add 1 tablespoon of salt and the penne. Cook, uncovered, over high heat until the pasta is tender but still firm to the bite.

WHILE the pasta is cooking, cut the tomatoes into small pieces. Heat the oil in a large skillet and add the cut-up tomatoes, with all their juice, and stir just long enough to heat them through. Drain the pasta and place it in the skillet. Stir in the parsley, and season lightly with salt and a bit of pepper. Mix everything quickly over low heat until the pasta and sauce are well combined. Serve at once.

Pennette with Speck, Peas, and Cream

PENNETTE CON SPECK, PISELLI, E PANNA

SPECK, A SMOKED *ham from the Alto Adige, is eaten all over Italy. I love its smoky taste, especially when paired with fresh sweet peas and a touch of cream. This is a basic quick pasta dish that lends itself to all sorts of creative variations. Try asparagus or young, small zucchini instead of peas, or all three together. For a light-tasting dish, use just enough cream to lend a smooth texture.*

SERVES 4 TO 6

1 cup shelled fresh peas or frozen
    peas, thawed
Salt
2 tablespoons unsalted butter
1–2 tablespoons olive oil
½ cup minced yellow onion

¼ pound speck (see Note, page
    15) or prosciutto, cut into
    ⅛-inch slices and diced
½ cup chicken broth (see page 33)
½ cup heavy cream
1 pound pennette (small penne)
½ cup freshly grated Parmigiano-
    Reggiano cheese

IF using fresh peas, bring a small saucepan of water to a boil over medium heat. Add the peas to the boiling water with a pinch of salt. Cook, uncovered, until tender, 5 to 10 minutes, depending on size. Drain and set aside.

continued

HEAT the butter and oil in a large skillet over medium heat. When the butter begins to foam, add the onion and cook, stirring, until the onion is lightly golden, 4 to 5 minutes. Add the speck and cook about 1 minute. Add the broth and the cream, season with salt, and cook until the sauce has a medium-thick consistency, 2 to 3 minutes. Add the peas, stir once or twice, and turn the heat off under the skillet.

MEANWHILE, bring a large pot of water to a boil. Add 1 tablespoon of salt and the pennette. Cook, uncovered, over high heat until the pasta is tender but still firm to the bite. Drain the pasta and place it in the skillet with the sauce. Add Parmigiano, and mix everything quickly over low heat until the pasta and the sauce are well combined. If pasta looks dry, stir in a bit more broth or cream. Serve with additional Parmigiano, if desired.

Rigatoni with Sausage and Porcini Mushrooms

RIGATONI AL RAGÙ DI SALSICCIA E PORCINI

THIS TYPICAL, EASY *ragù, which is made in many northern Italian homes, pairs tasty sausage and flavorful porcini mushrooms.*

SOMETIMES BEEF, VEAL, *or pork are used instead of sausage, and at other times pancetta or prosciutto lends its special texture and taste. Carrots and celery can add color and crunch to the flavorful onion base. And a small amount of milk or cream enriches the overall flavor of the sauce. All these everyday ingredients work well together and complement each other!*

THIS SAUCE IS *excellent tossed with penne and shells, and served on homemade tagliatelle or fettuccine.*

SERVES 4 TO 6

1 ounce dried porcini mushrooms,
soaked in 2 cups lukewarm
water for 20 minutes
1 tablespoon unsalted butter
2 tablespoons olive oil
⅓ cup minced yellow onion
½ pound mild Italian sausage,
casing removed and finely
chopped

3 cups canned imported Italian
plum tomatoes, with their
juice, put through a food mill
to remove the seeds
½ cup milk
Salt and freshly ground black
pepper to taste
1 pound rigatoni
⅓ cup freshly grated Parmigiano-
Reggiano cheese

DRAIN the porcini mushrooms and reserve the soaking water. Rinse the mushrooms well under cold running water and chop them roughly. Line a strainer with two paper towels and strain the liquid into a bowl to get rid of the sandy deposits. Set aside.

HEAT the butter and oil in a medium-size saucepan over medium heat. When the butter begins to foam, add the onion and cook, stirring, until the onion is lightly golden, 4 to 5 minutes. Raise the heat to high and add the sausage. Stir with a large spoon to break up the sausage. When sausage is lightly colored, add the mushrooms and stir for a minute or two. Add 1 cup of the reserved porcini soaking water, the tomatoes, and the milk. Season with salt and pepper. Bring the sauce to a boil, then reduce the heat to low and simmer, uncovered, 25 to 30 minutes.

MEANWHILE, bring a large pot of water to a boil. Add 1 tablespoon of salt and the rigatoni. Cook, uncovered, over high heat until the pasta is tender but still firm to the bite. Drain the pasta and place in a large, heated serving bowl. Add half of the sauce and the Parmigiano, and mix well. Add more sauce if needed. Taste and adjust the seasoning, and serve.

RISOTTO WITH ARTICHOKES, ASPARAGUS, AND PEAS

RISOTTO WITH ZUCCHINI AND SHRIMP

RISOTTO WITH SEA BASS

RISOTTO WITH SCALLOPS, PORCINI MUSHROOMS, AND SAFFRON

RISOTTO WITH CLAMS

RODRIGO'S SEAFOOD RISOTTO

RISOTTO WITH PROSCIUTTO AND FRESH TOMATOES

RISOTTO WITH SAUSAGES

BARLEY RISOTTO

BASIC POTATO GNOCCHI

POTATO GNOCCHI WITH CABBAGE AND FONTINA

POTATO GNOCCHI WITH ARUGULA

POTATO GNOCCHI WITH PORCINI MUSHROOMS, SAFFRON,
AND CREAM

POTATO GNOCCHI WITH EGGPLANT, MUSHROOMS,
AND ZUCCHINI

BASIC RICOTTA-PARMIGIANO GNOCCHI

RICOTTA-PARMIGIANO GNOCCHI WITH TOMATO AND CREAM

RICOTTA-PARMIGIANO GNOCCHI WITH PROSCIUTTO,
PEAS, AND CREAM

BASIC SPINACH-RICOTTA GNOCCHI

SPINACH-RICOTTA GNOCCHI WITH PORCINI MUSHROOMS
AND TOMATOES

SPINACH-RICOTTA GNOCCHI WITH THREE-MEAT RAGÙ

RICOTTA-CARROT GNOCCHETTI WITH PEAS AND PANCETTA

SPINACH, RICOTTA, AND MASCARPONE DUMPLINGS

BASIC POLENTA

Risotto, Gnocchi, and Polenta

NOW THAT MOST Americans know, enjoy, and appreciate pasta, they are beginning to discover some of the other staples of Italian first courses: risotto, gnocchi, and polenta.

RISOTTO is a northern Italian dish in which the rice is cooked gently with small, regular additions of broth, and stirred constantly. Shellfish, vegetables, cheeses, or herbs are added at different stages of cooking, giving the risotto its own unique identity.

I LOVE RISOTTO. I love the ritual of its cooking. The constant stirring, the small additions of aromatic broth, and the slow transformation of the rice, which turns large and plump as it cooks. It is wonderful to see raw materials change before your eyes to become a most pleasing, inviting dish. Even though in Italy risotto is traditionally a first course in a meal, for an everyday family dinner, risotto can become *the* meal, followed by a nice salad and some fruit or cheese.

IMAGINE TAKING COOKED potatoes, mixing them with flour into a basic dough, and turning them into delicious little dumplings. Legions of people in Italy grew up with gnocchi. And there are legions of Italian women who fed large families with this simple potato dish. While gnocchi was once considered a "poor man's dish," it isn't anymore. Today, gnocchi have been "rediscovered" by Italians who crave the good, honest food their mothers or grandmothers used to make.

POTATO GNOCCHI ARE the most popular variety, but they can also be made with ricotta, spinach, and bread, to mention a few variations. During a recent visit to Italy, I enjoyed gnocchi that were golden with saffron, orange with carrots, and green with spinach. Very special.

EVEN THOUGH technically polenta is not a first course, I have included it here because originally it was served at meals instead of pasta, rice, and bread. It was basic food, a staple in most northern Italian kitchens. A large bowl of polenta was often all that a peasant or laborer could afford to eat.

I CANNOT PREPARE this dish without seeing my mother at the stove, stirring the polenta with a long, wooden spoon. In our home polenta was made in the traditional large copper pot, called a *paiolo*, which had belonged to my grandmother. My mother would make lots of it, so that later she could bake it or fry it. She would cook the polenta with water and salt. At that time Parmigiano was too expensive, as was butter. Occasionally she would cook the polenta in milk, which gave it a creamy consistency.

POLENTA HAS NOW been updated and turned into a fashionable dish. I still like it prepared the old-fashioned way, using a mixture of coarsely ground cornmeal and fine cornmeal, which gives the polenta a nice texture. During the last minutes of cooking, I stir in freshly grated Parmigiano-Reggiano and sweet butter, which makes it nice and creamy. And, just like my mother, I make a large batch so that later I can fry, bake, and grill it, or layer it with a meat or vegetable sauce.

Risotto with Artichokes, Asparagus, and Peas

RISOTTO VERDE

I LOVE VEGETABLE *risottos. They are light and delicious, and have tremendous eye appeal. This recipe uses three "green" vegetables: artichokes, asparagus, and peas, which give the risotto a striking color and delicate taste.*

SERVES 4 TO 6

½ pound baby artichokes, cleaned, cooked, and cut into wedges as instructed on page 16
½ pound asparagus tips, appoximately 2¼ pounds asparagus
½ cup fresh shelled green peas or 1 cup frozen small peas, thawed
6 cups homemade chicken broth (see page 33) or 3 cups canned chicken broth and 3 cups water

4 tablespoons unsalted butter
½ cup minced yellow onion
2 cups imported Italian Arborio rice
1 cup dry white wine
Salt to taste
¼ cup freshly grated Parmigiano-Reggiano cheese

PREPARE the artichokes and set aside.

BRING a small saucepan with salted water to a boil. Add the asparagus tips and cook until tender but still firm to the bite, 1 to 2 minutes, depending on size. Drain asparagus and set aside.

IF using fresh peas, cook them in another small saucepan with salted boiling water until tender but still firm to the bite, about 5 to 10 minutes, depending on size. Drain peas and set aside. (Asparagus and peas can be cooked several hours ahead.)

HEAT the broth in a medium-size saucepan and keep warm over low heat.

HEAT 3 tablespoons of the butter in a large skillet over medium heat. When the butter foams, add the onion and cook, stirring, until onion begins to color, 3 to 4 minutes. Add the rice and stir until it is well coated with the butter and onion, about 1 minute. Add the wine and stir until it is almost all reduced. Add about ½ cup of hot broth, or just enough to barely cover the rice. Cook, stirring, until the broth has been absorbed almost completely. Continue cooking and stirring the rice in this manner, adding broth ½ cup at a time, for about 15 minutes. At this point the rice should be tender but still a bit firm to the bite.

STIR the artichokes, asparagus, and peas into the rice, and season lightly with salt. Add the remaining butter and the Parmigiano. Mix quickly for 1 to 2 minutes until the butter and the cheese are melted and the rice has a moist, creamy consistency. Taste and adjust the seasoning, and serve at once.

Risotto with Zucchini and Shrimp

RISOTTO CON ZUCCHINE E GAMBERI

EVEN THOUGH RISOTTO *can be made with a variety of ingredients, to me, risotto with seafood is a marriage made in heaven. This is a lovely, delicious dish that uses dry vermouth instead of wine, and made, as all seafood risottos should be, with fish broth.*

SERVES 4 TO 6

FOR THE ZUCCHINI AND SHRIMP

6 tablespoons extra-virgin olive oil
3 medium zucchini, about ¾ pound, washed and thinly sliced
1 pound medium-size shrimp, shelled and deveined
1 garlic clove, minced
1 cup dry white vermouth

FOR THE RISOTTO

1 medium leek
6 cups homemade fish broth (see page 135) or chicken broth (see page 33) or 3 cups canned chicken broth and 3 cups water
3 tablespoons unsalted butter
2 cups imported Italian Arborio rice
1–2 tablespoons chopped fresh flat-leaf Italian parsley or regular parsley
Salt to taste

Keep in mind that both homemade broth and canned broth are already seasoned. At the end of cooking, taste the rice and, if necessary, adjust the seasoning accordingly.

This dish can become superlative if the proper ingredients are used. Cooking the rice in fish broth instead of chicken broth will impart a unique flavor to the risotto.

In Italy risotto with seafood is generally prepared and served without adding cheese so as to preserve the flavor and aroma of the fish.

PREPARE THE ZUCCHINI AND SHRIMP: Heat 3 tablespoons of the oil in a medium-size skillet over medium-high heat. Add the zucchini, without crowding the skillet, and cook until they are lightly golden. Remove zucchini with a slotted spoon and transfer to a large platter lined with paper towels. Pat dry with more paper towels and set aside until ready to use. (Zucchini can be prepared several hours ahead.)

DISCARD the leftover oil and wipe the skillet clean with paper towels. Put the skillet back on medium-high heat with the remaining 3 tablespoons of oil. When the oil is hot, add the shrimp and cook, stirring, until they are lightly golden, 2 to 3 minutes. Discard some of the oil in the skillet, add the garlic, and sauté quickly a few times. (Keep in mind that the pan is very hot and the garlic will turn golden in no time at all.) Add ½ cup of the dry vermouth and cook, stirring, until it is reduced by half, 2 to 3 minutes. Turn the heat off under the skillet and set aside. (This step can be prepared an hour or two ahead.)

PREPARE THE RISOTTO: Cut off the root end of the leek and remove one third of the green stalk. Cut leek in half lengthwise and wash thoroughly under cold running water to remove all the grit clinging to the leaves. Chop the leek very fine.

HEAT the broth in a medium-size saucepan and keep warm over low heat.

HEAT the butter in a large skillet over medium heat. When the butter foams, add the leek and cook, stirring, until it is pale yellow and soft, 7 to 8 minutes. Add the rice and stir until it is well coated with the butter and the onion, about 1 minute. Stir in the remaining vermouth and cook until it is all reduced, about 2 minutes. Add ½ cup of the hot broth, or just enough to barely cover the rice. Cook, stirring, until the broth has been absorbed almost completely. Add more broth and continue cooking and stirring the rice in this manner, adding broth ½ cup at a time, for 15 to 16 minutes.

ADD the shrimp and all its juices to the risotto, and cook 1 to 2 minutes longer. Add the parsley and the zucchini, and mix quickly. Taste and adjust the seasonings, and serve at once.

Risotto with Sea Bass

RISOTTO CON BRANZINO

ONE OF MY *very favorite dishes in the world is risotto. This unique northern Italian specialty can be prepared in hundreds of ways, using basically the same cooking technique. I love fish and shellfish risottos for their lightness and delicate taste.*

SERVES 4 TO 6

FOR THE SEA BASS

2–3 tablespoons extra-virgin
    olive oil
1 pound fresh sea bass fillets, cut
    into ½-inch pieces
Salt to taste
1 garlic clove, finely minced
2 tablespoons chopped fresh flat-
    leaf Italian parsley or regular
    parsley
1 cup dry white wine

FOR THE RISOTTO

6 cups homemade fish broth (see
    page 135) or chicken broth,
    (see page 33) or 3 cups
    canned chicken broth and
    3 cups water
3 tablespoons unsalted butter
½ cup minced yellow onion
2 cups imported Italian
    Arborio rice
1 cup dry white wine
Salt to taste

PREPARE THE SEA BASS: Heat the oil in a large skillet over high heat. Add the fish and cook, stirring, until the pieces are lightly golden, 1 to 2 minutes. Add the garlic and parsley, and stir once or twice. Add the wine and cook, stirring, until wine is almost all reduced. Turn the heat off under the skillet.

PREPARE THE RISOTTO: Heat the broth in a medium-size saucepan and keep warm over low heat.

MELT the butter in a large skillet over medium heat. When the butter foams, add the onion and cook, stirring, until the onion begins to color, 3 to 4 minutes. Stir in the rice and cook until it is well coated with the butter and the onion, about 1 minute. Add the wine and stir until it is almost all reduced. Add about ½ cup of hot broth, or just enough to barely cover the rice. Cook, stirring, until the broth has been absorbed almost completely. Continue cooking and stirring the rice in this manner, adding the broth ½ cup at a time, for about 15 minutes. At this point the rice should be tender but still firm to the bite.

ADD the sea bass and all its juices to the risotto, and mix quickly for 1 to 2 minutes. Taste and adjust the seasoning, and serve at once.

Risotto with Scallops, Porcini Mushrooms, and Saffron

RISOTTO MARE E MONTI

IN MILANO THERE is a restaurant, Casa Fontana, that serves twenty-five different kinds of risotto. The one I enjoyed the most was made with scallops, fresh porcini mushrooms, and saffron. It came to the table looking like a large plate of golden nuggets, almost orange in color, steaming and inviting.

SERVES 4 TO 6

FOR THE PORCINI-SCALLOP SAUCE
1 ounce dried porcini mushrooms, soaked in 2 cups lukewarm water for 20 minutes
2–3 tablespoons unsalted butter
1 pound fresh sea scallops, the smallest you can find
1 large garlic clove, minced
Salt to taste

FOR THE RISOTTO
6 cups homemade fish broth (see page 135) or chicken broth (see page 33) or 3 cups canned chicken broth and 3 cups water

4 tablespoons unsalted butter
½ medium yellow onion, peeled and minced
2 cups imported Italian Arborio rice
1 cup dry white wine
¼ cup freshly grated Parmigiano-Reggiano cheese
2 tablespoons chopped fresh flat-leaf Italian parsley or regular parsley

continued

PREPARE THE PORCINI-SCALLOP SAUCE: Drain the porcini mushrooms and reserve the soaking water. Rinse mushrooms well under cold running water and chop them roughly. Line a strainer with two paper towels and strain the mushroom water into a bowl to get rid of the sandy deposits. Set aside.

HEAT the butter in a medium-size skillet over medium heat. When the butter foams, add the scallops and cook, stirring, until they are lightly golden, 1 to 2 minutes. Add the garlic and stir once or twice. Add the porcini and 1 cup of the reserved mushroom liquid and the saffron. Season with salt and cook, stirring a few times, until liquid is reduced approximately by half. Turn the heat off under the skillet. (This step can be prepared an hour or two ahead.)

PREPARE THE RISOTTO: Heat the broth in a medium-size saucepan and keep warm over low heat.

MELT the butter in a large skillet over medium heat. When the butter foams, add the onion and cook, stirring, until the onion begins to color, 3 to 4 minutes. Add the rice and cook until it is well coated with the butter and onion, about 1 minute. Add the wine and stir until it is almost all reduced. Add about ½ cup of hot broth, or just enough to barely cover the rice. Cook, stirring, until the broth has been absorbed almost completely. Continue cooking and stirring the rice in this manner, adding the broth ½ cup at a time, for about 15 minutes. At this point the rice should be tender but still firm to the bite.

ADD the porcini-scallop mixture, the Parmigiano, and the parsley to the rice. Mix quickly for 1 to 2 minutes until the cheese is melted and gives the rice a moist, creamy consistency. Taste and adjust the seasoning, and serve at once.

Risotto with Clams

RISOTTO CON VONGOLE

THIS RISOTTO HAS *a wonderfully rich concentrated clam flavor. To simplify, prepare the clams and their sauce a few hours in advance of serving.*

IF YOU USE *the homemade fish or chicken broth, prepare it several days beforehand and keep it refrigerated or frozen. All the other ingredients for the risotto can also be prepared somewhat in advance and kept on a tray next to the stove. So, at the last moment you will be able to give the risotto your undivided attention. Believe me, it's worth it!*

SERVES 4 TO 6

FOR THE CLAMS

3 pounds clams, the smallest you can find, thoroughly washed in several changes of water

2 tablespoons extra-virgin olive oil

2 garlic cloves, minced

2 tablespoons chopped fresh flat-leaf Italian parsley or regular parsley

Chopped fresh red chile pepper or dried red pepper flakes to taste

1 cup canned imported Italian plum tomatoes, with their juice, put through a food mill to remove the seeds

Salt to taste

FOR THE RISOTTO

5–6 cups homemade fish broth (see page 135) or chicken broth (see page 33) or 3 cups canned chicken broth and 3 cups water

¼ cup extra-virgin olive oil

½ cup minced yellow onion

2 cups imported Italian Arborio rice

1 cup dry white wine

1 tablespoon chopped fresh flat-leaf Italian parsley or regular parsley

Salt to taste

PREPARE THE CLAMS: Heat the oil in a medium-size sauté pan over medium heat. Add the garlic, parsley, and chile pepper. Cook, stirring, until the garlic begins to color, less than 1 minute. Add the tomatoes and bring to a boil. Reduce the heat to low and simmer, uncovered, 2 to 3 minutes. Season with salt.

continued

ADD the clams, cover the pan, and cook over medium heat until the clams open. Transfer them to a bowl as they open. Detach the clam meat from the shells and place it in a small bowl while you reduce the sauce. (At this point there will be considerably more sauce in the pan, since the clams will have released all their liquid.)

RAISE the heat under the pan and cook the sauce until it is reduced to about 1 cup. Stir the clam meat back into the sauce. Turn the heat off and set aside until ready to use.

PREPARE THE RISOTTO: Heat the fish broth in a medium-size saucepan and keep warm over low heat.

HEAT the oil in a large skillet over medium heat. Add the onion and cook, stirring, until the onion begins to color, 3 to 4 minutes. Add the rice and stir until it is well coated with the oil and the onion, about 1 minute. Add the wine, cook and stir until wine is almost all reduced. Add about ½ cup of the hot broth, or just enough to barely cover the rice. Cook, stirring, until the broth has been absorbed almost completely. Add more broth and continue cooking and stirring the rice in this manner, adding broth ½ cup at a time, for 14 to 15 minutes.

WHEN the broth is completely reduced and the rice looks somewhat dry, add the clams with all their sauce and the parsley to the rice, and stir quickly for a minute or two. Taste and adjust the seasoning, and serve at once.

Rodrigo's Seafood Risotto

IL RISOTTO AL FRUTTI DI MARE DI RODRIGO

RODRIGO IS A Bolognese restaurant that for the last thirty years has consistently served some of the finest pasta and risottos in Bologna. Every time I eat at Rodrigo, I order the great seafood risotto, which incorporates all kinds of fresh shellfish from the nearby Adriatic. At my restaurant in Sacramento, this risotto is always offered as a first course. When I make it for my family on Sunday, I serve it as a complete meal, followed by a large mixed green salad and some good cheese.

SERVES 4 TO 6

FOR THE SHELLFISH

4 tablespoons extra-virgin olive oil
1 cup dry white wine
½ cup water
2 pounds clams, the smallest you
    can find, thoroughly washed in
    several changes of water
½ pound fresh sea scallops, the
    smallest you can find, cut into
    ½-inch pieces
½ pound medium-size shrimp,
    peeled and cut into ½-inch
    pieces
1 garlic clove, minced
Chopped fresh red chile pepper or
    dried red pepper flakes to taste
Salt to taste

FOR THE RISOTTO

6 cups homemade fish broth (see
    page 135) or chicken broth
    (see page 33) or 3 cups
    canned chicken broth and
    3 cups water
3 tablespoons unsalted butter
½ cup minced yellow onion
2 cups imported Italian
    Arborio rice
1 cup dry white wine
1–2 tablespoons chopped fresh
    flat-leaf Italian parsley or
    regular parsley

PREPARE THE SHELLFISH: Heat 1 tablespoon of the oil in a large skillet over high heat. Add ½ cup of the wine and the water, and bring to a boil. Add the clams, cover the pan, and cook over medium heat until the clams open. Transfer clams to a bowl as they open. Detach the clam meat from the shells and place it in a small bowl. Line a strainer with two paper towels and strain the cooking liquid into another bowl to remove any sandy deposits. Set aside until ready to use.

WIPE the skillet clean with paper towels, add the remaining 3 tablespoons of oil, and place skillet on high heat. When the oil is hot, add the scallops and shrimp and cook, stirring, until shellfish is lightly golden, 1 to 2 minutes. Add the garlic and chile pepper, and season with salt. Stir quickly a few times. Add the remaining ½ cup wine. Cook and stir until wine is almost all reduced. Stir in the clams and turn the heat off under the skillet.

PREPARE THE RISOTTO: Heat the broth in a medium-size saucepan and keep warm over low heat.

MELT the butter in a large skillet over medium heat. When the butter foams, add the onion and cook, stirring, until the onion begins to color, 3 to 4 minutes. Add the rice and cook until it is well coated with the butter and the onion, about 1 minute. Add the wine and the reserved clam cooking liquid. Cook and stir until liquid is almost all reduced.

ADD about ½ cup of hot broth, or just enough to barely cover the rice. Cook and stir until the broth has been absorbed almost completely. Continue cooking and stirring the rice in this manner, adding broth ½ cup at a time, for about 15 minutes. At this point the rice should be tender but still firm to the bite.

ADD the clam-scallop mixture and all of its juices to the risotto. Stir in the parsley and mix quickly for a minute or two. Taste and adjust the seasoning, and serve at once.

Risotto with Prosciutto and Fresh Tomatoes

RISOTTO CON PROSCIUTTO E POMODORI

EVERY TIME I *make a risotto, I feel like a painter in front of a blank canvas. The possibilities are endless and they are limited only by the imagination. This recipe takes advantage of plump, ripe summer tomatoes. The tomatoes can be blanched in boiling water and peeled, or simply diced and tossed into the risotto during the last 5 minutes. The prosciutto, added to the onion at the beginning, lends rich flavor to this risotto.*

SERVES 4 TO 6

6 cups homemade chicken broth
   (see page 33) or 3 cups
   canned chicken broth and
   3 cups water
4 tablespoons unsalted butter
½ cup minced yellow onion
¼ pound prosciutto, cut into
   ⅛-inch slices and diced
2 cups imported Italian
   Arborio rice

1 cup dry white wine
1 pound ripe but firm plum
   tomatoes, seeded and diced
⅓ cup freshly grated Parmigiano-
   Reggiano cheese
2 tablespoons chopped fresh flat-
   leaf Italian parsley or 8–10
   fresh basil leaves, shredded
Salt to taste

HEAT the broth in a medium-size saucepan and keep warm over low heat.

MELT 3 tablespoons of the butter in a large skillet over medium heat. When the butter foams, add the onion and cook, stirring, until the onion begins to color, 3 to 4 minutes. Add the prosciutto and stir for a minute or two. Add the rice and cook until it is well coated with the butter and onion. Add the wine, cook and stir until it is almost all reduced.

ADD about ½ cup of hot broth, or just enough to barely cover the rice. Cook and stir until the broth has been absorbed almost completely. Continue cooking and stirring the rice, adding the broth ½ cup at a time, for 10 to 12 minutes.

ADD the tomatoes and cook 4 to 5 minutes longer. Stir in the remaining butter, the Parmigiano, and the parsley or basil. Mix quickly for a minute or so until the rice has a moist, creamy consistency. Taste and adjust the seasoning, and serve at once.

Risotto with Sausages

RISOTTO CON SALSICCE ALLA MANTOVANA

THERE WAS A *time when Italians made their own sausage, bread, prosciutto, salame, and wine, especially in rural areas. I remember my grandfather would spend many hours down in the cellar making wine. My brother, sister, and I would sneak down and sip the frothy liquid, until one day we were caught and the cellar became off-limits for us.*

TODAY, LIFESTYLES HAVE *changed considerably and most of the time we buy what we need rather than make it ourselves.*

THIS RISOTTO USES *good-quality Italian sausage, Arborio rice, robust red wine, and good Parmigiano-Reggiano cheese for a delicious, filling main dish. Check Italian markets and specialty food stores for high-quality sausage.*

SERVES 4 TO 6

6 cups homemade chicken broth
    (see page 33) or 3 cups canned
    chicken broth and 3 cups water
4 tablespoons unsalted butter
½ cup minced yellow onion
½ pound mild Italian sausage,
    casings removed and finely
    chopped
2 cups imported Italian
    Arborio rice

1 cup full-bodied red wine, such as
    Barbera or Zinfandel
2 tablespoons tomato paste, diluted
    in 1 cup chicken broth
¼ cup freshly grated Parmigiano-
    Reggiano cheese
2 tablespoons chopped fresh flat-
    leaf Italian parsley or regular
    parsley
Salt and freshly ground black
    pepper to taste

HEAT the broth in a medium-size saucepan and keep warm over low heat.

HEAT 3 tablespoons of the butter in a large skillet over medium heat. When the butter foams, add the onion and cook, stirring, until onion begins to color, 3 to 4 minutes. Add the sausage and stir with a large spoon to break up the meat. When the sausage loses its raw color, add the rice. Cook and stir until rice is well coated with the butter, onion, and sausage, about 1 minute. Add the wine.

When the wine is almost all reduced, add the diluted tomato paste. Cook, stirring, until the tomato paste and broth have been absorbed.

ADD about ½ cup of hot broth, or just enough to barely cover the rice. Cook, stirring, until the broth has been absorbed almost completely. Continue cooking and stirring the rice in this manner, adding ½ cup of broth at a time, for about 15 minutes. At this point the rice should be tender but still firm to the bite.

ADD the remaining butter, the Parmigiano, and the parsley. Mix quickly for 1 to 2 minutes until the butter and cheese have melted and the rice has a moist, creamy consistency. Taste and adjust the seasoning, and serve at once.

Barley Risotto

RISOTTO DI ORZO

IN FRIULI, IN *the northeastern corner of Italy, one finds oneself transported back in time, to a pleasant, unhurried pace of life, and to great local food. This recipe is a simplified version of a barley risotto created by the chef/owner of the Roma restaurant in the small town of Tolmezzo. Barley, speck, and fresh Parmigiano-Reggiano cheese combine to make a hearty dish for friends and family.*

SERVES 4

6–8 cups homemade chicken broth (see page 33) or 3–4 cups canned chicken broth and 3–4 cups water
4 tablespoons unsalted butter
½ cup minced yellow onion
2–3 ounces sliced speck (see Note, page 15) or prosciutto, diced

1 cup pearl barley
1 cup dry white wine
⅓ cup freshly grated Parmigiano-Reggiano cheese
2 tablespoons chopped fresh flat-leaf Italian or regular parsley

continued

HEAT the broth in a medium-size saucepan and keep warm over low heat.

MELT 3 tablespoons of the butter in a large skillet over medium heat. When the butter foams, add the onion and cook, stirring, until the onion begins to color, 3 to 4 minutes. Add the speck and stir for a minute or two. Add the barley and cook until it is well coated with the butter and onion. Add the wine, cook and stir until it is almost all reduced.

ADD about ½ cup of hot broth, or just enough to barely cover the barley. Cook and stir until the broth has been absorbed almost completely. Continue cooking and stirring in this manner, adding the broth ½ cup at a time until the barley is tender, 40 to 50 minutes. Add the remaining butter, Parmigiano, and parsley. Mix quickly for a minute or two, or until the barley has a moist, creamy consistency. Taste and adjust the seasoning, and serve at once.

Note: Since it takes approximately 40 to 50 minutes to make this barley risotto, you can begin making it a few hours ahead. Cook it for about 25 minutes, then finish the cooking at the last moment before serving.

The risotto can also be precooked a day ahead. Cook it for 25 minutes, then spread the precooked barley on a large cookie sheet and let it cool. Cover it with plastic wrap and refrigerate overnight. The next day resume cooking the risotto with small additions of hot broth.

Basic Potato Gnocchi

GNOCCHI DI PATATE

SERVES 4 TO 6

4 large boiling potatoes,
  approximately 2 pounds
1 tablespoon salt

1 large egg, lightly beaten in a
  small bowl
1½–2 cups unbleached all-purpose
  flour

PREHEAT the oven to 375°.

WASH and dry the potatoes. With a knife, make a long, deep incision in the potatoes. Put the potatoes in the oven and bake until they are tender, about 1 hour.

When cool enough to handle, peel potatoes and put them through a potato ricer or mash them with a fork. Put potatoes into a large bowl and season with salt. Add the egg and 1½ cups of the flour. Mix the potatoes and the flour together with your hands until the dough begins to stick together.

TRANSFER the mixture to a wooden board and knead lightly, gradually adding the remaining flour if the dough sticks heavily to the board and to your hands. Knead the dough for 3 to 4 minutes until it is smooth and pliable and just a bit sticky.

DIVIDE the dough into several equal pieces, about the size of an orange. Flour your hands lightly. Using both hands, roll out each piece of dough with a light back-and-forth motion into a roll about the thickness of your index finger. Cut each roll into 1-inch pieces.

HOLD a fork with its tines against a work board, the curved part of the fork facing away from you. Starting from the curved outside bottom of the fork, press each piece of dough with your index finger firmly upward along the length of the tines. Let the gnocchi fall back onto the work surface. Repeat with remaining pieces of dough until all the gnocchi have been formed. Place the gnocchi on a lightly floured platter or cookie sheet. They can be cooked immediately or stored in the refrigerator, uncovered, for several hours.

Note: Tips for making gnocchi:

- When you add the flour to the other ingredients, always start with just a bit less than the recipe suggests. You can always add more flour if the dough is too sticky, but you can't take it out once it is incorporated into the dough.
- Do not knead the gnocchi dough longer than a few minutes. The longer the dough is kneaded, the more flour it will absorb. The result will be heavier gnocchi.
- Before you prepare a whole batch of gnocchi, cook one to determine its consistency. If it is too soft or it falls apart in the water, you must knead a bit more flour into the dough. If the dumpling is heavy and chewy, you have probably added too much flour.
- Gnocchi, just like pasta, should be cooked in plenty of vigorously boiling water or they will stick together. Use 5 to 6 quarts of water for 4 portions of gnocchi.

Potato Gnocchi with Cabbage and Fontina

GNOCCHI DI PATATE COL CAVOLO E LA FONTINA

ITALY HAS A *great number of humble peasant dishes that can be assembled quickly with just a handful of ingredients. Potato gnocchi combined with slowly cooked cabbage, laced with melting fontina cheese, become a filling, satisfying first course.*

SERVES 4 TO 6

1 recipe Basic Potato Gnocchi
(see page 112)

2 tablespoons unsalted butter
2 tablespoons olive oil
¼ pound pancetta, cut into ⅛-inch slices and diced
2 large garlic cloves, minced

1 pound Savoy or curly cabbage,
cut into thin strips
1 cup chicken broth
Salt to taste
6 ounces fontina cheese, diced
⅓ cup freshly grated Parmigiano-Reggiano cheese
Freshly ground black pepper
to taste

PREPARE the potato gnocchi and set aside.

HEAT the butter and oil in a large skillet over medium heat. When the butter foams, add the pancetta and cook until pancetta is lightly golden, 2 to 3 minutes. Add the garlic and stir a few times. When the garlic begins to color, add the cabbage and cook, stirring, for a minute or two. Add the broth, partially cover the skillet, and reduce the heat to low. Cook until the cabbage is soft and the liquid in the skillet is almost all reduced, 6 to 7 minutes.

WHILE the sauce is cooking, bring a large pot of water to a boil. Add 1 tablespoon of salt and the gnocchi. Cook, uncovered, over high heat until gnocchi rise to the surface of the water, 1 to 2 minutes. Remove them with a large slotted spoon or a skimmer, draining off the excess water against the side of the pot. Place gnocchi in the skillet with the cabbage. Add the fontina and the Parmigiano, and season with salt and several grindings of pepper. Mix well over low heat until the cheese begins to melt, about 1 minute. Add a few tablespoons of the gnocchi cooking water if the dumplings seem dry. Serve at once.

Potato Gnocchi with Arugula

GNOCCHI DI PATATE CON LA RUCOLA

THIS IS A *classic example of good and uncomplicated Italian food. Potato gnocchi are cooked together with arugula leaves, then they are tossed with some pancetta, which has been browned in butter and oil. Nothing could be simpler or more delicious.*

SERVES 4 TO 6

1 recipe Basic Potato Gnocchi
   (see page 112)

2 tablespoons unsalted butter
1–2 tablespoons olive oil
¼ pound pancetta, cut into thick
   slices and diced

2 whole garlic cloves, peeled
Salt to taste
3 bunches arugula, tough stems
   removed
Freshly ground black pepper
   to taste

PREPARE the potato gnocchi and set aside.

HEAT the butter and oil in a large skillet over medium heat. When the butter foams, add the pancetta and the whole garlic. Cook until pancetta and garlic are lightly golden, 2 to 3 minutes. Discard the garlic and turn the heat off under the skillet.

Do not serve Parmigiano with this dish, since the cheese will overpower the delicate, peppery fresh taste of the arugula.

MEANWHILE, bring a large pot of water to a boil. Add 1 tablespoon of salt, the gnocchi, and the arugula. Cook, uncovered, over high heat until gnocchi rise to the surface of the water, 1 to 2 minutes. Remove gnocchi and arugula with a large slotted spoon or a skimmer, draining off the excess water against the side of the pot. Place gnocchi and arugula in the skillet with the pancetta. Season with salt and pepper, and mix over low heat until everything is well combined. Taste and adjust the seasoning, and serve.

Potato Gnocchi with Porcini Mushrooms, Saffron, and Cream

GNOCCHI DI PATATE CON PORCINI,
ZAFFERANO, E PANNA

POTATO GNOCCHI ARE *very popular all over northern Italy. My mother used to make wonderful gnocchi, and she was incredibly quick in shaping them on the fork. Gnocchi, just like pasta, can be paired with many sauces. They are easy to make, quick to cook, and irresistible.*

SERVES 4 TO 6

1 recipe Basic Potato Gnocchi
   (see page 112)

1 ounce dried porcini mushrooms,
   soaked in 2 cups lukewarm
   water for 20 minutes
3 tablespoons unsalted butter
1–2 garlic cloves, minced

½ cup dry white wine
1 cup heavy cream
Small pinch powdered saffron
Salt to taste
2 tablespoons chopped fresh flat-
   leaf Italian or regular parsley
½ cup freshly grated Parmigiano-
   Reggiano cheese

PREPARE the potato gnocchi and set aside.

DRAIN the mushrooms and reserve the soaking liquid. Rinse mushrooms well under cold running water and chop them roughly. Line a strainer with two paper towels and strain the mushroom liquid into a bowl to get rid of the sandy deposits. Set aside.

HEAT the butter in a large skillet over medium heat. When the butter begins to foam, add the mushrooms and the garlic. Cook, stirring, 1 to 2 minutes. Raise the heat to high and add the wine and 1 cup of the reserved mushroom liquid. Cook until the liquid is reduced by half, 5 to 6 minutes. Add the cream and the saffron, and season with salt. Reduce the heat to medium low and cook, stirring occasionally, until sauce has a medium-thick consistency, 3 to 4 minutes.

MEANWHILE, bring a large pot of water to a boil. Add 1 tablespoon of salt and the gnocchi. Cook, uncovered, over high heat until gnocchi rise to the surface of the water, 1 to 2 minutes. Remove them with a large slotted spoon or a skimmer, draining off the excess water against the side of the pot. Place gnocchi in the skillet with the sauce, add the parsley, and mix briefly over low heat until gnocchi and sauce are well combined. Taste and adjust the seasoning, and serve sprinkled with freshly grated Parmigiano.

Potato Gnocchi with Eggplant, Mushrooms, and Zucchini

GNOCCHI DI PATATE CON VERDURE AL FUNGHETTO

THERE ARE MANY *hundreds of classic pasta sauces in Italy that have stood the test of time. There are also a great many sauces that simply stem from the creativity of the cook. The method of preparing these vegetables is called al funghetto. This means a single vegetable or several vegetables are quickly sautéed in olive oil and seasoned with garlic and parsley. This funghetto preparation is a specialty of Liguria. Pasta or gnocchi, topped with healthy and tasty eggplant-mushroom-zucchini sauce, become irresistible.*

SERVES 4 TO 6

1 recipe Basic Potato Gnocchi
    (see page 112)

½ pound eggplant, peeled and cut
    into ½-inch cubes
Salt
¼–⅓ cup extra-virgin olive oil
½ pound white cultivated
    mushrooms, wiped clean and
    thinly sliced

½ pound zucchini, the smallest
    you can find, thinly sliced
2 garlic cloves, minced
2 tablespoons chopped fresh flat-
    leaf Italian parsley or regular
    parsley
½–1 cup chicken broth
Freshly ground black pepper
    to taste

PREPARE the potato gnocchi and set aside.

PREPARE THE VEGETABLES: Put the eggplant cubes in a pasta colander and sprinkle with salt. Mix well, place the colander over a bowl, and let it sit for about 1 hour. The salt will draw out the eggplant's bitter juices. Put the eggplant cubes on a large, clean kitchen towel and pat dry.

HEAT the oil in a large skillet or sauté pan over medium-high heat. Add the eggplant, mushrooms, and zucchini and cook, stirring, until vegetables have a nice golden color, 2 to 3 minutes. (Make sure not to crowd the skillet or the vegetables will be stewed instead of sautéed. If necessary, sauté the vegetables in a few batches.) Add the garlic and the parsley, and stir once or twice. Add the broth and cook, stirring, until broth is almost all evaporated and the vegetables are tender, 2 to 3 minutes. Turn the heat off under the skillet. At this point you should have in the pan only a few tablespoons of thickened wine and vegetable juices.

MEANWHILE, bring a large pot of water to a boil. Add 1 tablespoon of salt and the gnocchi. Cook, uncovered, over high heat until the gnocchi rise to the surface of the water, 1 to 2 minutes. Remove them with a large slotted spoon or a skimmer, draining off the excess water against the side of the pot. Place gnocchi in the skillet and mix well over low heat. Taste and adjust the seasoning, and serve.

Basic Ricotta-Parmigiano Gnocchi

GNOCCHI DI RICOTTA E PARMIGIANO

SERVES 4 TO 6

1 pound ricotta
½ cup freshly grated Parmigiano-
   Reggiano cheese
1–1½ cups all-purpose flour

2 teaspoons salt
1 large egg, lightly beaten in a
   small bowl

IN a large bowl combine all the ingredients except for ½ cup of the flour. With your hands mix everything until it sticks together in a dough. Put mixture on a wooden board and knead it lightly for 2 to 3 minutes, adding a bit of the reserved flour if the dough sticks heavily to the board and your hands. When the dough is soft, pliable, and just a bit sticky, divide it into several pieces of equal size.

FLOUR your hands lightly. Using both hands, roll out each piece of dough with a light back-and-forth motion into a roll about the thickness of your index finger. Cut each roll into 1-inch pieces.

HOLD a fork with its tines against a work board, the curved part of the fork facing away from you. Starting from the curved outside bottom of the fork, press each piece of dough with your index finger firmly upward along the length of the tines. Let the gnocchi fall back onto the work surface. Repeat with remaining pieces of dough until all the gnocchi have been formed. Place gnocchi on a lightly floured platter or cookie sheet. They can be cooked immediately or they can be kept in the refrigerator, uncovered, for several hours or overnight.

Ricotta-Parmigiano Gnocchi with Tomato and Cream

GNOCCHI DI RICOTTA E PARMIGIANO
AL BURRO E ORO

SOMETIMES THE LESS *fuss paid to the creation of a dish, the better it tastes. These light and delicate gnocchi are topped with a fresh-tasting, quickly cooked sauce of tomatoes to which a touch of cream is added. This dish is a traditional specialty of Emilia-Romagna.*

SERVES 4 TO 6

1 recipe Basic Ricotta-Parmigiano
    Gnocchi (see page 119)

3 tablespoons unsalted butter
2 cups canned imported Italian
    plum tomatoes, with their
    juice, put through a food mill
    to remove the seeds

¼ cup heavy cream
Salt to taste
½ cup freshly grated Parmigiano-
    Reggiano cheese

PREPARE the ricotta-Parmigiano gnocchi and set aside.

PREPARE THE SAUCE: Heat the butter in a large skillet over medium heat. When the butter begins to foam, add the tomatoes and the cream, and season with salt. Bring the sauce to a gentle boil, then reduce the heat to low and simmer, uncovered, stirring occasionally, 5 to 6 minutes, or until the sauce has a medium-thick consistency.

MEANWHILE, bring a large pot of water to a boil. Add 1 tablespoon of salt and the gnocchi. Cook, uncovered, over high heat until the gnocchi rise to the surface of the water, 1 to 2 minutes. Remove them with a large slotted spoon or a skimmer, draining off the excess water against the side of the pot. Place gnocchi in the skillet with the sauce and mix briefly over low heat. Taste and adjust the seasoning, and serve with a sprinkling of Parmigiano.

Ricotta-Parmigiano Gnocchi with Prosciutto, Peas, and Cream

GNOCCHI DI RICOTTA E PARMIGIANO AL PROSCIUTTO, PISELLI, E PANNA

RICOTTA GNOCCHI ARE *light and easy to prepare. In Emilia-Romagna they are paired with a Bolognese meat sauce or simply with sweet, melted butter and a sprinkling of good Parmigiano. My sister-in-law Emma serves them with this quick sauce for a creamy, mouth-watering dish.*

SERVES 4 TO 6

1 recipe Basic Ricotta-Parmigiano Gnocchi (see page 119)

1 cup fresh shelled green peas or 1 cup frozen small peas, thawed
3 tablespoons unsalted butter
½ cup minced yellow onion

¼ pound prosciutto, cut into ⅛-inch slices and diced
½ cup heavy cream
½ cup chicken broth
Salt and freshly ground black pepper to taste
½ cup freshly grated Parmigiano-Reggiano cheese

PREPARE the ricotta-Parmigiano gnocchi and set aside.

PREPARE THE SAUCE: If using fresh peas, cook them in boiling salted water until tender but still a bit firm to the bite. Drain and set aside.

HEAT the butter in a large skillet over medium heat. Add the onion and cook, stirring occasionally, until onion is pale yellow and soft, 4 to 5 minutes. Add the prosciutto and the fresh or thawed frozen peas. Cook, stirring, for 2 to 3 minutes. Add the cream and the broth, and simmer until sauce has a thick consistency, 2 to 3 minutes longer. Season with salt and pepper.

MEANWHILE, bring a large pot of water to a boil. Add 1 tablespoon of salt and the gnocchi. Cook, uncovered, over high heat until the gnocchi rise to the surface of the water, 1 to 2 minutes. Remove them with a large slotted spoon or a skimmer, draining off the excess water against the side of the pot. Place gnocchi in the skillet with the sauce and mix briefly over low heat. Taste and adjust the seasoning, and serve with a sprinkling of grated Parmigiano.

Basic Spinach-Ricotta Gnocchi

GNOCCHI DI SPINACI E RICOTTA

SERVES 4 TO 6

1 pound ricotta
½ cup freshly grated Parmigiano-
   Reggiano cheese
1–1½ cups unbleached all-purpose
   flour

2 teaspoons salt
⅓ cup very finely chopped fresh
   or frozen cooked spinach,
   mixed into 1 large beaten egg

IN a large bowl combine all the gnocchi ingredients except for ½ cup of the flour, and proceed to make the dough and roll out the gnocchi as instructed for Basic Ricotta-Parmigiano Gnocchi on page 119.

Spinach-Ricotta Gnocchi with Porcini Mushrooms and Tomatoes

GNOCCHI DI SPINACI E RICOTTA CON SALSA
DI FUNGHI E POMODORI

WHETHER IN THE *kitchen of my restaurant in Sacramento, or in my family's in Bologna, I am at my happiest when I can create a slightly new interpretation of a dish. Creativity is a very important part of cooking. Without it, we would probably eat the same ten dishes all our lives and become bored to death.*

IN THIS DISH *spinach-ricotta gnocchi are blanketed with a colorful sauce of aromatic porcini mushrooms and bright red, ripe tomatoes. When tomatoes are not at their best, use canned imported Italian tomatoes, diced, together with their juice.*

SERVES 4 TO 6

1 recipe Basic Spinach-Ricotta
    Gnocchi (see page 122)

4 fresh, ripe plum tomatoes
¼ cup extra-virgin olive oil
1 ounce dried porcini mushrooms,
    soaked in 2 cups lukewarm
    water for 20 minutes

2 garlic cloves, minced
½ cup dry white wine
Salt and freshly ground black
    pepper to taste
1 tablespoon unsalted butter,
    optional
½ cup freshly grated Parmigiano-
    Reggiano cheese

PREPARE the spinach-ricotta gnocchi and set aside.

PREPARE THE SAUCE: Bring a large pot of water to a boil. Cut a cross at the root end of the tomatoes and drop them into boiling water. Cook until the skin of the tomatoes begins to split, 1 to 2 minutes. Transfer the tomatoes to a bowl of iced water. Peel, seed, and dice the tomatoes, and place them in a bowl with all their juice.

DRAIN the mushrooms and reserve the soaking water. Rinse mushrooms well under cold running water and chop them roughly. Line a strainer with two paper towels and strain the mushroom liquid into a bowl to get rid of the sandy deposits and reserve it.

HEAT the oil in a large skillet over medium heat. Add the garlic and cook, stirring, until it begins to color, less than 1 minute. Add the mushrooms, and stir quickly for a minute or two. Raise the heat to high and add the wine. Cook until wine is almost all reduced, about 2 minutes. Add the tomatoes and ½ cup of the reserved mushroom soaking water. Season with salt and pepper. Cook, stirring, until the juices in the pan have thickened, 3 to 4 minutes. Stir in the butter, if using, and turn off the heat under the skillet.

MEANWHILE, bring a large pot of water to a boil. Add 1 tablespoon of salt and the gnocchi. Cook, uncovered, over high heat until gnocchi rise to the surface of the water, 1 to 2 minutes. Remove gnocchi with a large slotted spoon or a skimmer, draining off the excess water against the side of the pot. Place gnocchi in the skillet with the sauce, add Parmigiano, and mix briefly over low heat. Taste and adjust the seasoning, and serve with additional Parmigiano, if desired.

Spinach-Ricotta Gnocchi with Three-Meat Ragù

GNOCCHI DI SPINACI E RICOTTA CON RAGÙ DI CARNE MISTA

THE CELEBRATED ITALIAN *ragù alla Bolognese is made with vegetables, ground beef, tomato sauce, or tomato paste diluted in water and milk. My mother prepared it with veal instead of beef, and generally served it over homemade tagliatelle, but also over gnocchi or polenta.*

HERE THE RAGÙ *uses beef, pork, and veal, plus a little savory pancetta. The flavorful base consists of onion, celery, and carrots. Tomato sauce and milk are added, and everything cooks at the barest simmer for a few hours. The result is a highly flavorful and absolutely delicious ragù.*

SERVES 4 TO 6

1 recipe Basic Spinach-Ricotta
   Gnocchi (see page 122)

3 tablespoons unsalted butter
2 tablespoons olive oil
½ cup minced yellow onion
½ cup minced carrots
½ cup minced celery
½ pound ground veal, from the
   shoulder
½ pound ground pork, from the
   shoulder or sirloin

½ pound ground beef chuck
¼ pound pancetta, finely chopped
1 cup dry white wine
3 cups canned imported Italian
   plum tomatoes, with their
   juice, put through a food mill
   to remove the seeds
1 cup whole milk
Salt to taste
1 cup chicken broth
½ cup freshly grated Parmigiano-
   Reggiano cheese

PREPARE the spinach-ricotta gnocchi and set aside.

PREPARE THE MEAT SAUCE: Heat the butter and oil in a wide-bottomed saucepan over medium heat. Add the onion, carrots, and celery and cook, stirring, until

Since there will be a nice batch of sauce left over, you can refrigerate it in a tightly sealed container for a few days or freeze it.

Do not rush the cooking of this ragù. A good meat ragù needs slow, prolonged cooking to extract all the juices and flavor from the meat.

vegetables are soft and lightly colored, 6 to 8 minutes. Do not let vegetables turn too brown.

RAISE the heat to medium high, and add the meat and the pancetta. With a wooden spoon cook, stirring, to break up the meat and prevent it from sticking to the bottom of the pan. When the meat has lost its raw color, 7 to 8 minutes, add the wine and cook until wine has evaporated, 2 to 3 minutes. Add the tomato sauce and the milk, and season lightly with salt. Bring the sauce to a boil, then reduce the heat to low and partially cover the pot. Simmer very gently for 1½ to 2 hours, stirring occasionally. At the end of cooking, the sauce should have a medium-thick consistency. If too much liquid has evaporated, add broth or water and simmer a few minutes longer. You will have 3½ to 4 cups of sauce.

BRING a large pot of water to a boil. Add 1 tablespoon of salt and the gnocchi. Cook, uncovered, over high heat until gnocchi rise to the surface of the water, 1 to 2 minutes. Remove them with a slotted spoon or a skimmer, draining off the excess water against the side of the pot. Place the gnocchi in a large, heated serving bowl, add 3 or 4 large spoonfuls of sauce and a sprinkling of Parmigiano, and mix well. Taste and adjust the seasoning. Add a bit more sauce if necessary and serve at once with more Parmigiano, if desired.

Ricotta-Carrot Gnocchetti with Peas and Pancetta

GNOCCHETTI ROSA CON PISELLI E PANCETTA

GNOCCHETTI ARE SMALL *gnocchi and you can use a variety of ingredients when you make them.*

HERE, THE DOUGH *is made with ricotta, flour, Parmigiano, and pureed carrots. The carrots lend a light orange color and a sweet flavor to these dumplings. These gnocchetti do not have the "ridges" that are typical of traditional gnocchi; thus they are quicker to prepare.*

KEEP THE SAUCE *simple. It should complement the sweet taste of gnocchetti rather than overpower it.*

SERVES 4 TO 6

FOR THE GNOCCHETTI

2 medium carrots, 7–8 ounces
1 pound ricotta
½ cup freshly grated Parmigiano-
  Reggiano cheese
1–1½ cups unbleached all-purpose
  flour
2 teaspoons salt

FOR THE SAUCE

1 cup shelled fresh peas or frozen
  peas, thawed

Salt
2 tablespoons unsalted butter
2 tablespoons olive oil
2 ounces sliced pancetta, finely
  diced
1 cup chicken broth
½ cup freshly grated Parmigiano-
  Reggiano cheese

PREPARE THE GNOCCHETTI: Bring a medium-size saucepan of water to a boil. Add the carrots and cook, uncovered, until they are tender and cooked all the way through. Drain carrots, cool under cold running water, and puree them in a food processor or in a food mill.

IN a large bowl combine ricotta, Parmigiano, carrots, and 1 cup of the flour, and season with salt. Mix well with your hands until everything is thoroughly combined. (This step can also be done in an electric mixer using the paddle or the bread hook.) If the mixture is too sticky, knead in a bit more flour. Place dough in a lightly floured bowl, cover, and refrigerate about ½ hour to firm it up.

DIVIDE dough into several equal pieces. Flour your hands lightly. Using both hands, roll out each piece of dough with a light back-and-forth motion into a long, thin roll about the thickness of your little finger. Cut each roll into ½-inch pieces. When all the gnocchetti are made, place them on a lightly floured platter or cookie sheet. They can be cooked immediately or kept in the refrigerator, uncovered, for several hours.

PREPARE THE SAUCE: If using fresh peas, bring a small saucepan of water to a boil over medium heat. Add the peas to the water with a pinch of salt. Cook, uncovered, until tender, 5 to 10 minutes, depending on size. Drain peas and set aside.

HEAT 1 tablespoon of the butter and the oil in a large skillet over medium heat. Add the pancetta and cook, stirring, until pancetta is lightly golden, about 2 minutes. Add the peas and the broth, and season with salt. Cook until broth is reduced by half, 2 to 3 minutes. Add the remaining tablespoon of butter and stir briefly. Turn the heat off under the skillet.

MEANWHILE, bring a large pot of water to a boil. Add 1 tablespoon of salt and the gnocchetti. Cook, uncovered, over high heat until gnocchetti rise to the surface of the water, 1 to 2 minutes. Remove them with a large slotted spoon or a skimmer, draining off the excess water against the side of the pot. Place them in the skillet with the sauce and stir in a few tablespoons of Parmigiano. Mix briefly over low heat to combine. Taste and adjust the seasoning, and serve with additional Parmigiano, if desired.

Spinach, Ricotta, and Mascarpone Dumplings

MALFATTI

MALFATTI, LITERALLY TRANSLATED, *means "poorly made." These delicious spinach, ricotta, and Parmigiano dumplings originated in Lombardy. There are a few versions of this regional dish. My favorite uses not only ricotta but also mascarpone cheese and nutmeg. If mascarpone cheese is not available in your area, simply add a bit of additional ricotta.*

BECAUSE OF THE *nutmeg in the dough, the best topping for malfatti is melted sweet butter and freshly grated Parmigiano. If you omit the nutmeg, then you can top the dumplings with a light, fresh tomato sauce or sauté some prosciutto or pancetta in butter and fresh sage.*

SERVES 6

FOR THE MALFATTI

1 teaspoon salt

1½ pounds fresh spinach, stems removed and thoroughly washed, or two 10-ounce packages frozen spinach, thawed

2–3 tablespoons unsalted butter

½ pound ricotta

¼ pound mascarpone or, if unavailable, additional ricotta

½ cup freshly grated Parmigiano-Reggiano cheese

½ teaspoon freshly grated nutmeg

1½–2 cups unbleached all-purpose flour

1 large egg, lightly beaten

Salt to taste

Approximately 1 cup additional flour, spread on a sheet of aluminum foil, to coat the dumplings

FOR THE SAUCE

4 tablespoons unsalted butter

½ cup freshly grated Parmigiano-Reggiano cheese

Salt to taste

PREPARE THE MALFATTI: Bring a large pot of water to a boil. Add the salt and the spinach. Cook, uncovered, until spinach is tender, 3 to 4 minutes. If you are using frozen spinach, cook it according to the package directions. Drain spinach and rinse under cold running water. Squeeze the spinach dry, and chop it very fine.

MELT the butter in a medium-size skillet over medium heat. When the butter foams, add the spinach and mix well to coat thoroughly with the butter. Transfer the spinach to a large bowl and cool.

ADD the ricotta, mascarpone, Parmigiano, nutmeg, 1½ cups of flour, and the egg. Season with salt. Mix well with your hands until the ingredients are thoroughly combined. (If mixture is too sticky, knead in a bit more flour.) Place dough in a lightly floured bowl and refrigerate for about 1 hour to firm it up.

TAKE a small amount of the spinach mixture and shape it into a small ball about the size of a cherry tomato. Roll the ball lightly in the flour, and place on a lightly floured platter or cookie sheet. Repeat until all the mixture is rolled up. The dumplings can be cooked immediately or they can be refrigerated, uncovered, for a few hours.

TO COMPLETE THE DISH: Put the butter in a large, shallow serving dish and place in a low oven for about 10 minutes.

BRING a large pot of water to a boil over high heat. Add 1 tablespoon of salt and the dumplings. Cook, uncovered, until they rise to the surface of the water, 1 to 2 minutes. Remove the dumplings with a large slotted spoon or a skimmer, draining off the excess water against the side of the pot. Place the dumplings in the warm dish containing the melted butter. Season with salt and sprinkle generously with Parmigiano. Mix gently and serve at once.

Basic Polenta

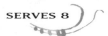

SERVES 8

9 cups cold water
2 tablespoons salt

2 cups coarsely ground cornmeal,
  mixed with 1 cup finely
  ground cornmeal

BRING the water to a boil in a medium-size heavy pot over medium heat. Add the salt and reduce the heat to medium low. As soon as the water begins to simmer, start pouring in the cornmeal by the handful in a thin stream, very slowly, and stir constantly with a long wooden spoon to prevent lumps from forming. When all the cornmeal has been incorporated, you can relax, but keep the water at a steady, low simmer and stir cornmeal frequently. (It is not necessary to stir constantly if the polenta is cooked gently.) Cook the polenta 25 to 30 minutes. As it cooks, the polenta will thicken considerably, and it will bubble and spit back at you. Keep stirring, crushing any lumps that form against the side of the pot. The polenta is cooked when it comes away effortlessly from the sides of the pan.

FOR SOFT POLENTA

SPOON polenta directly out of the pot into serving dishes.

FOR SOFT POLENTA PREPARED AHEAD

AS soon as the polenta is cooked, transfer it to a large bowl and place the bowl over a pot containing a few inches of slowly simmering water. The polenta will keep nice and soft for a few hours.

WHEN you are ready to serve it, stir the polenta energetically with a large wooden spoon. If it is a bit too firm, stir in some additional water, chicken broth, or milk.

FOR FIRM POLENTA

WHEN the polenta is cooked, pour it onto a large wooden board, shaping it with a large, wet spatula into a 2-inch round. Or spread the polenta in a 2-inch layer onto a baking sheet. Let the polenta firm up for 10 to 15 minutes (or longer), then cut it into slices and serve it with your favorite sauce or baked, grilled, or fried, as described below.

Polenta Cooked in a Double Boiler

BRING the water to a boil in a medium-size heavy pot over medium heat. Add the salt and reduce the heat to medium low. As soon as the water begins to simmer, start pouring in the cornmeal by the handful in a thin stream, very slowly, and stir constantly with a long wooden spoon to prevent lumps from forming.

For additional flavor, stir in some butter and freshly grated Parmigiano during the last few minutes of cooking. For extra-creamy polenta, add a bit of heavy cream.

When all the cornmeal has been incorporated, pour the polenta into a large stainless steel bowl and put the bowl over a large pot containing 3 to 4 inches of simmering water. Check that the bowl does not touch the water, then cover the bowl completely with foil and cook 1½ hours. Stir the polenta a few times during cooking with a wooden spoon or a spatula, and make sure that there is always enough simmering water in the pan. Add a bit more water if necessary. Serve polenta with sauce or as indicated below.

FOR BAKED POLENTA

CUT the firm cooled polenta into slices and place them in a buttered or oiled baking dish. Add the topping of your choice and bake in a preheated 375° oven until lightly golden.

FOR GRILLED POLENTA

CUT the firm cooled polenta into slices, brush slices with oil, and place on a hot grill or under a broiler until browned on both sides.

FOR FRIED POLENTA

CUT the firm cooled polenta into slices and fry them in a few inches of very hot oil until golden brown and crisp.

BASIC FISH BROTH

DEEP-FRIED CALAMARI

GRILLED PRAWNS AND POTATO SALAD

MONKFISH, LIVORNO STYLE

SEA BASS WITH FRESH TOMATOES AND OLIVES

DRIED SALT COD WITH TOMATO SAUCE AND POLENTA

POACHED HALIBUT WITH TOMATO-OLIVE SAUCE

SOLE WITH CRISP BREAD-HERB COATING

SHELLFISH "POLPETTE"

SOLE MARINATED WITH RED BELL PEPPERS, ONION,
AND VINEGAR

"DRUNKEN" TUNA

SEA BASS BAKED IN PARCHMENT

Seafood

FRESHNESS AND SIMPLICITY are the heart and soul of Italian fish cookery.

MY FAMILY USED to spend a few weeks each summer on the nearby Adriatic, where we would lodge in a simple family-style *pensione*. Once a day we would eat fish that had been freshly caught in the early morning by the owner of the pensione. It was always simply prepared. Often it was marinated in lemon juice, olive oil, salt, and pepper, and then coated very lightly with a mixture of bread crumbs and parsley. It might then be grilled to perfection; other times it was baked or poached, and served only with a few drops of oil and lemon juice. Even after all these years, I can still taste that wonderful fish!

THERE IS NO doubt that there is an undisputed pleasure in eating food at its source. Italians are quite fussy about this, especially when it comes to fish. If you look at the map of Italy you will see a long, thin peninsula squeezed between two great seas: the Adriatic to the east and the Mediterranean to the west, with the islands of Sicily and Sardinia floating around in it. It seems natural, then, that the people of a country that is practically surrounded by water, and with several thousand miles of coastline, would be great fish lovers.

NOW THAT ITALY has superhighways and fish can be transported quickly and safely from one part of the country to another, the popularity of fish has increased tremendously, especially inland. Still, for most Italians an important part of the pleasure of eating fish, fresh fish, is eating it at the source. Many will go out of their way to drive to the seacoast or to the lakes to do so. It is not unlike the Italian custom of buying seasonal produce only in its time or travelling to the countryside in search of freshly made cheeses and other local specialties. When Italians cook and eat, freshness is the number one priority.

THE BEST PLACE to see the abundance and variety of seafood in one swoop is at the local fish market. Every city or small town on the coast has one. Venezia has perhaps the best known and most celebrated fish market of all, the Rialto, where the incredible variety of fish caught daily in the Adriatic is displayed.

IN THIS CHAPTER I have tried to use fish that is available most of the time. Since most of us cannot hop in the car on the spur of the moment and drive to the nearest coast town to buy our fresh fish, it is important that we buy it from a good source. Read the tips below and use them as your guidelines for buying seafood.

TIPS FOR BUYING SEAFOOD

- Since seafood spoils quickly, make sure that you buy it from a good source. To determine how fresh it is, smell it. Fish should have a pleasant, clean odor, not a strong "fishy" one.
- The flesh of the fish should be firm to the touch. If it is soft and mushy, do not buy it. When buying a whole fish, look at the eyes. They should be clear, not cloudy, and the gills should be bright pink.
- Buy what is in season.
- Try to cook the fish the same day you buy it. If you must keep it a day or two, wrap it tightly in plastic wrap and store it in the coldest part of your refrigerator.
- Do not freeze the fish, if possible. Freezing will cause moisture loss. If you absolutely must freeze it, wrap it tightly in a few layers of plastic wrap.
- Thaw the frozen fish in the refrigerator and try to use it the same day.

Basic Fish Broth

BRODO DI PESCE

THIS IS A *great basic broth to have at hand, since it greatly improves the taste of any seafood risottos and fish stews. Divide the broth in several containers and freeze them for later use.*

MAKES APPROXIMATELY 8 CUPS

2½–3 pounds of fish frames
   (see Note)
1 large yellow onion, peeled and
   coarsely chopped
2 medium celery stalks, cut into
   pieces

2 small carrots, cut into pieces
3 fresh parsley sprigs
2 cups dry white wine
3 quarts cold water
Salt to taste

RINSE the fish frames under cold running water. Combine all the ingredients in a large saucepan and bring the water to a boil over medium heat. Reduce the heat to medium low and, with a slotted spoon or a skimmer, skim the scum that comes to the surface of the water. Simmer, uncovered, about 1 hour.

LINE a strainer with a few layers of paper towels, strain the broth into a bowl, and, if you are not planning to use it right away, cool it to room temperature. It can be refrigerated for a few days or frozen.

Note: Fish frames are a mixture of heads, bones, scales, etc., available in fish markets, sold for making fish broth or any fish-flavored liquid. You can assemble your own "fish frames" by accumulating and freezing any odd fish pieces.

Deep-Fried Calamari

CALAMARI FRITTI

IN THIS DELICIOUS *and simple seafood dish, the calamari are cleaned and cut into small rings, sprinkled lightly with flour, and dropped into very hot oil until golden and crunchy. I started serving this dish at my restaurant eight years ago, and it is still one of the most popular items on the menu.*

SERVES 4 AS AN ENTRÉE OR 6 AS AN APPETIZER

4 pounds squid, the smallest you
   can find
Vegetable oil for frying
1½ cups all-purpose flour

Salt to taste
Chopped fresh red chile pepper or
   dried red pepper flakes to taste

For perfectly crunchy yet tender calamari, make sure the oil is very, very hot—375° to 380°. When the oil just begins to smoke, add the squid.

If you do not have a thermometer to test the temperature of the oil, simply drop in a piece of squid. If it sizzles and turns golden in no time at all, the oil is hot enough. If the oil is not hot enough, the calamari will be soggy. If the calamari are cooked too long, they will become tough and rubbery.

TO clean the squid, hold it in one hand and gently pull away the tentacles. Cut the head off just below the eyes and discard it. Remove the little beak inside the tentacles. Remove the long cartilage from the squid body. Clean the squid body under cold running water, pulling out any matter that remains inside. Wash and peel away the grayish skin from the body and the tentacles and discard. Cut the squid body into ½-inch rings. Dry the squid well with paper towels.

FILL a heavy, medium-size saucepan halfway with oil and place over high heat. Place a handful or two of squid into a sieve and sprinkle liberally with flour. Mix the flour with the squid to coat well, then shake the sieve to remove excess flour, letting it fall onto a plate or piece of aluminum foil.

WHEN the oil is very hot and is just beginning to smoke, lower the squid carefully into the hot oil, making sure not to crowd the pan. Fry the squid until it has a nice golden color, less than 1 minute, then remove it with a slotted spoon and drain on paper towels. When all the squid has been fried, season it with salt and chile pepper, and serve piping hot.

Grilled Prawns and Potato Salad

INSALATA DI GAMBERI E PATATE

HERE THE PRAWNS *are prepared in the traditional manner of Emilia-Romagna. They are coated in a savory mixture of bread crumbs, parsley, olive oil, and lemon juice, and allowed to sit for a while before grilling. The bread crumb coating adds flavor and moisture. The grilled prawns then are tossed with peas, tomatoes, and young, tender potatoes to make an unusual and flavorful salad.*

SERVES 4

FOR THE PRAWNS
- ½ cup fine, plain dried bread crumbs
- 2 tablespoons chopped fresh flat-leaf Italian or regular parsley
- 3–4 tablespoons extra-virgin olive oil
- 2 tablespoons lemon juice
- Salt and freshly ground black pepper to taste
- 1 pound prawns, shelled and deveined

- 1 pound small, red new potatoes
- Salt
- 1 pound shelled fresh peas or one 10-ounce package frozen peas, thawed
- 2 medium ripe, firm tomatoes, 10–12 ounces, seeded and diced
- 2 tablespoons chopped chives
- Freshly ground black pepper to taste
- ⅓ cup extra-virgin olive oil
- 3 tablespoons red wine vinegar

IN a small bowl combine the bread crumbs, parsley, oil, and lemon juice into a moist mixture, and season with salt and pepper. Thread the prawns onto skewers and coat them lightly with the bread crumb mixture, pressing the coating into the prawns with the palms of your hands. Place the skewers on a platter and refrigerate, uncovered, for 30 to 40 minutes to allow the coating to dry.

PUT potatoes into a medium-size pot, cover with cold water, and bring to a boil over medium heat. Cook until potatoes are tender, 20 to 30 minutes, depending on size. Drain potatoes, cool them, and cut into thin, round slices. Place potatoes into a large salad bowl.

BRING a small saucepan of water to a boil. Add a pinch of salt and the fresh peas. Cook until tender, 5 to 10 minutes, depending on size. Drain peas and cool.

continued

PREHEAT the grill or the broiler, then place the skewers on the hot grill, or place them on a broiling sheet under the broiler. Cook until prawns are golden on all sides and are cooked all the way through, 5 to 6 minutes. Cool to room temperature, then remove prawns from skewers and add to the salad bowl with the potatoes.

ADD the peas, tomatoes, and chives, and season with salt and several grindings of pepper. Add the oil and the vinegar, and mix well. Taste and adjust the seasoning, and serve.

Monkfish, Livorno Style

CODA DI ROSPO ALLA LIVORNESE

THE FIRM, LEAN *white meat of the monkfish retains all its moisture when it is cooked gently with savory tomatoes. If monkfish is not available, you can substitute any other firm-fleshed white fish, such as orange roughy.*

SERVES 4

¼–⅓ cup extra-virgin olive oil
4 monkfish fillets, about 2 pounds
   (see Note)
Salt and freshly ground black
   pepper to taste
½ cup finely minced yellow onion
2 garlic cloves, minced
2 tablespoons chopped fresh flat-
   leaf Italian or regular parsley

1 cup Basic Fish Broth
   (see page 135)
2 cups canned imported Italian
   plum tomatoes, with their
   juice, put through a food mill
   to remove the seeds
1 tablespoon unsalted butter

HEAT the oil in a large skillet over medium-high heat. Season the fish fillets with salt and pepper and place in the skillet without crowding them. Cook until the fish is golden on both sides, 6 to 7 minutes. Transfer fish to a large dish.

REDUCE the heat to medium and add the onion, garlic, and 1 tablespoon of the parsley to the skillet. Cook, stirring, until onion is lightly golden and soft, 4 to 5 minutes. Add the fish broth and the tomatoes. Season with salt and pepper, and bring the sauce to a boil. Cook over medium heat, uncovered, stirring a few times, for 3 to 4 minutes.

RETURN the fish to the skillet, reduce the heat to low, and simmer, uncovered, until the fish is cooked all the way through, 3 to 4 minutes.

PLACE the fish on serving dishes and keep it warm in a low oven while you finish the sauce. Raise the heat under the skillet, and add the butter and the remainder of the parsley. Stir quickly until the butter is well incorporated with the sauce. Taste and adjust the seasoning. Spoon the sauce over the fish and serve.

Note: Monkfish, also known as anglerfish, is considered "the poor man's lobster," perhaps because its white, firm meat resembles cooked lobster tail meat. Most firm-fleshed white fish is suitable for this preparation.

Sea Bass with Fresh Tomatoes and Olives

IL BRANZINO AL POMODORO E OLIVE DEL
RISTORANTE COCCHI

AT THE COCCHI *restaurant in Parma, I was served a delicious sea bass with fresh tomatoes and olives, which I later reproduced at my restaurant in Sacramento. Try to select the freshest fish possible and the ripest tomatoes. In winter, when fresh tomatoes are not at their best, I add a tablespoon of sun-dried tomatoes to the sauce for extra flavor.*

SERVES 4

¼–⅓ cup extra-virgin olive oil
2 garlic cloves, peeled and left
    whole
4 sea bass fillets, about 2 pounds
Salt and freshly ground black
    pepper to taste
1 cup unbleached all-purpose flour,
    spread on a sheet of aluminum
    foil

1 cup dry white wine
4 medium ripe tomatoes, 1–1½
    pounds, seeded and diced
8 pitted black olives, minced
Juice of 1 lemon
1 tablespoon chopped fresh flat-
    leaf Italian parsley or regular
    parsley
1 tablespoon unsalted butter

HEAT the oil in a large skillet over medium-high heat. Add the garlic and cook until it is golden brown. Discard the garlic. Season the fish fillets with salt and pepper, coat them lightly with flour, and add them to the skillet. Cook until the fish is golden on both sides and is cooked all the way through, 6 to 8 minutes, depending on thickness. Transfer the fish to serving dishes and keep warm in a low oven while you finish the sauce.

DISCARD half of the fat in the skillet and add the wine. Cook, stirring, until the wine is reduced by half, 3 to 4 minutes. Add the tomatoes, olives, and lemon juice. Cook until tomatoes are soft and their watery juice is all evaporated, 2 to 3 minutes. Add the parsley and the butter, and stir a few times. Taste and adjust the seasoning. Spoon the sauce over the fish and serve at once.

Dried Salt Cod with Tomato Sauce and Polenta

BACCALÀ IN UMIDO CON POLENTA

ALMOST EVERY REGION *of Italy has a special way of preparing salt cod. My mother used to soak the cod for several days, then she would fry the pieces in oil and finish cooking them in a lovely tomato-based sauce. Today when I prepare this dish, I poach the cod instead of frying it, then I finish cooking it in a savory tomato sauce. And yes, just like my mother, I serve steaming-hot soft polenta alongside it.*

SERVES 4

FOR THE COD
1½ pounds dried salt cod
  (see Note)
1 cup dry white wine
2 dried bay leaves, crumbled
4–5 fresh parsley sprigs
½ yellow onion, peeled and cut
  into 2 or 3 pieces
1 tablespoon black peppercorns

FOR THE POLENTA
½ recipe Basic Polenta
  (see page 130)
¼ cup extra-virgin olive oil

½ cup minced yellow onion
2 garlic cloves, minced
3–4 anchovy fillets, chopped
Chopped fresh red chile pepper or
  dried red pepper flakes to taste
2 cups canned imported Italian
  plum tomatoes, with their
  juice, put through a food mill
  to remove the seeds
2–2½ cups cod poaching liquid
Salt to taste
2 tablespoons chopped fresh flat-
  leaf Italian parsley or regular
  parsley

TO soak the cod, place the salt cod in a large bowl and cover completely with cold water. Cover and refrigerate for 3 to 4 days, changing the water two or three times a day. Drain the softened cod and break it into large pieces.

TO poach the cod, fill a medium-size saucepan halfway with cold water. Add the wine, bay leaves, parsley, onion, and peppercorns, and bring to a gentle boil over medium heat. Simmer 20 to 25 minutes. Add the cold pieces, reduce the heat to low, and cook the fish at the barest simmer for 5 to 6 minutes. Scoop up the fish with a large skimmer and, when cool, remove skin and bones if any.

STRAIN the poaching liquid and reserve it.

PREPARE Basic Polenta and keep it soft, as instructed on page 130.

HEAT the oil in a large skillet over medium heat. Add the onion and cook, stirring, until it is lightly golden and soft, 4 to 5 minutes. Add the garlic, anchovies, and chile pepper, and stir for about 1 minute. Add the tomatoes and 2 cups of the reserved poaching liquid. Taste the sauce and, if necessary, season lightly with salt. Simmer, uncovered, until sauce has a medium-thick consistency, 10 to 15 minutes.

ADD the cod to the sauce, and simmer gently, shaking the pan occasionally, until the fish begins to break into large flakes when stirred with a wooden spoon, 5 to 6 minutes. Stir the parsley into the sauce, and taste and adjust the seasoning.

SPOON the cod and the sauce onto serving dishes, next to a generous helping of steaming soft polenta.

Note: Dried cod is generally cured in salt or in a brine solution, then it is dried on racks. Since dried salt cod is fairly expensive, I urge you to shop around. Look for it at Italian markets or at regular grocery stores.

Poached Halibut with Tomato-Olive Sauce

PESCE CON SALSA DI POMODORO E OLIVE

YEARS AGO, *when I taught cooking on the West Coast, this dish was one of my students' favorites. What they liked most was its quick, foolproof preparation and the way the fish tasted and looked after being cooked. The one thing to remember in preparing this recipe is to keep the sauce at a bare simmer. A fast-cooking sauce will overcook your fish.*

SERVES 4

¼ cup extra-virgin olive oil
½ cup minced yellow onion
2 garlic cloves, minced
2 anchovy fillets, chopped
2 tablespoons chopped fresh flat-leaf Italian or regular parsley
3 cups canned imported Italian plum tomatoes, with their juice, put through a food mill to remove the seeds

10–12 pitted black olives, halved
1 tablespoon capers
Salt and freshly ground black pepper
4 halibut or sea bass fillets, about 2 pounds

HEAT the oil in a large skillet over medium heat. Add the onion and cook, stirring, until onion is lightly golden and soft, 4 to 5 minutes. Add the garlic, anchovies, and 1 tablespoon of the parsley. Stir for about 1 minute. Add the tomatoes, olives, and capers, and season with salt and several grindings of pepper. Simmer the sauce 4 to 5 minutes.

PUT the sauce in the bowl of a food processor and process until smooth. Return the sauce to the skillet and bring it back to a simmer over medium-low heat. Taste and adjust the seasoning, then add the fish and cover the skillet. Simmer gently until the fish is cooked all the way through, 10 to 12 minutes.

SPOON some sauce in the center of serving dishes and place the fish over the sauce. Sprinkle fish with some of the remaining chopped parsley and serve.

Sole with Crisp Bread-Herb Coating

SOGLIOLA IMPANATA

IN THIS RECIPE *fillets of sole are dipped into eggs and coated with an aromatic mixture of finely chopped fresh white bread crumbs, freshly grated Parmigiano, chopped olives, and fresh herbs. The sole is then fried in butter and oil until the bread coating is golden and crisp.*

SERVE THE SOLE *accompanied by Oven-Baked Mixed Vegetables (page 204). Prepare the vegetables a day or so ahead, and serve them as a salad at room temperature, sprinkled with a bit of wine vinegar.*

SERVES 4

4 cups loosely packed pieces of white bread, chopped very fine

⅓ cup freshly grated Parmigiano-Reggiano cheese

10 pitted green olives, finely chopped

2 tablespoons chopped fresh flat-leaf Italian parsley or regular parsley

¼ cup loosely packed fresh oregano leaves, chopped, or 2 tablespoons chopped basil

3 large eggs, beaten in a medium bowl

Salt and freshly ground black pepper to taste

4 large fresh fillets of sole, about 1½ pounds

1 cup unbleached all-purpose flour, spread on a sheet of aluminum foil

2 tablespoons unsalted butter

3 tablespoons olive oil

Slices of lemon

IN a medium-size bowl combine the bread, Parmigiano, olives, parsley, and oregano, and mix well. Spread the mixture evenly on aluminum foil.

SEASON the eggs with salt and pepper. Coat the sole fillets lightly with flour and dip them into the eggs, letting the excess egg flow off the fish. Coat the fillets well with the bread crumb mixture, pressing the coating onto the fish with the palms of your hands. Place the fillets on a large platter and refrigerate, uncovered, for 30 minutes, so that the coating will settle and dry, and remain attached to the fish during cooking.

IN a large, heavy skillet, heat the butter and the oil over medium heat. When the butter foams, slip in the sole fillets without crowding them. Cook in two batches if necessary. Cook until the fish has a nice golden-brown color on both sides, about 6 minutes. If necessary, reduce the heat a bit so as not to burn the bread crumb coating.

TRANSFER the sole fillets to paper towels and pat dry to remove excess fat. Place fish on serving dishes and serve hot with slices of lemon.

Shellfish "Polpette"

POLPETTE DI PESCE

TRADITIONALLY POLPETTE ARE *made with meat. Today, however, Italians have discovered that fish and vegetable polpette are equally tasty. Here, sautéed shrimp and scallops are chopped in a food processor, then mixed together with soft cooked onion, eggs, and Parmigiano. Serve the polpette as an entrée with Roasted Pepper Salad (page 208) or as an appetizer.*

SERVES 4 AS AN ENTRÉE OR 6 AS AN APPETIZER

FOR THE SHELLFISH POLPETTE

⅓ cup extra-virgin olive oil

1 cup minced yellow onion

½ pound medium-size shrimp, peeled and deveined

½ pound sea scallops

2 large eggs, lightly beaten

⅓ cup freshly grated Parmigiano-Reggiano cheese

2 tablespoons fine, plain dried bread crumbs

2 tablespoons chopped fresh flat-leaf Italian or regular parsley

2 tablespoons heavy cream

Salt and freshly ground black pepper to taste

2 large eggs, lightly beaten

2 cups fine, plain dried bread crumbs

Oil for frying

HEAT 3 tablespoons of the oil in a medium-size skillet over medium heat. Add the onion and cook, stirring, until it is lightly golden and soft, 4 to 5 minutes. With a slotted spoon transfer onion to a bowl and cool.

continued

HEAT the remaining oil in a large skillet over high heat. Add the shrimp and the scallops, and cook until they are golden on all sides, about 2 minutes. With a slotted spoon transfer shrimp and scallops to a bowl and cool.

PLACE cooled fish and onion in the bowl of a food processor and chop them into very fine pieces (do not puree them). Put the mixture into a large bowl, and add the eggs, Parmigiano, bread crumbs, parsley, and cream. Season with salt and pepper. Mix everything well with a wooden spoon or with your hands until ingredients are thoroughly blended. (If the mixture seems too soft, add a few more tablespoons of Parmigiano or bread crumbs.)

TAKE 1 heaping tablespoon of the shellfish mixture, shape it into a small ball, then flatten it lightly between the palms of your hands. When all the polpette have been shaped, dip them into the eggs, and coat them with the bread crumbs.

HEAT 1 inch of oil in a medium-size skillet over medium heat. When the oil is very hot, lower a few polpette at a time into the oil with a slotted spoon. Cook until they are lightly golden, about 2 minutes, then turn them gently and cook the other side until golden. Remove with a slotted spoon to paper towels to drain. Serve piping hot.

Sole Marinated with Red Bell Peppers, Onion, and Vinegar

SOGLIOLA IN CARPIONE

THIS PREPARATION, CALLED in carpione, *is common to several Italian regions, in particular Sicily and the Veneto. Fillets of sole are browned in oil, then topped with a medley of sweet-and-sour soft cooked onion and red bell peppers, and left to marinate for several hours. Serve this at room temperature as an appetizer or as a light entrée.*

SERVES 4

⅓ cup, plus 2 tablespoons, extra-virgin olive oil

2 pounds firm-fleshed fillet of sole, such as Dover or yellow

Salt and pepper to taste

1 cup unbleached all-purpose flour, spread on a sheet of aluminum foil

2 tablespoons unsalted butter

2 garlic cloves, peeled and lightly crushed

1 large yellow onion, peeled and thinly sliced

2 red bell peppers, cored, seeded, and cut into thin strips

½ cup red wine vinegar

¼ cup granulated sugar

HEAT ⅓ cup of the oil in a large skillet over medium-high heat. Season the fish fillets with salt and pepper, dredge them in flour, and shake off the excess flour. Slip the fillets into the skillet without crowding them. Cook until they are golden on both sides, 6 to 7 minutes. Transfer fish to a deep serving dish.

HEAT the remaining oil and the butter in another large skillet over medium heat. When the butter foams, add the garlic cloves. Cook until they are golden brown. Discard the garlic, add the onion and pepper strips to the skillet, and cook, stirring occasionally, until the vegetables are lightly golden and soft, 10 to 12 minutes. Season with salt. Add the vinegar and the sugar. Cook and stir until the sugar is melted and the vinegar is reduced by half, is thick and glazy, and coats the vegetables.

SPOON the vegetables and all the juices over the fish and cool to room temperature. Cover the fish tightly and refrigerate for several hours or overnight. Bring the fish back to room temperature before serving.

"Drunken" Tuna

TONNO UBRIACO

THIS DISH COMES *from Le Marche, a beautiful region on the Adriatic Sea. The combination of fish and Marsala wine is unusual and delightful. The Marsala, when cooked to a thick essence, imbues the fish with mellow sweetness. The lemon juice, capers, and anchovies add bite and tanginess.*

SERVES 4

¼–⅓ cup extra-virgin olive oil
Four 1-inch-thick tuna or
    swordfish steaks, about
    2 pounds
Salt and freshly ground black
    pepper to taste
1 cup unbleached all-purpose flour,
    spread on a sheet of aluminum
    foil
1 cup dry Marsala wine, such as
    Florio or Pellegrino

½ cup Basic Fish Broth
    (see page 135)
1 tablespoon capers, rinsed
2 anchovy fillets, chopped
⅓ cup lemon juice
1 tablespoon unsalted butter
1 tablespoon chopped fresh flat-
    leaf Italian parsley or regular
    parsley

HEAT the oil in a large skillet over medium-high heat. Season the tuna steaks with salt and pepper, and coat them lightly with flour. Add the tuna steaks to the hot oil and cook until they are lightly golden on both sides, 2 to 3 minutes.

TILT the skillet gently and discard half of the oil. Place the skillet back on the heat and add the Marsala wine and the fish broth. As soon as the liquid comes to a boil, reduce the heat to medium low and simmer, uncovered, until tuna is cooked all the way through, 5 to 6 minutes. Transfer fish to serving dishes and keep warm in a low oven while you finish the sauce.

RAISE the heat to high under the skillet and add the capers, anchovies, and lemon juice. Season with salt and pepper. Cook the sauce for a few minutes until it has a medium-thick consistency. Add butter and parsley, and stir until sauce is thick and velvety, about 1 minute. Spoon sauce over fish and serve at once.

Sea Bass Baked in Parchment

IL BRANZINO AL CARTOCCIO

ONE OF THE *simplest ways to prepare moist, delicious fish is to cook it in parchment paper. In this preparation, sea bass fillets are topped with sliced fresh ripe tomatoes, scallions, capers, fresh basil, lemon juice, and good extra-virgin olive oil, wrapped in parchment, and baked. Cooking time of the fish is estimated at 10 minutes per inch of thickness. The bundles can be prepared several hours ahead and refrigerated. Just bring the fish back to room temperature before baking.*

SERVES 4

4 sheets of parchment paper or
    aluminum foil, cut into 12 ×
    16-inch rectangles
4 sea bass fillets, about 2 pounds
2–3 tablespoons extra-virgin
    olive oil
Salt and freshly ground black
    pepper to taste

Juice of 1 lemon
4 medium fresh, ripe tomatoes,
    sliced into ¼-inch rounds
3 scallions, white parts only, diced
1 tablespoon capers, rinsed
6–8 fresh basil leaves, thinly
    shredded, or 1 tablespoon
    chopped parsley

PLACE the sheets of parchment paper on a work surface and brush lightly with oil. Place the sea bass fillets in the center of one half of each parchment sheet. Season the fish with salt and pepper, and sprinkle with lemon juice. Top the fish with the tomato slices, scallions, capers, and basil, and drizzle with oil. Fold the other half of the parchment sheet over the fish, and tightly fold the edges of the paper to make a 1-inch border.

PREHEAT the oven to 400°. Place the parchment bundles on a baking sheet and bake 10 to 15 minutes, depending on the thickness of the fish. At this point the fish should be cooked all the way through and the bundles should have puffed up and have a dark brown color.

PLACE each bundle on a serving dish and carefully unwrap or cut the parchment with a knife or scissors. Serve the fish in its wrapping.

LAMB CHOPS WITH RED BELL PEPPERS

LAMB AND POTATO STEW

CHICKEN STEW WITH PUTTANESCA SAUCE

CRISP BREAST OF CHICKEN, MILANO STYLE

STUFFED CHICKEN BREASTS WITH WHITE WINE

STUFFED ROASTED TURKEY BREAST

ROASTED RABBIT WITH ARTICHOKES AND PEAS

RABBIT WITH PORCINI MUSHROOMS

STUFFED PORK BUNDLES WITH PORCINI MUSHROOMS,
MARSALA, AND TOMATOES

PANCETTA-WRAPPED PORK ROAST WITH ROASTED POTATOES

POACHED COTECHINO SAUSAGE WRAPPED IN TURKEY BREAST

PORK CHOPS WITH CABBAGE AND ONION

VEAL SCALOPPINE WITH ARTICHOKES AND LEMON

PAN-ROASTED VEAL STUFFED WITH MUSHROOMS

VEAL MEDALLIONS WITH PROSCIUTTO AND MARSALA WINE

VEAL SHANKS WITH FRESH TOMATOES AND PEAS

STUFFED BREADED VEAL CHOPS

VEAL STEW WITH ONION AND WHITE WINE

VEAL MEATBALLS AND SAUSAGE IN SAVORY TOMATO SAUCE

BOLOGNESE MEAT LOAF

BAKED POLENTA WITH MEAT SAUCE

Meat and Poultry

GIVEN THE GREAT enthusiasm that Italians have for their wonderful first courses—pastas, soups, risottos, and gnocchi—it is not surprising that they approach the *secondi*—meat and poultry—with a bit more restraint. That restraint has also been a function of expense. Until several decades ago, meat in Italy was expensive, particularly beef and veal, and therefore not widely consumed. When Italians could put meat on the table, they either opted for poultry, rabbit, and a variety of small birds, which they raised or hunted themselves, or less expensive meats, such as tripe, liver, and kidneys.

NOWADAYS, EVEN THOUGH most Italians can well afford to eat meat every day, they seldom do. And when meat is served, it is generally in small portions. One does not need to eat large amounts of food to enjoy its flavor.

THE DISHES I chose for this chapter are a mixture of traditional and contemporary. This is the food of *la buona cucina casalinga*, good home cooking. It is simple, wholesome food, with bold flavors, which depends strongly on excellent ingredients and centuries-old techniques. It is the food I grew up with and that I look for every time I go to Italy. As with many recipes in this book, some of these traditional dishes have been adapted for today's lighter eating.

THE INGREDIENTS FOR these recipes can be found most everywhere. Many of the meat and poultry dishes in this chapter are stewed and cooked slowly with savory sauces. Others are grilled, sautéed, and pan-roasted in the Italian manner.

A SIMPLE WAY to determine whether your chops, steaks, or chicken breasts are done is to press the meat with your fingertips. If the meat is very soft and yielding, it is rare. If the meat is medium soft, it is medium rare. If the meat is firm, it is well done.

TRY LAMB AND POTATO STEW (page 154), for your family, or Veal Meatballs and Sausage (page 179). (For me, this is Italian soul food!) For dinner with friends, make Stuffed Chicken Breasts with White Wine (page 158) or Veal Shanks with Fresh Tomatoes and Peas (page 174). If you want to impress someone close to your heart, do Lamb Chops with Red Bell Peppers (page 153) or Veal Medallions with Prosciutto and Marsala Wine (page 173). Serve these dishes attractively accompanied by nice, fresh vegetables, crusty Italian bread, and good wine. Then sit back and enjoy as you share this labor of love.

Lamb Chops with Red Bell Peppers

AGNELLO AI PEPERONI

IN THIS DISH *the young, tender lamb chops are quickly browned in oil, then finished in a savory sauce of onion, wine, broth, tomatoes, and grilled red bell peppers. The peppers impart a mellow sweetness to the sauce and to the lamb. On chilly days, I love to serve this dish over a few slices of grilled or fried polenta.*

SERVES 4

2 large red bell peppers, roasted and
  peeled as instructed on page 86
⅓ cup extra-virgin olive oil
8 single lamb chops, about 1½
  pounds, cut from the rib, each
  ½ inch thick
Salt and freshly ground black
  pepper to taste
⅓ cup finely minced yellow onion
1 garlic clove, minced
Chopped fresh red chile pepper or
  dried red pepper flakes to taste

¾ cup dry white wine
¾ cup canned imported Italian
  plum tomatoes, with their
  juice, put through a food mill
  to remove the seeds
¾ cup homemade chicken broth
  (see page 33) or canned
  chicken broth
1–2 tablespoons finely chopped
  fresh flat-leaf Italian parsley or
  regular parsley

CUT the bell peppers into ¼-inch strips and set aside.

HEAT the oil in a large skillet over medium-high heat. When the oil is hot, season the chops with salt and pepper and add to the skillet without crowding. Cook until chops are golden on both sides, about 2 minutes. (If necessary cook the chops in two batches.)

TRANSFER the chops to a platter. Discard half of the fat in the skillet. Reduce the heat to medium and add the onion. Cook, stirring, until onion is lightly golden, 2 to 3 minutes. Add the garlic and chile pepper, and stir less than 1 minute. Add the wine and cook, stirring, to pick up the bits and pieces stuck to the bottom of the skillet. When the wine is reduced by half, 2 to 3 minutes, add the tomatoes and the broth. Bring to a boil, stirring for a few minutes. Return the chops to the skillet and add the pepper strips. Cover the skillet partially, reduce the heat to low, and simmer 7 to 8 minutes.

PLACE the lamb chops on warm serving dishes. Raise the heat under the skillet and add the parsley. Cook until the sauce has a nice medium-thick consistency. Taste and adjust the seasoning, then spoon the sauce over the chops and serve at once.

Lamb and Potato Stew

SPEZZATINO DI AGNELLO CON PATATE

IN THE COUNTRYSIDE *of Emilia-Romagna, lamb is traditionally cooked on a spit or slowly stewed with garlic, herbs, and wine. Often, other ingredients are added to this basic preparation, such as pancetta or prosciutto, tomatoes, potatoes, or beans. However, the real secret of a good stew lies in its slow, long cooking, which allows the meat to be meltingly tender and extracts all the flavors of the ingredients.*

SERVES 6

1 pound boiling potatoes, peeled and cut into medium chunks
⅓ cup extra-virgin olive oil
3 pounds boneless lamb shoulder, all fat removed, cut into 2- to 3-inch pieces
1 cup all-purpose flour
2 ounces sliced pancetta, chopped
2 garlic cloves, minced
1 tablespoon finely chopped fresh rosemary or 1 teaspoon chopped dried rosemary

Salt and freshly ground black pepper to taste
1 cup light-bodied red wine, such as a Cabernet or Chianti Classico
1½ cups homemade meat broth (see page 32) or ½ cup canned meat broth and 1 cup water
1½ cups canned imported Italian plum tomatoes, with their juice, put through a food mill to remove the seeds

BRING a medium-size saucepan of water to a boil over medium heat. Add the potatoes and cook until they are tender but still firm to the bite, about 15 minutes. Drain potatoes and set aside.

Stews taste even better if they are prepared ahead of time. I often double this recipe and set aside what I need for supper. After the stew has cooled, I divide the remainder into separate bowls and refrigerate or freeze it. Then, I always have a meal ready and waiting.

Do not reduce the sauce too much, since the potatoes will absorb a lot of it. If that happens, add more broth or tomatoes.

HEAT the oil in a large skillet over medium-high heat. Place lamb in a large colander over a bowl and sprinkle with flour. Shake the colander to distribute the flour evenly. Add the lamb to the oil in the skillet in small batches and brown on all sides, 5 to 6 minutes. With a slotted spoon transfer lamb to a platter.

ADD the pancetta and stir quickly until pancetta is lightly golden, about 1 minute. Off the heat tilt the skillet and remove half of the fat. Place the skillet back over high heat and add the garlic and rosemary, and stir once or twice.

RETURN the lamb to the skillet, and season with salt and pepper. Stir for about a minute, and add the wine. Cook, stirring, until wine is reduced by half, 2 to 3 minutes. Add the broth and the tomatoes, and bring to a boil. Cover the skillet partially and reduce the heat to low. Simmer for about 1 hour, checking the stew and stirring it a few times during cooking.

ADD the potatoes to the lamb, and simmer 10 to 15 minutes longer. Taste and adjust the seasoning. Let the stew sit for 15 to 20 minutes before serving it hot.

Chicken Stew with Puttanesca Sauce

UMIDO DI POLLO ALLA PUTTANESCA

SPAGHETTI ALLA PUTTANESCA *is a well-known southern Italian dish. The sauce is a spicy blend of garlic, anchovies, tomatoes, capers, olives, and red chile pepper. Here, the chicken is browned in oil, then simmers in the savory puttanesca sauce.*

SERVES 4

⅓ cup extra-virgin olive oil

One 4-pound chicken, cut into 8
   serving pieces, washed and
   dried on paper towels

Salt to taste

4 anchovy fillets, chopped

1 garlic clove, minced

2–2½ cups canned imported
   Italian plum tomatoes, with
   their juice, put through a food
   mill to remove the seeds

Chopped fresh red chile pepper or
   dried red pepper flakes to taste

8–10 pitted black olives, thinly
   sliced

2 tablespoons capers, rinsed

HEAT the oil in a wide-bottomed casserole over medium heat. When the oil is very hot, slip in the chicken pieces without crowding them. Cook until the chicken is golden on both sides, 5 to 6 minutes. Transfer to a large platter.

DISCARD half of the oil in the casserole. Add the anchovies and the garlic, and stir quickly a few times. (Remember that the oil is very hot and the garlic will turn golden in no time at all.) Add the tomatoes and bring to a gentle boil. Season with salt and chile pepper. Return the chicken to the casserole, reduce the heat to low, and cover the pan partially. Simmer 30 to 40 minutes, turning the chicken pieces and stirring occasionally. Add the olives and the capers, and simmer 5 to 10 minutes longer. If the sauce is a bit thin, transfer the chicken pieces to a large platter, raise the heat under the pan, and boil the sauce down to a thicker consistency. Taste and adjust the seasoning, and serve.

Crisp Breast of Chicken, Milano Style

COTOLETTA DI POLLO ALLA MILANESE

BECAUSE VEAL IN *Italy is expensive, many cooks substitute chicken. Here, chicken breasts are dipped into beaten eggs, coated with a bread-crumb mixture, then sautéed in butter and oil until the meat is moist and tender and the top is crisp and golden brown. The cooking time is approximately 8 minutes.*

SERVES 4

4 chicken breasts, boned, skinned
    and left whole, pounded thin
2 large eggs, lightly beaten in a
    deep dish with salt to taste
1½ cups fine, plain dried bread
    crumbs, mixed with ⅓ cup
    freshly grated Parmigiano-
    Reggiano cheese, spread on a
    sheet of aluminum foil

1 tablespoon unsalted butter
3 tablespoons olive oil
Lemon wedges

One hot summer day in Rome, I was served a veal cutlet paired with a condiment of uncooked diced tomatoes, celery, scallions, and fresh basil, tossed with oil and vinegar—light but immensely satisfying.

DIP the chicken breasts into the beaten eggs, letting the excess egg fall back into the dish. Coat the chicken with the bread crumb mixture, lightly pressing the crumbs into the meat with the palms of your hands. (The chicken can be prepared up to this point 1 hour or so ahead and refrigerated.)

HEAT the butter and oil in a large skillet over medium heat. When the butter begins to foam, slide a few chicken cutlets at a time into the skillet and cook 3 to 4 minutes on each side, or until they have a nice golden-brown color. Transfer cutlets to a large platter and keep warm in a low oven while you cook the remaining cutlets. Sprinkle chicken lightly with salt and serve piping hot with lemon wedges.

Note: A cutlet is a slice of meat, fish, or vegetable that is cooked as in this recipe; it is not a dish per se.

Stuffed Chicken Breasts with White Wine

INVOLTINI DI POLLO IN PADELLA

I LOVE THE *mild flavor, firm texture, and versatility of chicken. In this preparation, chicken breasts are boned, skinned, and pounded to about half of their original thickness. Then they are stuffed with a mixture of chopped olives, bread, Parmigiano, grated lemon peel, and garlic, and rolled up into bundles. The bundles are browned in oil, then they finish cooking slowly in wine.*

SERVES 4

FOR THE FILLING

1 cup loosely packed white bread pieces, without crusts, soaked in 1 cup milk for 5 minutes

6 pitted black olives, finely chopped

1 tablespoon chopped fresh flat-leaf Italian parsley or regular parsley

1 small garlic clove, minced

Grated zest of 1 lemon

⅓ cup freshly grated Parmigiano-Reggiano cheese

1 medium-size egg, beaten

Salt and freshly ground black pepper to taste

FOR THE CHICKEN

4 whole chicken breasts, boned, skinned and split, pounded thin

¼ cup extra-virgin olive oil

Salt and freshly ground black pepper to taste

1 cup unbleached all-purpose flour, spread on a sheet of aluminum foil

1 cup dry white wine

2 tablespoons capers, rinsed

⅓ cup lemon juice

⅓ cup chicken broth

1 tablespoon unsalted butter

1 tablespoon chopped fresh flat-leaf Italian parsley or regular parsley

DRAIN the bread and squeeze it in your hands into a soft pulp. Put the bread in a medium-size bowl, together with the chopped olives, parsley, garlic, lemon zest, Parmigiano, and egg. Mix and season with salt and pepper.

LAY chicken breasts on a work surface and spread 1 large rounded teaspoon of filling on each breast, leaving a border free all around the chicken breast. Roll breasts into bundles. Secure each breast with a couple of wooden toothpicks or tie with string. (The chicken can be prepared up to this point several hours or a day ahead.)

HEAT the oil in a large skillet over medium heat. Season breasts with salt and pepper, and coat the bundles lightly with flour. When the oil is very hot, add the bundles to the skillet without crowding. Cook until the bundles are golden brown on all sides, 6 to 7 minutes. Discard half of the fat in the skillet, raise the heat to high, and add the wine. Cook, stirring, until wine is reduced by half, 2 to 3 minutes. Add the capers and the lemon juice. Cover the skillet partially, reduce the heat to low, and simmer until the chicken is cooked all the way through, 10 to 15 minutes. Stir the sauce and turn the breasts a few times during cooking. Add a little more wine, chicken broth, or water if the liquid in the skillet reduces too much.

REMOVE wooden toothpicks or string from the bundles and place them on serving dishes. Put the skillet back on high heat, and add the broth, butter, and parsley. Cook, stirring, for about 1 minute until the sauce has a medium-thick consistency. Taste and adjust the seasoning, spoon sauce over chicken, and serve.

Stuffed Roasted Turkey Breast

ARROSTO DI TACCHINO

IN ITALY TURKEY, *pork, and veal roasts very often are the centerpieces of casual or elegant meals. If I had to choose one dish to prepare for a leisurely Sunday dinner, this turkey breast roast would be it. The roast can be stuffed with a variety of ingredients. In summer I stuff it with savory small frittate or with roasted red bell peppers and serve it at room temperature. In winter I stuff it with prosciutto and fontina or Parmigiano and serve some of the pan juices on the side.*

SERVES 6 TO 8

FOR THE FRITTATE

6 large eggs

⅓ cup freshly grated Parmigiano-
 Reggiano cheese

2 tablespoons chopped fresh flat-
 leaf Italian parsley or regular
 parsley

8–10 basil leaves, minced

Salt and freshly ground black
 pepper to taste

1–2 tablespoons olive oil

1 cup minced red onion

FOR THE TURKEY

One 3½–4-pound boneless breast
 of turkey, butterflied and
 pounded thin

Salt and freshly ground black
 pepper to taste

¼–⅓ cup olive oil

½–1 cup dry white wine

PREPARE THE FRITTATE: In a medium bowl beat the eggs with the Parmigiano, parsley, and basil, and season with salt and pepper.

HEAT the oil in an 8-inch nonstick skillet over medium heat. Add the onion and cook, stirring, until it is lightly golden and soft, 8 to 10 minutes. With a slotted spoon scoop up the onion and stir into the eggs. Put the skillet back over medium heat and ladle in about one third of the egg mixture, or just enough to cover the bottom of the skillet. Cook until the bottom of the frittata is lightly golden and the top begins to solidify, 2 to 3 minutes. (Keep in mind that the frittata is very thin and it will cook quickly.) Put a large, flat plate over the skillet and turn the frittata onto the plate. Slide the frittata back into the skillet to cook the other side, 1 to 2 minutes. Make 2 more frittate, using the remaining egg mixture. Set aside to cool.

PREPARE AND COOK THE ROAST: Preheat the oven to 375°. Place the butterflied turkey on a work surface and season it with salt and pepper. Cover the turkey breast with the frittate, making sure to leave free about a 2-inch border all around. Roll up the turkey breast tightly and tie securely with string. Season the outside of the roast with salt and pepper.

HEAT the oil in a large, heavy casserole over medium-high heat. Add the turkey and cook until it is golden on all sides, 8 to 10 minutes. Place the casserole in the oven and cook 45 minutes to 1 hour. Baste the roast with its pan juices during cooking or with a bit of white wine. Transfer roast to a cutting board and let it settle for 5 to 10 minutes. Remove the string, slice the meat, and serve with some of the pan juices.

Roasted Rabbit with Artichokes and Peas

CONIGLIO ARROSTO

YOU SIMPLY HAVE got to try this! The vegetables, which are cooked separately and are swirled briefly into the pan juices, retain all their color and character while absorbing the flavor of the rabbit.

SERVES 4

⅓ cup extra-virgin olive oil
Salt and freshly ground black
  pepper
Two 3½- to 4-pound rabbits, cut
  into serving pieces (see Note)
1 garlic clove, minced
2–3 ounces sliced prosciutto, diced

2 pounds baby artichokes, cleaned
  and cooked as instructed on
  page 16
1 cup shelled fresh peas or frozen
  peas, thawed
⅓ cup red wine vinegar
⅓ cup dry white wine

PREHEAT the oven to 350°.

HEAT the oil in a large, heavy casserole over medium-high heat. Season the rabbit pieces with salt and pepper, and slip them into the hot oil without crowding. (If the casserole is not large enough, brown the meat in two batches.) Cook until the pieces are lightly golden on all sides, 5 to 6 minutes. Turn the heat off under the casserole, and add the garlic and the prosciutto. Stir quickly for less than 1 minute. Place the casserole in the oven and bake, 40 to 45 minutes. Baste the rabbit with the pan juices a few times during cooking. Add a bit of wine if the juices reduce too much.

WHILE the rabbit is cooking, prepare the artichokes. Cut the cooked artichokes into wedges and set aside.

IF you are using fresh peas, bring a small saucepan of water to a boil over medium heat. Add a pinch of salt and the peas. Cook, uncovered, until tender, 5 to 10 minutes, depending on size. Drain peas and set aside.

REMOVE casserole from the oven and transfer rabbit to a large, warm serving platter. Discard some of the fat in the casserole and put pan over medium heat. Add the vinegar and the wine, and stir quickly to dissolve the meat scraps sticking to the bottom of the casserole. As soon as the vinegar and the wine have reduced somewhat, and the pan juices are thick, add the artichokes and peas, and season lightly with salt and pepper. Stir until vegetables are well coated with the sauce, less than 1 minute. Spoon over rabbit and serve.

Note: Chicken can be used if you prefer it or if rabbit is unavailable.

Rabbit with Porcini Mushrooms

CONIGLIO CON FUNGHI PORCINI

ONE OF MY *favorite aunts used to have a small farm outside Bologna. Zia Rina's rabbit and chicken stews were memorable. Since porcini mushrooms were expensive, she would substitute large chunks of potatoes. These stews were made with plenty of sauce, so that she could use it over gnocchi or tagliatelle later on. And if she had any leftover tagliatelle, it would form part of a frittata for yet another meal.*

SERVES 4 TO 6

1 ounce dried porcini mushrooms, soaked in 2 cups lukewarm water for 20 minutes

6 tablespoons olive oil

1 cup unbleached all-purpose flour, spread on a sheet of aluminum foil

Two 3½- to 4-pound rabbits, cut into serving pieces

2 tablespoons unsalted butter

½ cup finely diced yellow onion

½ cup finely diced carrot

½ cup finely diced celery

¼ pound sliced pancetta, diced

½ cup dry white wine

2 cups canned imported Italian plum tomatoes, with their juice, put through a food mill to remove the seeds

Salt and freshly ground black pepper to taste

1 garlic clove, minced

2 tablespoons chopped fresh flat-leaf Italian parsley or regular parsley

Grated zest of a small lemon

DRAIN the mushrooms and reserve the soaking water. Rinse mushrooms well under cold running water and chop them roughly. Line a strainer with two paper towels and strain the mushroom liquid into a bowl to get rid of the sandy deposits. Set aside.

PREHEAT the oven to 375°. Heat 4 tablespoons of the oil in a wide-bottomed casserole over high heat. Flour the rabbit pieces lightly and when the oil is very hot, add them to the casserole without crowding them. Cook until rabbit is golden on both sides, 5 to 6 minutes. Transfer pieces to a large platter.

continued

If you do not care for the taste of rabbit, let it soak in cold water with 1 cup of white wine vinegar for a few hours. If you prefer, you can use chicken instead. Today cut-up fresh or frozen rabbit is widely available in butcher shops as well as Italian specialty stores.

DISCARD the oil and place casserole back on medium heat. Add the remaining 2 tablespoons of oil and the butter. As soon as the butter begins to foam, add the onion, carrot, celery, and pancetta. Cook, stirring, until pancetta and vegetables are lightly golden, 4 to 5 minutes. Add the porcini mushrooms and stir briefly.

RETURN rabbit to casserole, raise the heat to high, add the wine. Cook, stirring, until the wine is reduced by half, 1 to 2 minutes. Add the tomatoes and 1 cup of the reserved porcini soaking water. Season with salt and pepper, and bring the liquid to a boil. Cover the casserole loosely with some aluminum foil and place it in the oven. Cook until rabbit is tender and sauce has a medium-thick consistency, 50 minutes to 1 hour. Stir a few times during cooking.

REMOVE the casserole from the oven and place the rabbit on warm serving dishes. Add the garlic, parsley, and grated zest to the sauce, and stir over medium heat for 2 to 3 minutes. Taste and adjust the seasoning. Spoon the sauce over the rabbit and serve at once.

Stuffed Pork Bundles with Porcini Mushrooms, Marsala, and Tomatoes

INVOLTINI DI MAIALE IN UMIDO

TAKE A FEW *thin slices of pork, veal, or beef, top them with ham and a bit of grated cheese, roll them up into bundles, and cook them in a savory tomato- or wine-based sauce. The sauce can contain minced vegetables, mushrooms, or just a hint of herbs. There are many variations of this basic preparation, which can be served over soft or grilled polenta or simply by itself.*

SERVES 4

1½ pounds center-cut pork loin, cut into 12 slices and pounded thin into scaloppine

⅓ cup freshly grated Parmigiano-Reggiano cheese

¼ pound sliced speck (see Note, page 15) or prosciutto

¼–⅓ cup extra-virgin olive oil

½ cup minced yellow onion

½ ounce dried porcini mushrooms, soaked in 2 cups lukewarm water for 20 minutes

1 cup dry Marsala wine, such as Florio or Pellegrino

1½ cups canned imported Italian plum tomatoes, with their juice, put through a food mill to remove the seeds

Salt and freshly ground black pepper to taste

PLACE the pork scaloppine on a work surface. Spread 1 teaspoon of Parmigiano over each piece and top it with a small slice of speck. (Cut the slices of speck in half if they are too large.) Roll the scaloppine into bundles and secure with one or two wooden toothpicks.

HEAT the oil in a large skillet over medium heat. When the oil is hot, slip the pork bundles into the skillet without crowding them. (If necessary, brown the bundles in a couple of batches.) Cook until the meat is lightly golden on all sides, 2 to 3 minutes. Transfer bundles to a platter.

continued

ADD the onion to the skillet. Cook, stirring quickly, for 2 to 3 minutes. Add the porcini and stir once or twice. Raise the heat to high and add the Marsala wine. Cook, stirring, until the sauce begins to thicken and wine is reduced approximately by half. Add the tomatoes and 1 cup of the reserved porcini soaking liquid. Season with salt and pepper. Bring the sauce to a boil, then reduce the heat to low, and return the bundles to the skillet. Cover the pan partially and cook gently for 10 to 15 minutes, stirring and turning the bundles a few times. Remove toothpicks and serve hot.

Pancetta-Wrapped Pork Roast with Roasted Potatoes

ARROSTO DI MAIALE AL FORNO CON PATATE

IN THIS DISH *a pork roast is wrapped with pancetta, threaded with fresh rosemary, and cooked until the pancetta turns crisp and golden. The result is one of the juiciest, tenderest roasts you've ever tasted. Add large chunks of potatoes and garlic cloves to the pan and serve the roast with Sweet and Sour Onions with Balsamic Vinegar (page 197) for a memorable meal.*

SERVES 4

One 2½-pound center-cut
    boneless pork loin (see Note)
Salt and freshly ground black
    pepper to taste
¼ pound sliced pancetta

5–6 sprigs fresh rosemary
⅓ cup extra-virgin olive oil
5–6 whole garlic cloves, peeled
2 pounds boiling potatoes, peeled
    and cut into large chunks

PREHEAT the oven to 350°.

SEASON the pork loin with salt and pepper. Place the slices of pancetta on a work surface, place the roast over the pancetta, and wrap the pancetta around the pork. Tie the roast securely with string, and tuck the sprigs of rosemary securely under the string.

HEAT the oil in a large, heavy casserole over medium heat. Add the roast and brown it very lightly all over, about 2 minutes. Keep turning the meat to avoid burning the rosemary. When the roast has a pale golden color, turn the heat off under the casserole and add the potatoes and the garlic. Season the potatoes and garlic with salt and pepper and mix them with the oil.

PLACE the casserole in the oven and bake 40 to 45 minutes. Baste the roast with its pan juices a few times during cooking. Check the roast for doneness by piercing it with a thin knife. If the juices that come out are clear or just barely pink, the roast is done. If the juices are visibly pink, cook the roast a bit longer.

TRANSFER the roast to a cutting board and let it settle 5 to 10 minutes. Meanwhile, tilt the casserole slightly away from you and remove as much fat as possible.

REMOVE the string around the roast, slice the meat, and serve with the potatoes and some of the pan juices.

Note: Pork loin roasts are generally prepared with two center-cut loins tied together, thus making them "double loin roasts." For this preparation, you need a single, 2½-pound boneless center-cut pork loin.

Poached Cotechino Sausage Wrapped in Turkey Breast

COTECHINO IN GALERA

COTECHINO IN GALERA, *a classic dish of Emilia-Romagna, literally means "imprisoned" or "jailed" cotechino. The large cotechino sausage is enclosed, or imprisoned, in a large slice of beef, then either roasted or boiled. In this version, turkey is used instead of beef, and the large bundle is slowly simmered with water, wine, and vegetables. The result is a much lighter, tender preparation. It is equally delicious served warm, or at room temperature, along with Emma's Peppers and Tomatoes in a Skillet (page 203) and rice or mashed potatoes.*

SERVES 6

One 1- to 1½-pound cotechino sausage (see Note)

One 3-pound turkey breast, bone and skin removed, butterflied and pounded thin

Salt and freshly ground black pepper to taste

1 small medium yellow onion, peeled and cut into large pieces

1 medium carrot, cut into large pieces

1 celery stalk, cut into large pieces

Several fresh parsley sprigs

1½ cups dry white wine

BRING a large saucepan filled halfway with water to a boil over medium heat. Puncture the cotechino in several places with a fork and slip the cotechino into the water. When the water begins to bubble again, reduce the heat to low and simmer cotechino 25 to 30 minutes. Remove cotechino from the water and gently remove the skin when cool.

PLACE the butterflied turkey breast on a work surface and season with salt and pepper. Place the cotechino on the turkey. Roll up the turkey breast tightly around the cotechino and tie securely with kitchen string.

PLACE the large bundle in a wide saucepan. Add all the remaining ingredients. Cover with cold water and bring to a gentle boil over medium heat. Cover the pot and reduce the heat to low. Cook about 1 hour to 1¼ hours, or until the meat and cotechino are cooked all the way through.

TRANSFER meat to a cutting board and let it settle for 5 to 10 minutes. Remove the string, slice the meat, and serve.

Note: Cotechino is a large, fresh pork sausage that is boiled and served as a part of the classic bollito misto, or simply by itself. Look for it at your Italian market or specialty food store.

Pork Chops with Cabbage and Onion

COSTOLETTE DI MAIALE E VERZE IN PADELLA

ONE OF MY *favorite restaurants in Mantova, in Lombardy, is Trattoria Martini, which serves wonderful traditional dishes like sausage with stewed cabbage, accompanied by grilled polenta. Instead of using sausage, I have prepared this dish with 1-inch-thick, perfectly marbled pork chops. First, I stew the cabbage very slowly with the pancetta and the onion until they are all very soft. I cook the chops separately, splash on a bit of red wine vinegar, and serve them over a layer of meltingly tender Savoy cabbage.*

SERVES 4

½ cup extra-virgin olive oil
2 cups thinly sliced yellow onion
2 ounces sliced pancetta, minced
1 pound Savoy cabbage, cut into
    thin strips

½ cup red wine vinegar
4 pork rib or loin chops, cut
    1 inch thick
Salt and freshly ground black
    pepper to taste

HEAT ¼ cup of the oil in a large skillet over medium heat. Add the onion and the pancetta and cook, stirring, until onion is lightly golden, 3 to 4 minutes. Add the cabbage and stir for a minute or two until cabbage is well coated with the savory base. Add ⅓ cup of the vinegar and stir once or twice. Cover the skillet partially, reduce the heat to low, and cook until the cabbage is soft, 50 to 55 minutes. Stir the cabbage a few times during cooking, adding a bit of water or chicken broth if the pan juices have reduced too much.

TRIM off the excess fat from the pork chops. Heat the remaining oil in a large sauté pan. Season the chops on both sides with salt and pepper and add them to

Make sure to brown the chops and cook them over gentle heat or they will be tough. Overcooking also toughens the chops. To test for doneness, cut a small slit in a chop. If the meat is barely pink, the chop is done.

the hot oil. Reduce the heat to medium low and brown the chops gently, 4 to 5 minutes on each side. When done, the chops should be fairly firm to the touch and the meat when cut through should be just barely pink.

TASTE and adjust the seasoning of the cabbage, arrange some on individual serving dishes, and place the chops over the cabbage.

PUT the pan in which the chops were cooked back on high heat and add the remaining vinegar. Stir quickly until only 1 or 2 tablespoons of thick, concentrated pan juices are left in the pan. Pour over the chops and serve at once.

Veal Scaloppine with Artichokes and Lemon

SCALOPPINE DI VITELLO AI CARCIOFI

SCALOPPINE ARE A *delicious, quick Italian meat dish generally made with veal. However pork, chicken, and turkey scaloppine are also popular. When cooking scaloppine all you have to keep in mind is a few basic rules (see Note).*

SERVES 4

1 pound baby artichokes, cleaned and cooked as instructed on page 16
¼ cup olive oil
1½ pounds veal scaloppine from the top round, sliced ⅛ inch thick and pounded thin
Salt to taste

1 cup dry white wine
Juice of 1 lemon
1 tablespoon unsalted butter
2–3 tablespoons heavy cream
1 tablespoon chopped fresh flat-leaf Italian parsley or regular parsley

PREPARE the artichokes, cut them into thin wedges, and set aside.

HEAT the oil in a large, heavy skillet over high heat. When the oil is hot, add the scaloppine, making sure not to crowd the skillet. (If necessary, cook the veal in two batches.) Season with salt and cook until the veal is lightly golden on both sides, about 2 minutes. Transfer the veal to a plate.

DISCARD the fat in the skillet and put it back on high heat. Add the wine and lemon juice, and stir quickly to dissolve any meat particles stuck to the bottom of the skillet. Add the butter, cream, and artichokes, and season lightly with salt. Cook, stirring, until sauce has a medium-thick consistency, 2 to 3 minutes.

RETURN the scaloppine and any juices on the plate to the skillet. Reduce the heat to medium and mix briefly until the veal is well coated with the sauce, 30 to 40 seconds. Arrange the scaloppine on serving dishes, and taste and adjust the seasoning. Spoon the sauce and the artichokes over the veal, and serve at once.

Note: Tips for cooking scaloppine:

- Use a large, heavy skillet that can take and retain high heat well.
- Always cook the scaloppine over high heat. The meat should be golden outside and pink and juicy inside.
- Do not crowd the skillet or the veal will not brown properly. If necessary, cook meat in a few batches.
- After they are cooked, the scaloppine should not be held before being served, or they will keep on cooking and will be dry when reheated.
- Do not make this dish for a crowd unless you are a whiz at handling several skillets at the same time.
- Have all ingredients ready on a tray, so at the last moment everything will be at hand.

Pan-Roasted Veal Stuffed with Mushrooms

ARROSTO DI VITELLO AI FUNGHI

ITALIAN CUISINE REJOICES *in a great number of "stuffed" dishes: pastas and roasts; large and small birds; veal, pork chops, and vegetables; and even fruit. All these dishes are beautiful to behold, delicious, and yes, even simple to prepare. Here is a stuffed veal roast that after the first 10 or 15 minutes of preparation cooks all by itself and demands only an occasional basting from the cook. Serve it warm or at room temperature. It can feed a crowd.*

SERVES 6

½ cup extra-virgin olive oil
½ pound white cultivated
    mushrooms, wiped clean
    and thinly sliced
1 garlic clove, minced
2 tablespoons chopped fresh flat-
    leaf Italian or regular parsley
⅓ cup freshly grated Parmigiano-
    Reggiano cheese

1 small egg, lightly beaten
Salt and freshly ground black
    pepper to taste
2½ pounds veal shoulder roast,
    butterflied and pounded thin
¼ pound sliced prosciutto
1 cup imported dry Marsala wine
    (see Note)

HEAT ¼ cup of the oil in a large skillet over high heat. Add the mushrooms without crowding the skillet, and cook, stirring, until the mushrooms are lightly golden, 2 to 3 minutes. Add the garlic and the parsley, and stir quickly once or twice. Scoop up the mushrooms with a slotted spoon and place in a bowl to cool. Chop the mushrooms very fine, by hand or with a food processor, and place in a medium-size bowl. (If using a food processor, make sure not to puree the mushrooms.) Mix the mushrooms with the Parmigiano and the egg, and season with salt and pepper.

PLACE the veal on a work surface and season it with salt and pepper. Cover the meat with the slices of prosciutto, and spread the mushroom mixture evenly over the prosciutto, making sure to leave free about a 2-inch border all around. Roll up the veal tightly and tie securely with string. Season the outside of the meat with salt and pepper.

HEAT the remaining oil in a large, heavy casserole over medium-high heat. When the oil is hot, add the roast and cook until it is golden on all sides, 8 to 10 minutes. Add the Marsala wine and when the wine begins to bubble, reduce the heat to low and cover the pot partially. Simmer the roast, basting it occasionally with the pan juices or a little more wine, until the meat is tender, about 1 hour, or until the juices run clear when the meat is pierced with a knife. Transfer the roast to a cutting board and let it settle for about 10 minutes. Remove the string, slice the meat, and serve with the pan juices.

Note: Marsala is an aromatic wine from Sicily used extensively in cooking. Look for imported Marsala, such as Florio or Pellegrino, available in Italian markets and wine shops. It comes in both dry and sweet versions. Use dry Marsala when cooking white meats, and sweet Marsala for desserts.

Veal Medallions with Prosciutto and Marsala Wine

VITELLO AL PROSCIUTTO E MARSALA

THIS QUICK, ELEGANT *dish is prepared the same way as veal scaloppine except that in this lighter version the flour is omitted and the veal is cooked in oil instead of butter. Deglazing the skillet with wine and adding just a little butter will thicken the sauce and impart a fresh taste to it.*

SERVES 4

¼ cup extra-virgin olive oil
1¼ pounds veal loin, cut into
    ¼-inch medallions
Salt to taste

1 cup dry Marsala wine (see Note)
1 tablespoon unsalted butter
2 ounces sliced prosciutto, cut
    into short strips

HEAT the oil in a large, heavy skillet over high heat. When the oil is hot, add the veal, making sure not to crowd the skillet. Season with salt and cook until the veal is golden brown on both sides, 2 to 3 minutes. Transfer veal to a plate.

continued

DISCARD the fat and put the skillet back on high heat. Add the Marsala wine and stir quickly to dissolve any meat particles sticking to the bottom of the skillet. Add the butter and the prosciutto, and season lightly with salt. Cook, stirring, until sauce has a medium-thick consistency, 2 to 3 minutes.

RETURN the veal and any juices on the plate back into the skillet. Reduce the heat to medium and mix briefly until the veal is well coated with the sauce, 30 to 40 seconds. Arrange the veal medallions on serving dishes, and taste and adjust the seasoning of the sauce. Spoon the sauce over the veal and serve at once.

Note: Look for imported dry Marsala wine, such as Florio or Pellegrino, which has a light sugar content and is perfect for this preparation.

Veal Shanks with Fresh Tomatoes and Peas

OSSOBUCO CON POMODORI E PISELLI

IN ITALY THERE *are many ossobuco preparations, of which the best known is the classic ossobuco alla Milanese. A good ossobuco should begin with meaty, milk-fed veal. In this preparation veal shanks are browned in oil and cooked slowly with a flavorful base of onion, pancetta, wine, and broth until they are meltingly tender. Fresh tomatoes and peas are stirred into the sauce during the last 10 minutes of cooking for added color and taste.*

SERVES 4

8 medium-size veal shanks, approximately 4 pounds, cut about 1½ inches thick
2 cups unbleached all-purpose flour, spread on a sheet of aluminum foil
⅓ cup olive oil
2 tablespoons unsalted butter
2–3 ounces sliced pancetta, minced
1 cup minced yellow onion

1 cup dry white wine
Salt and freshly ground black pepper to taste
2½–3 cups homemade chicken broth (see page 33) or 1½ cups canned chicken broth and 1½ cups water
½ pound fresh, ripe tomatoes, seeded and diced
1 cup shelled fresh peas or frozen peas, thawed

DREDGE the veal shanks in flour and shake off any excess. Heat the oil in a large skillet over medium heat. When the oil is very hot, add the veal and cook until golden on both sides, 6 to 8 minutes. Transfer the veal to a dish. Discard some of the fat in the skillet if necessary, and add the butter. When the butter begins to foam, add the pancetta and the onion. Cook, stirring, for 2 to 3 minutes until they begin to color.

RETURN veal to the skillet, raise the heat to high, and add the wine. Cook until the wine is reduced by half and the sauce has thickened a bit, 2 to 3 minutes. Add the broth and bring to a boil. Season with salt and pepper. Reduce the heat to low and cover the skillet partially. Cook, checking the meat and stirring the sauce a few times, until the meat is tender, 1 to 1½ hours. Add some more broth if sauce reduces too much.

STIR in the tomatoes and the fresh peas if using. Put the cover back on the skillet and simmer 10 to 15 minutes longer. (If you use thawed frozen peas, add them to the skillet during the last couple of minutes of cooking.) Taste and adjust the seasoning, and serve piping hot with a few slices of grilled, fried, or soft polenta (pages 130–131).

Stuffed Breaded Veal Chops

COSTOLETTE DI VITELLO FARCITE

THIS DISH TAKES *its inspiration from a classic Milanese recipe. Veal chops are stuffed with a mixture of soft leeks, prosciutto, and Parmigiano, then they are coated with bread crumbs and gently sautéed in butter and oil. For perfectly crisp chops, cook them on medium heat, so the coating will not burn and turn too dark. Then finish the chops in a 350° oven until they are cooked all the way through. I love to serve these chops with Swiss Chard Salad (page 210) or with sautéed Broccoli Rabe with Garlic, Oil, and Hot Chile Pepper (page 196).*

SERVES 4

FOR THE FILLING

1 large leek

3–4 tablespoons extra-virgin olive oil

¼ pound sliced prosciutto or baked ham, finely minced

2 tablespoons finely chopped flat-leaf Italian parsley or regular parsley

⅓ cup freshly grated Parmigiano-Reggiano cheese

1 large egg, lightly beaten

Salt and freshly ground black pepper to taste

Four ¾-inch-thick veal chops, about 2½ pounds, cut from the loin, with the bones cleaned

2 large eggs, lightly beaten in a bowl with a pinch of salt

1 cup fine, plain dried bread crumbs, mixed with ⅓ cup freshly grated Parmigiano-Reggiano cheese, spread evenly over a sheet of aluminum foil

1 tablespoon unsalted butter

3 tablespoons olive oil

Lemon wedges

CUT off the root of the leek and remove one third of the green stalk. Cut leek in half lengthwise and wash well under cold running water, making sure to remove all the dirt trapped between the leaves. Cut the leek into fine dice.

HEAT the oil in a medium skillet over medium-low heat. Add the diced leek and cook, stirring, until it is lightly golden and soft, 6 to 7 minutes. With a slotted spoon transfer leek to a bowl. Add the prosciutto, parsley, Parmigiano, and egg, and season with salt and pepper. Mix well to combine.

PREHEAT the oven to 350°.

MAKE a pocket in each chop by cutting a horizontal slit as far as the bone. Fill each pocket with some of the stuffing and secure each chop with two or three wooden toothpicks. Dip the veal chops into the beaten eggs, letting the excess egg fall off into the bowl. Coat the chops with the bread crumbs, lightly pressing the crumbs into the meat with the palms of your hands. (The chops can be prepared up to this point 1 hour or so ahead and refrigerated.)

IN a large, heavy ovenproof skillet, heat the butter and the oil over medium heat. When the butter begins to foam, slide the veal chops into the skillet and cook 2 to 3 minutes on each side until they are lightly golden. Place the skillet in the oven and cook 6 to 7 minutes longer. Serve piping hot with lemon wedges.

Veal Stew with Onion and White Wine

VITELLO IN TEGAME

THIS IS ANOTHER dish that I love to cook in winter. Cooking large batches of stew is very heartwarming and relaxing. It is so gratifying to see how raw ingredients can become transformed into a fragrant dish in such a short amount of time.

SERVES 6

⅓ cup extra-virgin olive oil
2 large yellow onions, peeled and
    thinly sliced
3 pounds veal shoulder, cut into
    2- to 3-inch pieces
1 cup all-purpose flour
1 cup dry white wine
2 cups homemade chicken broth
    (see page 33) or 1 cup canned
    chicken broth and 1 cup water

Salt and freshly ground black
    pepper to taste
1 garlic clove, minced
2 tablespoons chopped fresh flat-
    leaf Italian parsley or regular
    parsley
Grated zest of 1 lemon

continued

For meltingly tender veal, make sure to simmer the stew very gently. If at the end of cooking the sauce seems a bit thin, raise the heat slightly and cook the stew uncovered for a few minutes.

HEAT the oil in a large skillet over medium heat. Add the onion and cook, stirring, until onion begins to color, 3 to 4 minutes. With a slotted spoon transfer the onion to a dish, draining the excess oil against the side of the skillet.

PLACE the veal in a large strainer over a bowl and sprinkle with flour. Shake the strainer to distribute the flour evenly. Add the veal to the skillet without crowding it, and brown on all sides, 5 to 6 minutes. (If necessary, brown the veal in a couple of batches.)

RETURN the onion to the skillet and add the wine. Stir energetically with a wooden spoon to pick up the bits and pieces that are sticking to the bottom of the skillet. As the wine begins to bubble and thicken, add the broth, season with salt and pepper, and bring to a boil. Cover the skillet partially and reduce the heat to low. Simmer for about 1 hour, checking the stew and stirring it a few times during cooking. Add a bit more broth if the sauce reduces too much.

WHEN the veal is tender, add the garlic, parsley, and grated lemon zest, and cook 5 to 10 minutes longer. Taste and adjust the seasoning, and serve piping hot.

Veal Meatballs and Sausage in Savory Tomato Sauce

POLPETTE E SALSICCE IN UMIDO

IN THIS DISH *we have a perfect example of* la buona cucina casalinga, *good home cooking. Meatballs are very popular in Italy. They can be made with almost any kind of meat and many kinds of other ingredients, such as prosciutto, pancetta, and Parmigiano. The meatballs can be round or flattened like small patties. They are usually crisply pan-fried and served alone. Or cooked in a flavorful sauce with beans, potatoes, or vegetables, they can make a heaty entrée. This dish tastes even better when made several hours ahead. Serve it with soft, baked, or grilled polenta (pages 130–131).*

SERVES 4

FOR THE SAUSAGE AND POLPETTE

1 pound mild Italian sausage
2 slices Italian bread without crusts, broken into pieces and soaked in 1 cup milk for 5 minutes
1 pound ground veal
2 small eggs, lightly beaten
½ cup freshly grated Parmigiano-Reggiano cheese
2 tablespoons chopped fresh flat-leaf Italian parsley or regular parsley
Salt and freshly ground black pepper to taste
2 cups fine, plain dried bread crumbs, spread evenly over a sheet of aluminum foil
Oil for frying

FOR THE SAUCE

¼–⅓ cup extra-virgin olive oil
1 cup minced yellow onion
2 garlic cloves, minced
1 tablespoon chopped fresh sage or 1 teaspoon dried sage, broken into small pieces
½ cup dry white wine
1½ cups canned imported Italian plum tomatoes, with their juice, put through a food mill to remove the seeds
1½ cups homemade chicken broth (see page 33) or ¾ cup canned chicken broth and ¾ cup water
Salt and freshly ground black pepper to taste
1 tablespoon chopped fresh flat-leaf Italian parsley

continued

PRECOOK THE SAUSAGE: Bring a medium-size saucepan of water to a boil over medium heat. Puncture the sausage skin in a few places with a fork and place into the boiling water. Cook for 4 to 5 minutes, to allow the sausage to lose some of its fat. Drain the sausage and set aside.

PREPARE THE POLPETTE: Drain the pieces of bread and squeeze them with your hands into a soft pulp. Put the bread in a medium-size bowl together with the veal, eggs, Parmigiano, and parsley. Season with salt and pepper. Mix well with your hands or with a large spoon until the ingredients are well combined.

TAKE 1 heaping tablespoon of the veal mixture between the palms of your hands and shape it into a ball the size of a small egg. Flatten the ball a bit. When all the polpette have been shaped, coat them with the bread crumbs. (Polpette can be prepared up to this point several hours or a day ahead, covered, and refrigerated.)

HEAT 1 inch of oil in a heavy medium-size skillet over medium heat. When the oil is hot, lower a few polpette at a time into the oil with a slotted spoon and cook until lightly golden on both sides, about 2 minutes. Transfer them to paper towels to drain. (The polpette can be prepared up to this point a few hours ahead.)

PREPARE THE SAUCE: Heat the oil in a large skillet over medium heat. When the oil is hot, add the onion and cook until it begins to color, 2 to 3 minutes. Add the garlic and sage, and cook 1 to 2 minutes longer. Add the wine. Cook and stir until wine is reduced by half, about 2 minutes. Add the tomatoes and the broth, and season with salt and pepper. Bring the sauce to a boil, then reduce the heat to low, and add the polpette and the sausage. Cover the skillet partially, and simmer 25 to 30 minutes, checking the stew and stirring occasionally. Stir in the parsley, taste and adjust the seasoning, and serve hot.

Bolognese Meat Loaf

POLPETTONE ALLA BOLOGNESE

MEAT LOAF, OR POLPETTONE, *is homey, simple food, and when prepared in the manner of Bologna, it becomes something special. In this recipe, ground beef is mixed with savory pancetta, grated Parmigiano, and grated lemon zest, shaped into a loaf, browned in oil, then cooked gently in the oven. The bread soaked in milk lends soft-ness and creaminess to the polpettone, and onion, which is added to the pot during the last 30 minutes of cooking, imparts its sweetness. Serve the meat loaf with fluffy, Parmigiano-enriched mashed potatoes, for a truly memorable meal.*

SERVES 4 TO 6

2 cups loosely packed pieces of
    white bread without crusts,
    soaked in 2 cups milk for 5
    minutes
2 pounds ground beef
¼ pound sliced pancetta, chopped
2 large eggs, lightly beaten
Grated zest of 1 lemon
½ cup freshly grated Parmigiano-
    Reggiano cheese

3 tablespoons chopped fresh flat-
    leaf Italian or regular parsley
Salt and freshly ground black
    pepper to taste
2 cups fine, plain dried bread
    crumbs, spread evenly over a
    sheet of aluminum foil
¼ cup extra-virgin olive oil
2 large yellow onions, peeled and
    thinly sliced

PREHEAT the oven to 350°.

DRAIN the bread and squeeze it with your hands into a soft pulp. Put the bread in a large bowl together with the ground beef, pancetta, eggs, grated lemon zest, Parmigiano, and parsley. Season with salt and pepper. Mix well with your hands or with a large spoon until the ingredients are well combined. Shape the meat into a large rectangular loaf and coat the polpettone with the bread crumbs.

HEAT the oil in a large, heavy oven-proof casserole over medium heat. When the oil is hot, add the polpettone and cook until the bottom is golden, 2 to 3 minutes. Carefully tilt the pan, with the oil away from you, and with a large metal spatula flip the meat over toward you. Brown the polpettone 2 to 3 minutes longer.

continued

DISCARD some of the fat and watery juices of the polpettone, and place the casserole in the oven. Bake about 30 minutes. Baste the polpettone a few times during cooking with the pan juices. Add the sliced onion, mix well with the pan juices, and bake 25 to 30 minutes longer.

TRANSFER the polpettone to a cutting board and let it settle 5 to 10 minutes. Cut the meat into slices and serve topped by some of the sliced cooked onion.

Baked Polenta with Meat Sauce

POLENTA PASTICCIATA

POLENTA PASTICCIATA IS *a dish found in many northern Italian households. Freshly prepared polenta, or cold leftover polenta, is layered with a meat sauce and baked, the sauce changing according to the region. In this recipe sausage, pork, onion, porcini mushrooms, wine, and broth are slowly simmered into a flavorful, rich-tasting sauce.*

THIS IS A *wonderful rustic dish that calls for cold weather and big appetites. Use any left-over sauce over tagliatelle, rigatoni, or gnocchi.*

SERVES 8 TO 10

1 recipe Basic Polenta
  (see page 130)
1 ounce dried porcini mushrooms,
  soaked in 2 cups lukewarm
  water for 20 minutes
1 pound mild Italian sausage
2 tablespoons unsalted butter
3 tablespoons olive oil
1 cup finely minced yellow onion
1 pound ground pork, preferably
  from the Boston butt
1 cup dry white wine

2 cups homemade chicken broth
  (see page 33) or 1 cup canned
  chicken broth and 1 cup water
3 tablespoons tomato paste
Salt and freshly ground black
  pepper to taste
Butter for the baking dish
1 cup freshly grated Parmigiano-
  Reggiano cheese
2 tablespoons unsalted butter, cut
  into small pieces

PREPARE the polenta. Spread it ½ inch thick on a large platter or cookie sheet, and let cool.

DRAIN the porcini mushrooms and reserve the soaking water. Rinse mushrooms well under cold running water and chop them roughly. Line a strainer with two paper towels and strain the mushroom liquid into a bowl to get rid of the sandy deposits. Set aside.

REMOVE the casing from the sausage and chop sausage very fine.

HEAT the butter and the oil in a medium-size saucepan over medium heat. When the butter foams, add the onion and cook, stirring, for 3 to 4 minutes until onion is pale yellow. Add the mushrooms and stir once or twice. Add the sausage and ground pork. Cook, stirring to break up the meat with a large spoon, until the meat loses its raw color, 4 to 5 minutes. Add the wine and cook until it is almost all reduced, 3 to 4 minutes.

STIR the tomato paste into the broth and add to the saucepan, together with 1 cup of the reserved mushroom liquid. Season with salt and pepper. Bring the liquid to a boil and reduce the heat to low. Simmer, uncovered, stirring occasionally, until the sauce has a medium-thick consistency, 1 to 1½ hours. If sauce reduces too much, add a bit more of the reserved mushroom liquid. (The sauce can be prepared up to this point several hours or a day ahead.)

PREHEAT the oven to 400°. Butter a 9 × 12-inch baking dish generously.

CUT the cooled polenta into slices 3 inches wide and 6 inches long and place them tightly together in the baking dish. Spread a generous layer of meat sauce over the polenta and sprinkle with the Parmigiano. Repeat with one more layer of polenta, meat sauce, and Parmigiano. Dot with butter. Bake 15 to 20 minutes, or until the polenta has a nice golden-brown color. Let the polenta settle for 5 minutes and serve.

POTATO AND SMOKED MOZZARELLA CAKE

CAULIFLOWER AND BROCCOLI WITH BREAD CRUMBS, OIL,
AND CHILE PEPPER

POTATO, CHEESE, AND PROSCIUTTO CAKE

BEANS WITH PROSCIUTTO AND ONION

POTATO, ONION, AND TOMATO GRATIN

NEAPOLITAN EGGPLANT PARMIGIANA

ARTICHOKES, PEAS, AND STRING BEANS IN A SKILLET

STUFFED BAKED PEPPERS

BROCCOLI RABE WITH GARLIC, OIL, AND HOT CHILE PEPPER

SWEET AND SOUR ONIONS WITH BALSAMIC VINEGAR

MUSHROOM SALAD WITH PECORINO RICOTTA

MARINATED SPICY EGGPLANT

BRAISED STUFFED ARTICHOKES

CRISP POTATO-CHEESE CAKE

EMMA'S PEPPERS AND TOMATOES IN A SKILLET

OVEN-BAKED MIXED VEGETABLES

STRING BEANS WITH SUN-DRIED TOMATOES

TAMBURINI'S MOZZARELLA, CHERRY TOMATO,
AND ARUGULA SALAD

BEANS AND GRILLED SHRIMP SALAD

ROASTED PEPPER SALAD

CAULIFLOWER AND GREEN OLIVE SALAD

SWISS CHARD SALAD

Vegetables and Salads

ONE OF THE first things I do when I go to Italy is visit the great medieval open-air food market of Bologna, filled to capacity with mounds of multicolored vegetables and fruit. This is where I can best feel the pulse of my city. It is a most incredible sight!

VEGETABLES ARE AN essential part of an Italian meal, and they are chosen with the same attention that some people give to prized wines. They are inspected, smelled, poked, and discussed. When the season changes and the *primizie*, the first produce of the season, reach the market, Italian cooks are out in full force to take advantage of tender, perfect asparagus, beautifully blossomed artichokes, or bright green peas.

THE ITALIAN WAY with vegetables follows the same basic theory of all good Italian cooking: Keep things simple. That's the best way for the true taste of vegetables to prevail over any other component of the dish. Also be sure that you begin your cooking at the market. Select your vegetables well, and choose, where possible, those that are in season. If you choose an eggplant that is soft and spongy, no amount of attention will revive its original fresh taste.

VEGETABLES CAN PLAY many roles. They can be served as splendid antipasti or side dishes: They are essential to hundreds of soups. They are wonderful paired with pasta and risottos, and equally so served alone. Now, more than at any other stage of my life, I find a plate of pasta topped by vegetables, or a large platter of grilled mixed vegetables, makes a completely satisfying meal.

IN THIS CHAPTER you will find vegetables that are sautéed, baked, roasted, stuffed, grilled, and braised. There is a delicious Potato and Smoked Mozzarella Cake (page 187); a dish of Cauliflower and Broccoli with Bread Crumbs, Oil, and Chile Pepper (page 188), which can be served as a vegetable or as a topping for pasta—also immensely appetizing; a great traditional Neapolitan Eggplant Parmigiana (page 192) that is unusually light; and mouth-watering Oven-Baked Mixed Vegetables (page 204). That's just to mention a few.

ITALIAN SALADS ARE also innumerable and extremely varied. There are leafy green salads dressed only with good extra-virgin olive oil, vinegar, and salt. (In a traditional Italian meal these salads follow the entrée.) There are rice salads, seafood salads, and cooked vegetable salads in which fish or meat might be added. These salads can be served interchangeably as *antipasti*, a first course (*primo*) or a second course (*secondo*). The salads in this chapter are all *secondi* and can be served at different stages of a meal or, as in the case of Beans and Grilled Shrimp Salad (page 207) and Tamburini's Mozzarella, Cherry Tomato, and Arugula Salad (page 206), they can become the whole meal.

BASIC GUIDELINES FOR DRESSING A SALAD PROPERLY:

- Season the salad lightly with salt and pepper, if indicated in the recipe.
- Drizzle just enough oil to coat the salad but not too much to drown it.
- Drizzle the vinegar judiciously. You can always add a bit more if needed.
- Toss the salad well. Then taste and adjust the seasoning to your liking.
- Serve the salad at once, unless otherwise stated in the recipe.

Potato and Smoked Mozzarella Cake

TORTINO DI PATATE E MOZZARELLA AFFUMICATA

POTATOES PLAY AN *important role in rustic country cooking. With a few potatoes and a handful of savory ingredients, one can whip up a most appetizing dish. One of my favorites is a tortino, or potato cake. In this recipe potatoes are layered with smoked mozzarella and Parmigiano, dotted with butter, and baked until the cheese is melted and the top is golden.*

SERVES 8

7 large boiling potatoes, 3½ to
    4 pounds
Butter for the baking dish
¼ pound smoked mozzarella,
    grated or shredded

½–¾ cup freshly grated
    Parmigiano-Reggiano cheese
¼ cup plain dried bread crumbs
2–3 tablespoons unsalted butter,
    cut into small pieces

Keep in mind that smoked mozzarella and Parmigiano are already a bit salty, so go easy with the salt. If smoked mozzarella is unavailable, use regular mozzarella or Italian fontina cheese.

PUT the potatoes in a large pot and cover with cold water. Bring the water to a boil and cook, uncovered, over medium heat until potatoes are tender but still firm to the touch. Drain the potatoes and set aside to cool. Peel potatoes and cut them into ¼-inch rounds.

PREHEAT the oven to 400°. Butter a 9 × 13-inch baking pan generously. Line the bottom of the pan with the potato slices, slightly overlapping each other. Season lightly with salt and sprinkle the potatoes with the smoked mozzarella and half of the Parmigiano. Repeat with one more layer of potatoes, mozzarella, and Parmigiano. Sprinkle potatoes with bread crumbs and dot with butter. (The cake can be prepared up to this point several hours or a day ahead. Keep it tightly covered in the refrigerator.)

PUT the cake in the oven and bake until the top has a nice golden color, 15 to 20 minutes. Let it sit for 5 to 10 minutes and serve.

Cauliflower and Broccoli with Bread Crumbs, Oil, and Chile Pepper

CAVOLFIORE E BROCCOLI "ALLA POVERELLA"

I LOVE BROCCOLI *prepared in the southern Italian manner, tossed with a bit of garlic and oil, a few anchovies, and lots of chile pepper. My kind of food, basic, simple, but tasty and satisfying. This dish also features tender cauliflower, tangy sun-dried tomatoes, and bread crumbs. Frying the bread crumbs in the hot oil creates a light, crisp coating for the vegetables.*

SERVES 6 TO 8

1 small head cauliflower, about 2 pounds, broken into florets
Salt
1 bunch broccoli, about 1½ pounds
¼–⅓ cup extra-virgin olive oil
2 garlic cloves, minced

1 tablespoon diced sun-dried tomatoes
Chopped fresh chile pepper or dried red pepper flakes
2 anchovy fillets, chopped
1 tablespoon plain dried bread crumbs

BRING a medium-size pot of water to a boil. Wash the cauliflower florets under cold running water and add to the boiling water with 1 teaspoon of salt. Cook, uncovered, until tender but still firm to the bite, 3 to 5 minutes. Drain and rinse the florets under cold running water and set aside.

WASH the broccoli. Remove and discard the bottom third of the stalks. Separate the florets from the stalks. Peel remaining stalks, exposing the white, tender part, and cut into rounds. Bring another medium-size pot of water to a boil. Add 1 teaspoon of salt and the florets and sliced stalks. Cook until broccoli is tender but still firm to the bite, 3 to 4 minutes. Drain and rinse under cold running water and set aside. (These steps can be done several hours or a day ahead.)

HEAT the oil in a large skillet over medium heat. Add the garlic, sun-dried tomatoes, chile pepper, and anchovies. Cook, stirring, for about 1 minute. Do not let the garlic turn dark or it will be bitter. Raise the heat and add the bread crumbs. Stir quickly. As soon as the bread crumbs turn lightly golden, less than 1 minute, add the cauliflower and the broccoli. Season with salt and stir just long enough to heat the vegetables through. Taste and adjust the seasoning, and serve.

Potato, Cheese, and Prosciutto Cake

TORTINO DI PATATE, FORMAGGIO, E PROSCIUTTO

THIS POTATO CAKE *was a favorite in my family. Rounds of cooked potatoes were layered with slices of prosciutto and Parmigiano-Reggiano cheese and baked to a golden, crisp consistency. Today, when I make this tortino, I add sautéed sweet onions for extra taste. The potato cake can be served as a side dish with roasted meat or poultry, or all by itself.*

SERVES 6

6 medium boiling potatoes, about
    2½ to 3 pounds
5 tablespoons unsalted butter
2 medium yellow onions, about 1
    pound, peeled and thinly sliced
Butter for the baking pan
2–3 tablespoons plain dried bread
    crumbs

Salt to taste
½ cup freshly grated Parmigiano-
    Reggiano cheese
½ pound thinly sliced prosciutto
    or baked ham

PUT the potatoes in a large saucepan and cover them generously with cold water. Bring the water to a boil over medium heat and cook until tender but firm to the bite, 35 to 40 minutes. Drain the potatoes and peel them as soon as they are cool enough to handle. Cut them into ¼-inch rounds.

MELT 3 tablespoons of the butter in a large skillet over medium heat. Add the onions and cook, stirring, until onions are lightly golden and soft, 5 to 6 minutes.

continued

PREHEAT the oven to 375°. Butter a 10-inch springform cake pan and coat it lightly with bread crumbs.

LINE the bottom of the pan with the potato slices, slightly overlapping each other, and season lightly with salt. Cover the potatoes with a layer of onions and top with a few tablespoons of Parmigiano. Add a layer of prosciutto. Repeat with a layer of potatoes, onions, Parmigiano, and prosciutto. Finish the tortino with one final layer of potatoes. Season the potatoes lightly with salt, sprinkle with remaining Parmigiano, and dot with remaining butter.

BAKE until the cake has a nice golden color, 15 to 20 minutes. Remove from the oven and cool for 10 to 15 minutes. Serve warm or at room temperature.

Beans with Prosciutto and Onion

FAGIOLI CON PROSCIUTTO E CIPOLLA

THIS RECIPE IS *a variation on a Florentine dish called* piselli alla Fiorentina, *in which fresh, early peas are cooked together with onions and prosciutto.*

SERVES 4 TO 6

1 cup dried cannellini beans,
    cooked as instructed on
    page 18
⅓ cup extra-virgin olive oil
1 cup loosely packed yellow
    onion, thinly sliced

¼ pound prosciutto, cut into 2
    thick slices and diced
Salt and freshly ground black
    pepper to taste

COOK the beans and set aside until ready to use.

HEAT the oil in a large skillet over medium heat. Add the onion and cook, stirring a few times, until onion turns lightly golden, 4 to 5 minutes. Add the prosciutto and stir for 1 to 2 minutes. Add the beans, and season with salt and several grindings of pepper. Cook 2 to 3 minutes. Taste and adjust the seasoning, and serve.

Potato, Onion, and Tomato Gratin

TORTINO DI PATATE, CIPOLLE, E POMODORI

IN ITALY THIS *type of dish is called a tortino, or gratin. Vegetables, seasoned with a soffritto (garlic, parsley, pancetta, onion, or tomatoes), are layered into a pan and baked in the oven. A tortino can consist of several vegetables or only a few; it can be embellished with leftover cooked meats, or with cheese, or potatoes, prosciutto, or salame. Many of these dishes stem from local traditions. Others are new variations on a classic theme. At the trattoria Il Piedone in Rome, I had a delicious potato cake layered with slices of smoked mozzarella (page 187). Potato cakes are perfect for casual dinner parties, because you can put them together ahead of time and bake them at the last moment.*

SERVES 8

7 large boiling potatoes, 3½ to 4 pounds

2–3 tablespoons unsalted butter

2 tablespoons olive oil

2 medium yellow onions, about 1 pound, peeled and thinly sliced

5 fresh, ripe plum tomatoes, about 1 pound, seeded and diced

2 garlic cloves, minced

Salt to taste

Butter for the baking dish

½–¾ cup freshly grated Parmigiano-Reggiano cheese

2–3 tablespoons unsalted butter, cut into small pieces

The dish can be prepared up to just before baking several hours or a day ahead. Keep dish tightly covered in the refrigerator, then bring back to room temperature before baking it.

PUT the potatoes in a large pot and cover with cold water. Bring the water to a boil and cook, over medium heat, until potatoes are tender but still firm to the bite, 40 to 50 minutes. Drain the potatoes and set aside to cool. Peel potatoes and cut them into ¼-inch rounds.

HEAT the butter and the oil in a skillet over medium heat. When the butter begins to foam, add the onions and cook, stirring, until they are lightly golden, 4 to 5 minutes. Add tomatoes and garlic, and cook 3 to 4 minutes longer. Season lightly with salt.

PREHEAT the oven to 400°. Butter a 9 × 13-inch baking pan generously. Line the bottom of the pan with the potato slices, slightly overlapping each other, and season lightly with salt. Spread some onion-tomato mixture over the potatoes and sprinkle with half of the Parmigiano. Repeat with one more layer of potatoes, onion, tomatoes, and Parmigiano. Dot potatoes with butter.

PUT the potato cake in the oven and bake until the top has a nice golden color, 15 to 20 minutes. Let the cake sit for 5 to 10 minutes, and serve.

Neapolitan Eggplant Parmigiana

LA PARMIGIANA DI MELANZANE

WHEN PROPERLY MADE, *Eggplant Parmigiana is a tribute to the creativity of southern Italian cooking (see Note).*

SERVES 8

4 medium eggplants, 3½ to
    4 pounds
Salt
Oil for frying
1 cup unbleached all-purpose
    flour, spread on a sheet of
    aluminum foil
3 tablespoons extra-virgin olive oil
2 garlic cloves, peeled and left
    whole

4 cups canned imported Italian
    plum tomatoes, with their
    juice, put through a food mill
    to remove the seeds
½ pound thinly sliced fresh
    mozzarella
¾ cup freshly grated Parmigiano-
    Reggiano cheese

If you are on a restricted diet, grill eggplant instead of frying. However, be warned, some of the unique, delicious taste of this dish will be sacrificed.

PEEL the eggplants and cut lengthwise into ¼-inch slices. Place slices on a large dish and sprinkle with salt. Let stand 30 minutes. The salt will draw out the eggplant's bitter juices. Pat the slices dry with paper towels.

HEAT 1 inch of oil in a medium-size skillet over medium heat. Coat the eggplant slices lightly with flour and slip them, a few

The traditional Neapolitan way of eating eggplant Parmigiana is at room temperature. This dish tastes even better after it sits for several hours or a day. If prepared a day in advance and refrigerated, bring it back completely to room temperature before serving.

at a time, into the hot oil. Cook until they are lightly golden on both sides, about 2 minutes. Repeat with remaining eggplant slices and drain on paper towels.

HEAT the oil in a small saucepan over medium heat. Add the garlic cloves and let them turn a golden brown, then discard them. Add the tomatoes and season with salt. As soon as the tomatoes come to a boil, reduce the heat to low and simmer, stirring occasionally, for 6 to 8 minutes, or until the sauce has a medium-thick consistency.

PREHEAT the oven to 350°.

SPREAD a few heaping tablespoons of sauce on the bottom of a 12 × 9-inch baking dish, and cover with a layer of fried eggplant slices, slightly overlapping each other. Spread some more sauce over the eggplant and cover with a layer of mozzarella and a sprinkling of Parmigiano. Repeat with one more layer of eggplant, tomatoes, mozzarella, and Parmigiano.

ADD a final layer of eggplant and tomatoes, and sprinkle with Parmigiano. Place the dish in the oven and bake 30 to 35 minutes. Remove from oven and let the dish settle for 15 to 20 minutes before serving.

Note: To make perfect Eggplant Parmigiana every time, all you need to do is to follow some simple, basic rules:

- Be sure to sprinkle the eggplant with salt before cooking so as to draw off the bitter juices.
- After frying the eggplant slices, pat them thoroughly with paper towels so they won't taste greasy.
- Do not overcook the tomato sauce or it will lose its fresh taste.
- Choose the freshest mozzarella possible. The rubbery mozzarella sold in supermarkets will not complement the dish.
- Invest in a large chunk of imported Parmigiano-Reggiano cheese and do not substitute any other type of cheese.

Artichokes, Peas, and String Beans in a Skillet

PADELLATA DI CARCIOFI, PISELLI, E FAGIOLINI ALLA PANCETTA

THIS DELICOUS DISH *combines three of my favorite vegetables; artichokes, peas, and string beans. The vegetables are cooked separately, then sautéed together in extra-virgin olive oil along with crisp, golden diced pancetta. Precook your vegetables several hours ahead, and toss them together at the last minute.*

SERVE 4 TO 6

1½ pounds baby artichokes, cleaned and cooked as instructed on page 16
1 pound unshelled fresh peas, or one 10-ounce package frozen peas, thawed
Salt

½ pound string beans, the smallest you can find
¼–⅓ cup extra-virgin olive oil
2–3 ounces pancetta, cut into thick slices and diced
Freshly ground black pepper to taste

COOK the artichokes and cut them into wedges. Set aside.

IF you are using fresh peas, bring a medium-size saucepan of water to a boil. Shell the peas and add them to the water with a pinch of salt. Cook, uncovered, until tender, 5 to 10 minutes, depending on size. Drain the peas and set aside.

SNAP off both ends of the string beans and wash beans under cold running water. Bring a medium-size saucepan of water to a boil. Add beans to the water with a pinch of salt. Cook, uncovered, until tender, 5 to 10 minutes, depending on size. Drain beans and set aside.

HEAT the oil in a large skillet over medium heat. Add the pancetta and cook, stirring, until it is lightly golden and crisp, about 2 minutes. Add all the vegetables, and season with salt and several grindings of pepper. Cook and stir until the vegetables are well coated with the oil and are heated all the way through. Serve hot.

Stuffed Baked Peppers

PEPERONI IMBOTTITI

STUFFED BAKED VEGETABLES *are a staple preparation in Italian homes. The choice of vegetable and stuffing varies from cook to cook, but the method of cooking is basically the same. Here red bell peppers are stuffed, then lined up in a lightly oiled baking dish, sprinkled with oil, and baked slowly in a preheated low oven for a long time until their skin wrinkles and softens completely. The long, slow cooking intensifies the sweetness of the red bell peppers.*

SERVES 4

2 tablespoons olive oil for the
    baking dish
4 large red bell peppers
1 cup loosely packed white bread
    pieces, without crusts
2 garlic cloves, minced
2 anchovy fillets, chopped

2 tablespoons chopped fresh flat-
    leaf Italian parsley or regular
    parsley
⅓ cup extra-virgin olive oil
Salt and freshly ground black
    pepper to taste

PREHEAT the oven to 325°. Coat a baking dish lightly with oil.

WASH and dry the bell peppers, and cut them into fourths lengthwise. Core and seed them, and remove the white membranes.

IN a small bowl combine the bread, garlic, anchovies, parsley, and olive oil. Season with salt and pepper. Mix everything well to combine. Taste and adjust the seasoning. At this point the mixture should be nice and moist. Add a bit more oil if necessary. Spoon some of the filling on the cut part of the peppers.

LINE the peppers in the baking dish and drizzle them with some olive oil. Place the dish in the oven and bake 40 to 45 minutes, or until the peppers are soft and a bit wrinkled. Serve hot or at room temperature.

Broccoli Rabe with Garlic, Oil, and Hot Chile Pepper

BROCCOLI RAPE CON AGLIO, OLIO, E PEPERONCINO

ITALIANS LOVE VEGETABLES *that are slightly bitter, such as broccoli rabe. This delicious, simple preparation comes from Tuscany. The broccoli are boiled until tender, then quickly tossed with extra-virgin olive oil, garlic, pepper. For a memorable meal, serve them along with Pancetta-Wrapped Pork Roast (page 166).*

SERVES 4

2 pounds broccoli rabe
Salt
¼ cup extra-virgin olive oil

2 garlic cloves, minced
Chopped fresh red chile pepper or
    dried red pepper flakes to taste

TRIM and discard any large woody stalks and wilted leaves from the broccoli. Wash the broccoli well under cold running water.

BRING a large pot of water to a boil over medium heat. Add 2 teaspoons of salt and the broccoli, and cook until tender, 5 to 7 minutes. Drain and plunge the broccoli into a large bowl of iced water. (This will stop the cooking and will help retain the bright green color of the broccoli.) When cool, drain again and press the broccoli with a large spoon to remove as much water as possible. (These steps can be done several hours ahead.)

HEAT the oil in a large skillet over medium heat. Add the garlic and the chile pepper, and cook, stirring, less than 1 minute. Add the broccoli, season with salt, and stir just long enough to coat the broccoli with the oil and to heat through. Taste and adjust the seasoning, and serve hot.

Sweet and Sour Onions with Balsamic Vinegar

CIPOLLINE GLASSATE AL BALSAMICO

IN THIS DISH, *balsamic vinegar works magic by coating the onions with its unique mellow taste. This is one of the simplest of all vegetable dishes to prepare. Try to obtain a good-quality balsamic vinegar. Remember, the older the vinegar is, the less you need to use.*

SERVES 4 TO 6

2 pounds small white boiling onions

2 tablespoons unsalted butter

Salt to taste

1 tablespoon granulated sugar

¼ cup balsamic vinegar (see Note)

BRING a large saucepan of water to a boil over medium heat. Cut a cross at the root end of each onion and add to the boiling water. Cook for 2 to 3 minutes, then drain the onions, peel them, and remove the dangling tails. (The onions can be prepared up to this point several hours or a day ahead.)

MELT the butter in a large skillet over medium heat. When the butter begins to foam, add the onions and season with salt. Cook, stirring occasionally, until the onions are lightly golden, 4 to 5 minutes. Add the sugar and the balsamic vinegar. Cook and stir until vinegar is almost all reduced and the onions are brown and glazed, about 2 minutes. Serve hot.

Note: Balsamic vinegar is an aromatic, concentrated product made from the boiled-down must of white Trebbiano grapes, and it is produced in Emilia-Romagna. Balsamic vinegar falls into two categories: artisan made and commercially made.

It takes decades to produce artisan-made balsamic vinegar. The boiled-down must is aged for many years in a series of barrels of different woods; the contents of the barrel are moved to other barrels of diminishing size and different types of wood, after part of the vinegar has evaporated. This process is repeated approximately every ten years until the vinegar has acquired its special thick, velvety, highly aromatic quality. If you can find a ten- or fifteen-year-old balsamic, and if price is no object, buy it.

continued

Most balsamic vinegar available in the United States is commercially made and does not resemble artisan-made balsamic vinegar. However, it is reasonably flavorful. Some good brands are Fini, Giuseppe Giusti, and Cavalli.

Mushroom Salad with Pecorino Ricotta

INSALATA DI FUNGHI CON RICOTTA PECORINA SALATA

IN THIS SALAD *mushrooms are tossed with chives, extra-virgin olive oil, and vinegar, and sprinkled with ricotta salata cheese. The slightly tangy flavor of the ricotta marries very well with the mild mushrooms. If ricotta salata is not available, substitute small chunks of a mild Gorgonzola or thinly slivered Parmigiano.*

SERVES 4

1 pound white cultivated mushrooms
2 tablespoons minced chives
Salt and freshly ground black pepper to taste

¼–⅓ cup extra-virgin olive oil
2 tablespoons red wine vinegar
2 ounces ricotta pecorina salata cheese (see Note), in a single piece

CLEAN the mushrooms thoroughly with a damp towel and cut into thin slices. Place the mushrooms in a salad bowl. Add the chives, and season with salt and several twists of the peppermill. Add the oil and the vinegar. Taste and adjust the seasoning.

SPOON mushrooms into mounds on salad plates, crumble the cheese over the mushrooms, and serve.

Note: Ricotta pecorina salata is a sheep's milk cheese to which salt had been added as a preservative. The consistency of this cheese is considerably drier than regular ricotta, and its taste varies from mild to assertive. A good brand of ricotta salata available in the United States is Locatelli.

Marinated Spicy Eggplant

MELANZANE IN SALSA PICCANTE

THE FIRST TIME *I had a dish similar to this was at the house of one of my husband's relatives in Salerno, a beautiful city south of Rome. The eggplants had been fried, not grilled, then they had been marinated for several hours in a mixture of oil, vinegar, garlic, and fresh oregano.*

CHOOSE FAIRLY SMALL *eggplants that are firm and compact with a shiny skin. Prepare the dish several hours ahead and serve it to accompany grilled lamb or chicken, or as a delicious, county-style appetizer.*

SERVES 4 TO 6

2 medium eggplants, about 1½
    pounds
Salt
2 garlic cloves, minced
1 tablespoon chopped fresh flat-
    leaf Italian or regular parsley

4 anchovy fillets, chopped
Chopped fresh red chile pepper or
    dried red pepper flakes to taste
⅓ cup extra-virgin olive oil
⅓ cup red wine vinegar

CUT off the ends of the eggplants and cut them lengthwise into ¼-inch slices. Sprinkle the slices with salt, place them in a large dish, and let stand 30 minutes. The salt will draw out the eggplant's bitter juices.

PREHEAT the grill or the broiler.

PAT the eggplant slices dry with paper towels, brush them lightly with oil, and place on the hot grill. Or put the slices on a broiler rack and place under the broiler for 2 to 3 minutes. When the slices are golden on both sides, place them, slightly overlapping, in a large, deep serving dish.

IN a small bowl combine the garlic, parsley, anchovies, chile pepper, oil and vinegar, and mix well to blend. Season the eggplant with salt and pour the oil-vinegar mixture over the slices. Cover and marinate at room temperature for a few hours.

Braised Stuffed Artichokes

CARCIOFI RIPIENI

WHEN MY DAUGHTERS, *Carla and Paola, were young, I prepared artichokes often because it was one of the few vegetables they liked. Perhaps what they loved most was the stuffing: the bread soaked in oil, the hint of garlic, and the flavor of the chopped pancetta.*

THE ARTICHOKES CAN *be served as a side dish, a light luncheon entrée, or as an appetizer. For a totally vegetarian dish, omit the pancetta and add a few chopped anchovies to the bread mixture for extra piquancy. Serve the artichokes at room temperature so as to enjoy their flavor fully.*

SERVES 6

6 large globe artichokes
1 lemon, cut in half
Juice of 1 lemon
1 tablespoon extra-virgin olive oil
¼ pound sliced pancetta, chopped
3 cups loosely packed white bread pieces, chopped fine
3 tablespoons chopped fresh flat-leaf Italian parsley or regular parsley

2 garlic cloves, minced
⅓ cup freshly grated Parmigiano-Reggiano cheese
½ cup extra-virgin olive oil
Salt and freshly ground black pepper to taste

REMOVE and discard the tough outer leaves of the artichokes. Cut the remaining leaves halfway with scissors until you reach the central cone of leaves. Cut off the green tips of the cone. Gently open the artichokes and remove the fuzzy chokes with a spoon or a melon ball scoop. Rub the lemon halves over the cut edges of the artichokes to prevent discoloration.

CUT the stalks of the artichokes off at the base and, with a small knife, trim off the outer green part of the artichoke bottoms. Rub lemon over the cut parts. Trim away the greener outer fibrous part of the artichoke stalks, exposing the white inner parts. Cut the stalks into 1-inch pieces. Put the stalks and the artichokes as you clean them into a large bowl of water together with the lemon juice.

HEAT 1 tablespoon of oil in a small skillet over medium heat. Add the pancetta and stir for 1 to 2 minutes until pancetta turns lightly golden. Scoop up the pancetta with a slotted spoon and drain on paper towels.

IN a medium bowl combine the bread, parsley, garlic, Parmigiano, pancetta, and ⅓ cup of the olive oil. Season with salt and pepper. Push the stuffing between the artichoke leaves and into each cavity.

PLACE the artichokes, cut part facing up, in a pot that can accommodate them snugly. Add the artichoke stalks, the remaining oil, and enough water to come halfway up the sides of the artichokes. Bring the liquid to a boil, then reduce the heat to low, and cover the pot. Cook until the artichokes are tender and the water in the pot is almost all reduced, about 1 hour.

PLACE the artichokes on a large serving platter and cool. Raise the heat to high under the pot and cook the liquid, stirring, until it is reduced to about ½ cup. Spoon over each artichoke and serve.

Crisp Potato-Cheese Cake

FRICO DI PATATE E FORMAGGIO

FRICO IS A *small pan-fried cake that is a specialty of the Friuli region. The most popular version is made with potatoes and cheese or only with cheese. The first time I had this golden, crunchy potato cake was at the trattoria Al Grop, outside Udine. When I asked the waitress to suggest some typical dishes of the area, she brought this golden, crunchy potato cake, which was absolutely delicious.*

SERVE FRICO AS *a side dish to roasted or grilled meat or fish. It also make an excellent appetizer, and can form part of a Sunday brunch.*

SERVES 4

1½ pounds boiling potatoes, peeled and shredded or finely diced

½ pound Asiago cheese or fontina cheese, shredded or diced
Salt to taste
2–3 tablespoons unsalted butter

Even though frico is crisper if cooked at the last moment, you can cook it a few hours ahead and reheat it briefly in the oven or broiler. It is still quite delicious.

When I make frico, I use a 6-inch nonstick skillet. Frico can also be prepared as a single large cake. In that case, increase the cooking time.

PLACE the shredded or diced potatoes in a large bowl, add the cheese, and season with salt. Mix the potatoes well with the cheese. Divide the potato mixture into 4 equal portions.

HEAT ½ tablespoon of the butter in a 6-inch or 8-inch nonstick skillet over medium-low heat. Add 1 portion of potatoes to the skillet, making sure to cover the bottom of the skillet tightly with the potatoes. Flatten the potatoes with a spatula and shape the edges into a round. Let the potatoes cook gently, without mixing them, until the bottom is lightly golden, 8 to 10 minutes. Shake the skillet occasionally and make sure that the potatoes do not stick to the pan or burn. Raise the heat a bit and let the bottom turn golden brown and crunchy.

INVERT the potato cake onto a flat plate, add about a teaspoon or so of butter to the skillet, and slide the cake back into the skillet to cook the other side. Cook 6 to 7 minutes longer, shaking the skillet occasionally. When the bottom of the cake is lightly browned, raise the heat a little and cook until the bottom turns golden brown and crunchy. Transfer the cake to a large platter and keep it warm in a low oven while you cook the other potato cakes. Sprinkle the cakes lightly with salt and serve warm.

Emma's Peppers and Tomatoes in a Skillet

LA PEPERONATA DI EMMA

MY SISTER-IN-LAW *Emma, who lives in Bologna, is a wonderful cook. Her food is not overly complicated, very regional, and quite creative. This is her version of the classic peperonata, a medley of peppers, tomatoes, and onion, to which she adds a touch of balsamic vinegar and a bit of chile pepper. Serve peperonata hot or at room temperature as an accompaniment to roasted or boiled meat.*

SERVES 6

⅓ cup extra-virgin olive oil
5 large red bell peppers, about
    2 pounds
5 medium firm, ripe tomatoes,
    about 2 pounds, seeded and
    diced
Chopped fresh red chile pepper or
    dried red pepper flakes to taste

2 tablespoons tomato paste,
    diluted in 1½ cups cold water
Salt to taste
2 tablespoons chopped fresh flat-
    leaf Italian parsley or regular
    parsley
¼ cup balsamic vinegar

HEAT the oil in a large skillet over medium heat. Add the bell peppers and cook, stirring, 4 to 5 minutes. Add the fresh tomatoes, chile pepper, and diluted tomato paste. Season with salt. Reduce the heat to low and cook, uncovered, stirring occasionally, until the peppers are soft and tender and the juices in the skillet have thickened, 20 to 25 minutes. Add parsley and balsamic vinegar, stir for a minute or two, and serve hot or at room temperature.

Oven-Baked Mixed Vegetables

VERDURE MISTE AL FORNO

ROASTED VEGETABLES ARE *versatile; they can be served hot to accompany a main dish, or at room temperature as a salad with eye and taste appeal.*

SERVES 4 TO 6

1 small firm eggplant, about 1 pound, cut into 2-inch cubes

3 large red bell peppers, about 1½ pounds, cored and seeded, cut into 1-inch strips

2 medium yellow onions, peeled and quartered

½ pound small white cultivated mushrooms, wiped clean

4 whole garlic cloves, peeled

Salt and freshly ground black pepper to taste

⅓ cup extra-virgin olive oil

1 cup cold water

1–2 tablespoons chopped fresh flat-leaf Italian parsley or regular parsley

¼ cup strong red wine vinegar

PREHEAT the oven to 350°.

PLACE all the vegetables and the whole garlic cloves in a large baking pan and season generously with salt and pepper. Add the oil and the water, and mix well.

COVER the pan tightly with aluminum foil and place in the oven. Bake 20 to 25 minutes, then remove and discard the foil, and stir vegetables. Bake 20 to 30 minutes longer, or until all the water in the pan is evaporated and the vegetables have a golden-brown color. Stir once or twice during cooking.

TO serve the vegetables hot, scoop them up with a slotted spoon and serve immediately. If you plan to serve them as a salad, transfer them with a slotted spoon to a salad bowl, add the parsley and the vinegar, and toss. Cool to room temperature and serve.

String Beans with Sun-dried Tomatoes

FAGIOLINI CON POMODORI SECCHI

THIS IS ANOTHER *dish that embodies the simplicity of Italian cooking, and stresses the importance of good basic ingredients. Fresh string beans, extra-virgin olive oil, garlic, anchovies, and sun-dried tomatoes are quickly sautéed together into a supremely flavorful dish.*

SERVES 4 TO 6

1½ pounds green beans, the
    smallest you can find
3–4 tablespoons extra-virgin
    olive oil
2 garlic cloves, minced

2 anchovy fillets, chopped
1 tablespoon minced sun-dried
    tomatoes
Salt and freshly ground black
    pepper to taste

SNAP off both ends of the beans and wash them under cold running water. Bring a medium-size saucepan half full of salted water to a boil over medium heat. Add the beans and cook, uncovered, until tender but still a bit crunchy, 2 to 4 minutes, depending on size. Drain and immediately plunge the beans in a large bowl of ice water to stop the cooking and to set their green color. Drain and set aside.

HEAT the oil in a large skillet over medium heat. Add the garlic, anchovies, and sun-dried tomatoes. Stir for about 1 minute, making sure not to let the garlic turn too dark. Add the green beans, season with salt and pepper, and stir just long enough to heat the beans through, 1 to 2 minutes. Taste and adjust the seasoning, and serve.

Tamburini's Mozzarella, Cherry Tomato, and Arugula Salad

L'INSALATA DI OVOLINE DI TAMBURINI

WHENEVER I AM in Bologna, I make a ritual visit to Tamburini, the most glorious food store in my city, offering a breathtaking array of hams, sausages, cheeses, pasta, and tantalizing takeout dishes.

THIS RECIPE IS based on one of the delicious salads purveyed by Tamburini. Small white fresh mozzarella balls (ovoline) are paired with ripe, red cherry tomatoes and green, peppery arugula, then tossed in a flavorful dressing of extra-virgin olive oil, vinegar, and anchovies. Make sure to have some good crusty bread on hand to sop up the dressing.

SERVES 4

1 large bunch of arugula, about
   ½ pound (see Note)
10 ounces cherry tomatoes
½ pound small mozzarella balls
   (ovoline)

2 anchovy fillets, chopped
¼ cup extra-virgin olive oil
2–3 tablespoons red wine vinegar
Salt and freshly ground black
   pepper to taste

DISCARD the stems of the arugula. If the leaves are large, tear them in 2 or 3 pieces. Wash arugula well under cold running water and pat dry thoroughly with paper towels.

WASH the cherry tomatoes, dry them and, if tomatoes are large, cut them in half or into fourths. Place the tomatoes in a large bowl and add the mozzarella and the arugula.

IN a small bowl combine the anchovies with the oil and vinegar. Season the salad with salt and several grindings of black pepper, and toss with the dressing. Taste and adjust the seasoning, and serve.

Note: Arugula is a slightly bitter, peppery green that often appears in Italian mixed-leaf salads. Even though arugula is popular, it is not always available in supermarkets. You can substitute watercress or fresh small-leaf spinach.

Beans and Grilled Shrimp Salad

INSALATA DI FAGIOLI E GAMBERI ALLA GRIGLIA

THIS TASTY SALAD *has appeared on the menu of my restaurant several times, sometimes as a lunch entrée, sometimes as part of an antipasto misto. It is a perfect salad to serve to a large gathering, since the preparation can be done a day in advance. I keep all the prepared ingredients in separate bowls, and combine and dress them just before serving.*

SERVES 4

1 cup dried cannellini beans, cooked as instructed on page 18

1 pound medium-size shrimp, shelled and deveined

½ cup fine, plain dried bread crumbs, mixed with 2 tablespoons olive oil

2 red bell peppers, roasted and peeled as instructed on page 86, cut into short, thin strips

½ medium red onion, thinly sliced

1 tablespoon chopped fresh flat-leaf Italian parsley or regular parsley

Salt and freshly ground black pepper to taste

¼–⅓ cup extra-virgin olive oil

2–3 tablespoons strong red wine vinegar

COOK the beans and set aside until ready to use.

PREHEAT the grill or the broiler.

THREAD the shrimp on skewers, coat them lightly with the bread crumb–oil mixture, and place on the hot grill. Or put the skewers on a broiler rack and place them under the broiler. Cook until the shrimp are golden on all sides, 3 to 4 minutes. Cool, then remove shrimp from the skewers and place in a salad bowl.

ADD the beans, pepper strips, onion, and parsley, and season generously with salt and pepper. Add the oil and the vinegar, and toss well. Taste and adjust the seasoning.

SPOON salad into mounds on salad plates, arranging the shrimp on top of the salad, and serve.

Roasted Pepper Salad

PEPERONI ARROSTITI IN INSALATA

FOOD NEEDS BOTH *to taste good and look good, and this salad fits the bill. Bright red and yellow roasted peppers, tossed with green fresh basil leaves, and lightly bathed in fragrant olive oil, capers, and anchovies, create a most colorful and appetizing dish.*

SERVES 4 TO 6

3 large red bell peppers and 3
  large yellow bell peppers,
  roasted and peeled as
  instructed on page 86
2 tablespoons capers, rinsed and
  chopped
10–12 fresh basil leaves, shredded
  or 2 tablespoons chopped fresh
  flat-leaf Italian parsley or
  regular parsley

1 garlic clove, minced
3 anchovy fillets, minced
Salt and freshly ground black
  pepper to taste
¼ cup extra-virgin olive oil
2 tablespoons red wine vinegar

CUT the bell peppers into ½-inch strips and place in a large salad bowl. Add the capers and the basil or parsley.

IN a small bowl combine the garlic and anchovies with the oil and the vinegar. Pour the dressing over the peppers, and season lightly with salt (remember, the anchovies are already salty) and several grindings of pepper. Toss everything well and serve.

Cauliflower and Green Olive Salad

CAVOLFIORE IN INSALATA

CAULIFLOWER IS PAIRED *with a handful of green olives and capers, some fresh oregano, and just a bit of chopped garlic, and everything is tossed together with olive oil and good, full-bodied red wine vinegar. Make sure to have a large loaf of bread on hand to sop up the delicious dressing.*

SERVES 4

1 head of cauliflower, 2 to
    2½ pounds
Salt
Freshly ground black pepper to
    taste
8–10 small pitted green olives,
    quartered
1 garlic clove, minced

⅓ cup loosely packed fresh
    oregano leaves or 2
    tablespoons chopped fresh flat-
    leaf Italian parsley or regular
    parsley
¼ cup extra-virgin olive oil
2–3 tablespoons red wine vinegar

REMOVE all the leaves from the cauliflower except the small tender ones. Cut a cross at the stem of the cauliflower.

BRING a large pot of water to a boil over medium heat. Add 2 teaspoons of salt and the cauliflower. Cook, uncovered, until cauliflower can be pierced easily at the root end with a thin knife, 15 to 20 minutes. Drain cauliflower and place in a bowl of iced water to stop the cooking. (The cauliflower can be cooked several hours or a day ahead and kept tightly covered in the refrigerator.)

SEPARATE the florets and the leaves, and place them in a salad bowl. Season with salt and pepper. Add olives, garlic, and oregano or parsley, and toss with the oil and the vinegar. Taste and adjust the seasoning, and serve.

Swiss Chard Salad

INSALATA DI BIETE

IN THIS REFRESHING *salad, the slightly bitter undertone of the Swiss chard is comple-mented by fruity olive oil and tangy lemon juice. Don't be stingy with the dressing; season the salad generously with salt and pepper to enjoy the chard flavor at its fullest.*

WHEN YOU DON'T *feel like cooking, a large Swiss chard salad, a slice of pecorino or fontina cheese, a piece of bread, and a glass of chilled white chardonnay make a wonderfully simple and satisfying meal.*

SERVES 4

2 bunches Swiss chard, about
   2 pounds
Salt to taste
Freshly ground black pepper to
   taste

¼ cup extra-virgin olive oil
2–3 tablespoons freshly squeezed
   lemon juice

REMOVE the Swiss chard leaves from the stems, and reserve the stems for another use (see Note). Wash the leaves thoroughly in several changes of cold water. Put them in a large saucepan with 1 cup of cold water and a generous pinch of salt. Bring the water to a boil over medium heat and cook, uncovered, until the leaves are tender, 2 to 3 minutes.

DRAIN the chard and gently press the leaves lightly with a large spoon to remove as much water as possible. Place the chard in a salad bowl and cool to room temperature. (These steps can be prepared several hours or a day ahead.)

SEASON the chard with salt and several grindings of pepper, toss with olive oil and lemon juice, and serve.

For Swiss Chard with Parmigiano, cook the Swiss chard as instructed and squeeze out as much water as possible. Melt 3 to 4 tablespoons of butter in a large skillet, add the Swiss chard, and sprinkle on some freshly grated Parmigiano-Reggiano cheese. Season with salt and mix well, just long enough to heat the Swiss chard through, and serve.

Note: To use the Swiss chard stems, boil the stalks until tender. Drain and place them in a buttered baking dish, top with grated Parmigiano, and dot with butter. Bake for 10 to 15 minutes in a 350° oven, or until the cheese is melted and lightly golden.

Pizza, Calzoni, Savory Breads, and Focaccia

FLOUR, WATER, AND yeast are the basic ingredients for some of the legendary dishes of Italy, such as pizza, calzoni, savory breads, and focaccie. These rustic, unpretentious preparations with humble origins perhaps were created out of necessity.

PIZZA, A SPECIALTY of Naples, has become one of the most loved dishes in the world. The first pizzas were probably flavored only with oil, salt, and garlic, since the tomato did not arrive in Italy from the New World until the sixteenth century. When the first woodburning-oven pizzeria opened in Naples in 1830, pizza became what it is today, and Naples became its undisputed capital. Although pizza can be prepared with a variety of toppings, I prefer one that uses fresh-tasting ingredients and is made with a light hand. The trick really lies in the crust, which should be golden brown and crisp.

A CALZONE IS an extension of pizza, for the same dough is used to wrap around a delicious filling. The pizza dough is rolled out into a large circle, the filling is put in the center of the circle, and the dough is folded over the filling and sealed. The baking of the calzone, just like pizza, should be done in a very hot oven to ensure a crisp, brown crust.

EVERY REGION OF Italy has its own savory breads: crescenta or crescentina in Emilia-Romagna; schiacciata in Tuscany; focaccia in Liguria; crescia in Le Marche, and pizza and calzone in Campania and Puglia. These specialties are all members of the same family, since they comprise the same basic ingredients. The flavorings change according to area, tradition, and the cook's imagination.

MY MOTHER USED to make a thick-crusted crescenta, laden with pancetta and fresh rosemary. It was often stuffed with prosciutto and mortadella and became a most succulent school lunch.

Basic Pizza Dough

1½ cups unbleached all-purpose
   flour
1 package active dry yeast,
   dissolved in ½ cup plus 2
   tablespoons lukewarm water

1 tablespoon olive oil
1 teaspoon salt

MADE BY HAND

PUT all the ingredients in a medium-size bowl and mix well with your hands until incorporated. Put the dough on a work surface and knead 5 to 6 minutes, or until the dough is smooth and pliable. If it seems a bit sticky, knead in a little more flour. Dust the dough lightly with flour and place in a large bowl.

For a fast-rising dough, place the covered bowl in an unlit oven.

Cover the bowl with a moist kitchen towel or with plastic wrap, and put it in a warm, draft-free place to rise, 1 to 1½ hours. At this point the dough should have doubled in volume, be springy, and have small gas bubbles all over its surface.

MADE IN AN ELECTRIC MIXER

PUT the flour in the bowl of an electric mixer. Add the dissolved yeast, oil, and salt and, with the dough hook, mix well at medium-low speed until all ingredients are incorporated. Increase the speed to high and knead the dough 4 to 5 minutes. Dust the dough lightly with flour and place it in a large bowl. Cover the bowl with a moist kitchen towel or with plastic wrap, and let it rise in a warm, draft-free place for 1 to 1½ hours.

MADE WITH A FOOD PROCESSOR

PUT the flour and the salt in a food processor fitted with the metal blade. Add the dissolved yeast and the oil, and pulse the machine on and off until the dough is loosely gathered around the blade. Remove the dough and knead it by hand 2 to 3 minutes. Dust the dough lightly with flour and place it in a large bowl. Cover the bowl with a moist kitchen towel or with plastic wrap, and let it rise in a warm, draft-free place for 1 to 1½ hours.

continued

FINISHING THE PIZZA

PREHEAT the oven to 450° about 30 minutes before baking.

FLATTEN the dough down with your hands. Roll out the dough into a 12-inch circle, making sure to leave the edges a bit thicker than the center so that the filling won't spill over.

BRUSH a 12-inch flat pizza pan with a bit of olive oil and spread the dough onto the pan with your fingertips. Top with your favorite filling and bake until golden, 15 to 20 minutes.

Note: For a crisp crust, place a large baking stone or unglazed terra-cotta tile in the middle of the oven and preheat the oven to 450° about 30 minutes before baking. The pizza can be cooked directly on the baking stone or in its own pizza pan placed over the stone. If you don't have a baking stone, make sure that the oven is very hot.

Dissolve the yeast in lukewarm water, not in hot water. Too much heat will kill the yeast. Test the water on the inside part of your wrist if you don't have a thermometer. If you test the water with a thermometer, the temperature should be between 100° and 120°.

Even though active dry yeast is quite reliable, it is a good idea to proof the yeast. Add a pinch of sugar to the dissolved yeast, and if tiny bubbles appear on the surface of the water, the yeast is okay. Make sure always to check the expiration date on the yeast package before using it.

Pizza dough can also be made with a combination of all-purpose flour and finely ground semolina (hard wheat durum) flour or only with semolina flour.

Neapolitan Calzoni

CALZONI NAPOLETANI

THE DOUGH FOR *calzoni is rolled out into 2 large circles, and filled with a savory mixture of ricotta, salame, and pecorino cheese. The calzoni, just like pizza, are baked at a very high temperature so that the dough turns golden brown and crisp.*

MAKES 2 CALZONI

1 recipe Basic Pizza Dough (see pages 215–216)

FOR THE FILLING

2 large eggs

6 ounces sliced salame, cut into strips

¼ pound mozzarella, grated or diced

½ pound whole-milk ricotta

2–3 tablespoons grated pecorino Romano or ½ cup freshly grated Parmigiano-Reggiano cheese

2 tablespoons chopped fresh flat-leaf Italian parsley or regular parsley

Salt and freshly ground black pepper to taste

1 large egg, lightly beaten, to brush over the calzoni

PREPARE the pizza dough and let it rise.

PREHEAT the oven to 450° about 30 minutes before baking.

BEAT the eggs in a large bowl. Add all the filling ingredients, season with salt and pepper, and mix well to combine. Taste and adjust the seasoning.

DIVIDE the dough into 2 equal parts and roll out 2 circles, approximately 8 inches in diameter. Place half of the filling in the center of each circle of dough, and fold the dough over so that the edges meet. Fold the edges slightly to form a border. Press the tines of a fork over the folded dough to seal.

PLACE the calzoni on a baking sheet and brush them with the beaten egg. Bake until the crust is golden brown, 15 to 20 minutes. Cool slightly and serve.

Calzoni with Onions, Olives, and Tomatoes

CALZONI CON CIPOLLE, OLIVE, E POMODORI

YEARS AGO, MY *husband and I spent a dream vacation in a beautiful seaside resort near Vieste, in Puglia. The food at the resort was quite good, but we found ourselves seeking out small trattorie that served traditional regional food. I still have memories of that wonderful uncontrived, honest food, prepared with the freshest ingredients.*

THE CALZONE IS *typical of rustic Pugliese cuisine. The filling of onion, tomatoes, anchovies, olives, capers, and sun-dried tomatoes is positively addictive.*

MAKES 2 CALZONI

1 recipe Basic Pizza Dough (see pages 215–216)

FOR THE FILLING

3–4 tablespoons extra-virgin olive oil

1 large yellow onion, about 1 pound, peeled and thinly sliced

1 pound ripe, firm tomatoes, peeled and diced

4 anchovy fillets, chopped

2 tablespoons capers, rinsed

10 pitted black olives, thinly sliced

1 tablespoon minced sun-dried tomatoes

¼ cup grated pecorino Romano cheese or 3/4 cup freshly grated Parmigiano-Reggiano cheese

2 tablespoons chopped fresh flat-leaf Italian parsley or regular parsley

Salt and freshly ground black pepper to taste

1 large egg, lightly beaten, to brush over the calzoni

PREPARE the pizza dough and let it rise.

PREHEAT the oven to 450° about 30 minutes before baking.

PREPARE THE FILLING: Heat the oil in a large skillet over medium heat. Add the onion and cook, stirring, until it is lightly golden, 4 to 5 minutes. Add the diced tomatoes, anchovies, capers, olives, sun-dried tomatoes, and parsley, and cook until the juices of the tomatoes are nice and thick, 5 to 6 minutes.

WITH a slotted spoon transfer the contents of the skillet to a bowl and cool. Add the cheese to the cooled mixture, season with salt and pepper, and mix well to combine. Taste and adjust the seasoning.

DIVIDE the dough into 2 equal parts and roll out 2 circles, approximately 8 inches in diameter. Place half of the filling in the center of each circle of dough, and fold the dough over so that the edges meet. Fold the edges slightly to form a border. Press the tines of a fork over the folded dough to seal.

PLACE the calzoni on a baking sheet and brush them with the beaten egg. Bake until the crust is golden brown, 15 to 20 minutes. Cool slightly and serve.

Small Fried Calzoni

CALZUNCIEDDI PUGLIESI

LARGE OR SMALL, *baked or deep fried, calzoni are specialties of the Puglia region.*

THESE CALZONI, CALLED *calzuncieddi, are made with a basic pizza dough, are filled with sautéed onion, ripe tomatoes, and fresh mozzarella, then fried to a golden-crisp consistency, absolutely irresistible.*

MAKES 16 CALZONI

1 recipe Basic Pizza Dough (see pages 215–216)

FOR THE FILLING
2–3 tablespoons extra-virgin olive oil
½ cup minced yellow onion
2 medium ripe tomatoes, 6–7 ounces, seeded and diced

1 small garlic clove, minced
Salt to taste
¼ pound mozzarella, diced

Vegetable oil for fying
Salt

PREPARE the pizza dough and let it rise.

PREHEAT the oven to 450° about 30 minutes before baking.

continued

PREPARE THE FILLING: Heat the oil in a medium-size skillet over medium heat. Add the onion and cook, stirring, until it is lightly golden, 4 to 5 minutes. Add the tomatoes and the garlic, and season with salt. Cook until the juices of the tomatoes are thick. Transfer the tomato mixture to a bowl and cool. Mix the mozzarella into the cooled tomatoes.

ON a lightly floured surface, roll out the dough to pie-dough thickness. With a large glass or cookie cutter, cut the dough into 4-inch circles. Put 1 heaping teaspoon of filling in the center of each circle of dough and fold the dough over the filling so that the edges meet. Press the edges of the dough firmly to seal.

HEAT 2 inches of oil to 375° in a medium heavy pot over medium-high heat. With a slotted spoon carefully lower 3 or 4 small calzoni at a time into the oil. When one side of the calzoni is golden, 20 to 30 seconds, turn them over to cook the other side. Drain on paper towels, sprinkle lightly with salt, and serve hot.

VARIATION

To bake the small calzoni, preheat the oven to 450°. Place the calzoni on a baking sheet and bake until they have a nice golden color, 12 to 14 minutes.

Four Seasons Pizza

PIZZA ALLE QUATTRO STAGIONI

WHENEVER I GO *to Italy, I must have a pizza fix. One of my favorites is* pizza alle quattro stagioni, *pizza with four different toppings. Traditionally this pizza should include at least one type of shellfish, better yet two. However, quattro stagioni pizza can become the canvas for one's creativity. Try this version, then experiment on your own.*

SERVES 2

1 recipe Basic Pizza Dough (see pages 215–216)

1½ pounds clams, thoroughly washed in several changes of water

1 pound mussels, thoroughly washed and scrubbed, with beards removed

Salt and freshly ground black pepper to taste

2–3 tablespoons extra-virgin olive oil

One 6-ounce jar small artichokes, marinated in oil

1 tablespoon minced sun-dried tomatoes

2–3 fresh, ripe tomatoes, cut into thin, round slices

PREPARE the pizza dough and let it rise.

PREHEAT the oven to 450° about 30 minutes before baking.

HEAT a small amount of water in a large skillet over medium heat. Add the clams and the mussels, and cover the skillet. Cook just until the clams and mussels open. Transfer them to a bowl as they open. Detach the valves from the shells, and place the mussels and clams separately in 2 small bowls. Season them with salt and pepper, and drizzle with 1 to 2 tablespoons of olive oil. Set aside.

DRAIN most of the oil from the artichokes and cut them into small pieces. Place them in a bowl, add the sun-dried tomatoes, and season lightly with salt and pepper.

continued

ROLL out the dough into a 12-inch circle and place it on the oiled pizza pan. With the tip of a knife, make a light cross in the dough, forming 4 wedges. Brush the dough lightly with oil, and arrange the clams, mussels, artichokes, and sliced fresh tomatoes separately on each wedge. Season lightly with salt and drizzle with remaining oil. Bake until the dough is golden brown, about 15 minutes. Serve hot.

Pizza with Mushrooms and Tomato

PIZZA CON FUNGHI E POMODORO

SERVES 2

1 recipe Basic Pizza Dough (see
    pages 215–216)
3–4 tablespoons extra-virgin
    olive oil
½ pound white cultivated
    mushrooms, wiped clean and
    thinly sliced

1 garlic clove, minced
Salt to taste
3 fresh, ripe tomatoes, about 10
    ounces, cut into thin rounds
6 ounces mozzarella, cut into thin
    rounds

PREPARE the pizza dough and let it rise.

PREHEAT the oven to 450° about 30 minutes before baking.

HEAT 2 to 3 tablespoons of the oil in a large skillet over high heat. Add the mushrooms and cook, stirring, until they are lightly golden, 2 to 3 minutes. Add the garlic and stir once or twice. Season with salt. Transfer mushrooms to a bowl and cool.

ROLL out the dough into a 12-inch circle and place on the oiled pizza pan. Brush the dough lightly with oil. Cut the slices of mozzarella in half. Arrange the tomatoes and the mozzarella alternatingly in 2 large circles, drizzle with the remaining oil, and season lightly with salt. Fill the center of the pizza with the mushrooms. Bake until the dough is golden brown, about 15 minutes. Serve hot.

Onion Focaccia

FOCACCIA CON CIPOLLE

THERE IS NOTHING *that appeases hunger and gives more satisfaction than a large plate of steaming pasta, or freshly baked bread or focaccia. This is the kind of food that begs to be eaten, savored, and enjoyed.*

MAKES ONE 15 × 12-INCH FOCACCIA

FOR THE FIRST RISING

1 teaspoon active dry yeast, dissolved in ½ cup lukewarm water
1 cup unbleached all-purpose flour

FOR THE SECOND RISING

2 teaspoons active dry yeast, dissolved in 1 cup lukewarm water

2½ cups unbleached all-purpose flour
1 tablespoon salt
2 tablespoons olive oil

3–4 tablespoons extra-virgin olive oil
2 large yellow onions, about 1¼ pounds, peeled and thinly sliced
Salt to taste

FOR THE FIRST RISING: Put all the ingredients in a large bowl or in the bowl of an electric mixer fitted with the dough hook, and mix well. Knead 6 to 7 minutes by hand, or 3 to 4 minutes by machine, until the dough is smooth and pliable. Put the dough in a lightly oiled bowl, cover tightly with plastic wrap, and let it rise until doubled in volume, 1 to 1½ hours.

FOR THE SECOND RISING: Put all the ingredients in a large bowl or in the bowl of an electric mixer fitted with the dough hook, and mix well. Add the dough from the first rising and knead 4 to 5 minutes by machine, 8 to 10 minutes by hand. The dough should be smooth and elastic. If it is too sticky, work in some additional flour.

LIGHTLY oil a 15 × 12-inch baking sheet. Place the dough on the sheet and, with your fingers, starting from the center, push the dough out to fit the baking sheet. Cover the dough loosely with plastic wrap and let it rise again until it has doubled in size, 40 to 45 minutes.

continued

TO COMPLETE THE DISH: While the dough is rising, heat the oil in a large skillet over medium-low heat. Add the onions and cook, stirring occasionally, until they are completely soft, 30 to 35 minutes. Season lightly with salt. Do not let the onions color; they should be white, soft, and translucent.

PREHEAT the oven to 400° about 30 minutes before baking.

BRUSH the top of the dough lightly with oil and season with salt. With your fingertips, make small indentations all over the dough, then cover the dough with the soft onions. Bake 20 to 25 minutes, or until the dough and the onions have a nice golden color. Cool 5 to 10 minutes, then remove the focaccia from the pan, and place it on a cutting board. Serve warm or at room temperature.

Bolognese Savory Fried Dough

LE CRESCENTINE BOLOGNESI

THERE IS A *whole category of Italian food that conjures up comforting images. Street food, country food, deliciously homey and appetizing, this is what crescentine are. In country trattorie all over Emilia-Romagna, crescentine come to the table sprinkled with salt, generally accompanied by a large platter of prosciutto and salame. You drink a glass of wine, top a crescentina with a slice of prosciutto, and wait for the rest of the meal to arrive. It is then that you realize you are not hungry anymore because you have devoured a whole plate of these delicious, crisp crescentine.*

MAKES 14 TO 16 CRESCENTINE

1½ cups unbleached all-purpose flour
2 tablespoons olive oil
2 tablespoons unsalted butter, melted

½ package active dry yeast, dissolved in ½ cup lukewarm milk
1 teaspoon salt

PUT the flour, oil, butter, and salt in a medium bowl. Add the dissolved yeast and mix all the ingredients well with a wooden spoon or with your hands until

The dough can be prepared several hours ahead and kept refrigerated. Bring it back to room temperature before rolling it out.

Like most fried food, crescentine should be eaten immediately after they are fried or they will become soggy.

You can serve crescentine as an appetizer for a rustic meal, or as a snack.

they are incorporated. Put the dough on a work board and knead 2 to 3 minutes. Add a bit of flour if the dough seems sticky. Wrap the dough with plastic wrap and let it rest for about 30 minutes.

LIGHTLY flour a wooden board or other work surface, and roll out the dough into a large, thin rectangle. With a fluted pastry wheel, cut the sheet of dough into 5-inch wide strips, and zigzag each strip into large triangles. Lay the triangles on a tray lined with a clean kitchen towel.

HEAT 1 inch of oil in a medium-size skillet over medium-high heat. When the oil is very hot, slide a few pieces of dough into the skillet and fry a few at a time. When they are golden on one side, 20 to 30 seconds, turn them to fry the other side. Transfer to paper towels to drain. Sprinkle the crescentine lightly with salt and serve piping hot, by themselves or accompanied by slices of prosciutto or salame.

BASIC PIE DOUGH

FIG AND JAM TART

APPLE, FIG, AND DATE ROLL

PEAR, HONEY, AND WALNUT PIE

APPLE AND AMARETTI CAKE

APRICOT CAKE

BOLOGNESE JAM CAKE

DEEP-FRIED SWEET PASTRY BALLS

ST. JOSEPH'S DAY RICE FRITTERS

OVEN-TOASTED BREAD WITH GORGONZOLA AND HONEY

SWEET FLAT BREAD WITH GRAPES

HOMEMADE PANETTONE

MASCARPONE-ZABAGLIONE MOUSSE

STRAWBERRY-LEMON GELATO

BLACK CHERRY GRANITA

ESPRESSO GRANITA

PEAR SORBET

STRAWBERRIES IN RED WINE

MARINATED ORANGES

BAKED PEARS

Desserts

THERE ARE TWO distinct types of Italian desserts simple; traditional sweets created at home, and rich, elaborate desserts made mainly by pastry cooks and showcased in *pasticcerie*, pastry shops, throughout Italy.

WHEN I WAS a child in Bologna, the only desserts my mother would make on a regular basis were basic and uncomplicated. Rice, apples, chestnut, and pastry fritters were the treats that would greet us when we returned home from school. Often we would help our mother by dropping a spoonful of rice batter into the hot oil, or rolling out the sweet pastry dough. We would slice apples for the apple cake, or help prepare baked apples for the evening meal. On Sunday my mother would branch out a bit and would bake a ciambella or a pinza, both traditional Bolognese desserts, made with leavened sweet dough. Only on very special occasions would a more elaborate dessert, such as zuppa inglese, be prepared. Sweets were generally consumed throughout the day, as midmorning or midafternoon snacks, rather than at the end of a meal, when we usually had fruit. On special occasions, when we entertained family members or guests, we would go to the pastry shop to buy *paste miste*, assorted pastries, which we displayed on a large platter in all their glory.

WHILE LIFE IN Italy has changed greatly since I was a child, traditional desserts are still made at home, even though less frequently now that many women work outside the home. Today, just as years ago, fresh fruit completes the family dinner, and when sweets *are* served, they are often fruit-based.

THE DESSERTS IN this chapter are easy to make, and many stem from regional traditions. For a special children's treat, try St. Joseph's Day Rice Fritters (page 239). For a light ending to an elegant meal, make Pear Sorbet (page 248) or, my favorite, Oven-Toasted Bread with Gorgonzola and Honey (page 240). Two desserts that keep well for several days are Apricot Cake (page 236) and Apple, Fig, and Date Roll (page 231). For a hot summer night, whip up some refreshing Espresso Granita (page 247). And always keep some fresh fruit handy. Spur-of-the-moment desserts can be created by marinating strawberries in wine; try sliced oranges, sprinkled with walnuts and drizzled with lemon juice; and poached pears. In the kitchen, creativity and fantasy are just as important as good recipes and good ingredients.

Basic Pie Dough

2 cups unbleached all-purpose flour

5 ounces unsalted butter, at room temperature for hand mixing, or cold, cut into small pieces for the food processor

2 tablespoons granulated sugar

1 large egg, lightly beaten

4–5 tablespoons chilled dry white wine

1 large egg, lightly beaten, to brush over pastry

IN a medium-size bowl, or in a food processor fitted with the metal blade, mix the flour and the butter until crumbly. Add the sugar, egg, and wine, and mix into a soft dough. (If you use a food processor, remove the dough when it is loosely gathered around the blade.) Shape the dough into 1 or 2 balls, depending on the recipe, wrap in plastic wrap, and refrigerate for 1 hour or until ready to use.

Fig and Jam Tart

CROSTATA DI FICHI E MARMELLATA

JAM TARTS ARE *very popular all over Italy, and in Bologna every bread store and pastry store has a large display of them. Even though the jam, which is often homemade, is the main ingredient, dried fruits sometimes are also added to the filling. In this recipe dried figs, soaked in Marsala wine and cooked to a soft consistency, are stirred into the jam. Serve a thin slice of this delicious tart with a cup of espresso to top off a meal.*

SERVES 6 TO 8

1 recipe Basic Pie Dough (see
    page 229)

1 pound dried figs, stems removed,
    minced
1½ cups dry Marsala wine, such
    as Florio or Pellegrino

Juice of 1 lemon
Grated zest of 1 lemon
One 10-ounce jar fig jam
1 large egg, lightly beaten in a
    small bowl

PREPARE the pie dough. Shape into 2 balls and refrigerate for 1 hour.

PREPARE THE FILLING: In a medium bowl combine the figs with the Marsala wine and let them sit for about 1 hour. In a small saucepan combine figs, wine, lemon juice, and grated lemon zest. Bring the liquid to a boil, then lower the heat to medium low and simmer until figs are soft and all the wine in the pan is evaporated, 10 to 12 minutes. Stir a few times during cooking. Transfer figs to a bowl and cool completely. Add the jam to the cooled figs and mix well to combine.

PREHEAT the oven to 375°. Butter a 10-inch tart pan that has a removable bottom.

ON a lightly floured surface, roll out 1 ball of the dough to a 12-inch circle. Place the dough into the prepared tart pan and press gently and evenly into the pan. Trim the edges of the dough with scissors, leaving some hanging over the rim. Fold the dough under to form a border and pinch it with your fingertips to seal. Prick the bottom of the pastry shell in several places with a fork. Pour the filling into the shell and spread it evenly with a spatula.

ROLL out the second ball of dough and, with a pastry wheel, cut it into six to eight ½-inch wide strips.

LAY the pastry strips across the tart to make a lattice top. Brush the dough with the beaten egg and place the tart in the oven. Bake until crust is golden brown, 20 to 25 minutes. Cool tart to room temperature before serving.

Apple, Fig, and Date Roll

STRUCOLO DI MELE, FICHI, E DATTERI

IN TRENTINO—ALTO ADIGE *they call this dessert* strudel; *in neighboring Friuli–Venezia Giulia,* strucolo. *A large sheet of delicate, crisp pastry or phyllo dough is stuffed with all manner of sweet ingredients: apples, dates, figs, walnuts, pine nuts, and jam. This is a great dessert to serve guests or family at Thanksgiving or Christmas.*

SERVES 10 TO 12

1 recipe Basic Pie Dough (see page 229)

¼ pound dried figs, stems removed
¼ pound dates
1½ cups dry Marsala wine, such as Florio or Pellegrino
6 large Golden Delicious apples, about 2½ pounds, peeled, cored, and thinly sliced
½ cup granulated sugar

Grated zest of 1 lemon
Grated zest of 1 orange
½ cup golden raisins, soaked in lukewarm water for 20 minutes and drained
⅓ cup pine nuts
One 10-ounce jar plum jam
½ cup walnuts, finely chopped
1 large egg, lightly beaten in a small bowl
Powdered sugar

PREPARE the pie dough. Shape into a ball and refrigerate for 1 hour.

continued

PREPARE THE FILLING: Chop the figs and the dates by hand or in a food processor, and soak them in the Marsala wine for 20 minutes. Put the figs, dates, and the soaking wine in a large skillet and cook, uncovered, over medium heat until the wine is all evaporated, 8 to 10 minutes. Add the apples, sugar, and grated lemon and orange zest. Cook and stir until the juice from the apples has all evaporated, 4 to 5 minutes. Transfer mixture to a bowl, and stir in the raisins and pine nuts. Set aside to cool. Fold the jam into the cooled mixture and refrigerate until ready to use.

PREHEAT the oven to 375°. Lightly butter a 15 × 12-inch baking sheet and line it with parchment paper. Butter the parchment paper lightly.

ON a lightly floured surface, with a rolling pin roll out the dough into a large, thin rectangle, about 20 inches long and 10 to 12 inches wide. With a fluted pastry wheel or a sharp knife, trim the edges of the pastry into straight lines.

SPREAD a large kitchen towel on the work surface. Roll the pastry loosely over the rolling pin and unroll the pastry over the towel. Spread the walnuts over the pastry dough, leaving free about a 2-inch border on three sides, and a 4-inch border on the side near you. Spread the apple mixture evenly over the walnuts. Fold the empty 4-inch border over the apple filling, then pick up the edges of the towel and roll the pastry over loosely, jelly-roll fashion, until it is completely rolled up. Pinch the two ends of the roll with your fingers to seal.

PICK up the pastry roll with the towel, and carefully slide it over the buttered baking sheet with the seam facing up. If necessary, trim the roll to fit the baking sheet. Brush the pastry roll with the beaten egg and place in the oven. Bake until the pastry is golden brown, 40 to 50 minutes.

REMOVE from the oven and cool to room temperature. With 2 large metal spatulas, carefully pick up the pastry roll and transfer it to a large serving platter. Dust with powdered sugar and serve.

Pear, Honey, and Walnut Pie

TORTA DI PERE, MIELE, E NOCI

ONE OF MY *favorite desserts is a honey-walnut pie from Bologna called "La Bonissima."* *One day while I was getting ready to make it, I decided to add pears and Amaretti* *cookies to the classic filling, with wonderful results. The amaretti add crunch and the* *pears lend their autumnal sweetness to the moist, dense filling.*

SERVES 6 TO 8

1 recipe Basic Pie Dough (see page 229)

2 tablespoons unsalted butter
8 firm Bosc pears, about 3 to 3½ pounds, peeled, cored, and cut into small chunks
¼ cup granulated sugar
½ teaspoon cinnamon
Grated zest of 1 lemon

1 cup dry Marsala wine, such as Florio or Pellegrino
½ cup honey
1 cup walnuts, finely chopped
8 amaretti di Saronno cookies, finely crumbled
2 tablespoons unbleached all-purpose flour
1 large egg, lightly beaten in a small bowl

PREPARE the pie dough. Shape into 2 balls, one a bit larger than the other, and refrigerate for 1 hour.

PREPARE THE FILLING: Heat the butter in a large skillet over medium heat. Add the pears, sugar, cinnamon, grated lemon zest, and Marsala wine. Cook, uncovered, stirring ocassionally until the wine is all reduced and the pears are tender but still firm to the bite, 8 to 10 minutes. Transfer pears to a bowl and cool completely. Add the honey, walnuts, amaretti, and flour to the cooled pears, and mix well to combine. Refrigerate mixture until ready to use.

PREHEAT the oven to 375°. Butter a 10-inch tart pan that has a removable bottom.

ON a lightly floured surface, roll out the larger ball of dough to a 12-inch circle. Place the dough into the prepared tart pan, and press gently and evenly into the pan. Let the excess dough hang over the rim of the pan. Prick the bottom of the pastry shell in several places with a fork so that the pastry will not puff up while it is baking. Fill the pastry shell with the pear mixture and smooth the top with a spatula.

ROLL out the remaining ball of dough and lay it over the filling. Trim the excess dough with scissors if necessary. Combine the edges of the bottom and top dough and fold them over to form a border. Pinch the border with your fingers to seal. Brush the dough with the beaten egg and prick it with a fork in several places to allow the steam to escape while pie is baking.

BAKE until the crust is golden brown, 30 to 35 minutes. Remove pie from oven and let stand for 15 to 20 minutes, then remove from the pan and place on a serving platter. Let cool completely before serving.

Apple and Amaretti Cake

TORTA DI MELE E AMARETTI

THIS LIGHT, DELICIOUS *cake can be put together in a short amount of time. The amount of flour used is minimal, just enough to bind the mixture of apples, amaretti cookies, and raisins. Dust the cake with powdered sugar, and serve it by itself or with ice cream, custard cream, or zabaglione.*

SERVES 6 TO 8

Butter for the baking pan
2–3 tablespoons plain dried bread crumbs to coat the baking pan
1 cup golden raisins, soaked in lukewarm water for 20 minutes
2 tablespoons unsalted butter
1 cup dry Marsala wine, such as Florio or Pellegrino

½ cup granulated sugar
3 pounds Golden Delicious apples, peeled, cored, and thinly sliced
⅓ cup all-purpose flour
½ cup plain dried bread crumbs
8 amaretti di Saronno cookies, finely crumbled (see Note)
3 large eggs, lightly beaten
Powdered sugar

PREHEAT the oven to 350°. Butter and coat with bread crumbs a 10-inch spring-form cake pan with a removable bottom.

DRAIN raisins and pat them dry with paper towels.

HEAT the butter in a large skillet over medium heat. Add the Marsala wine, sugar, and apples. Raise the heat to high and cook, stirring, until the apples begin to soften, 3 to 5 minutes.

SCOOP up the apples with a large slotted spoon, letting the excess juices fall back into the skillet, and place apples in a strainer. Put the apples in a large bowl. Over high heat, cook down the juices left in the skillet until you have about ¼ cup of thick sauce. Stir the sauce into the apples.

ADD the flour, bread crumbs, amaretti, raisins, and eggs to the apples, and mix well to combine. Place the apple mixture in the buttered baking pan and level top with a spatula. Shake the pan lightly to distribute the batter evenly. Bake 30 to 40 minutes, or until the top of the cake is golden brown and a thin knife inserted in the center of the cake comes out just slightly moist. Cool to room temperature and serve.

Note: Amaretti di Saronno are delicious almond cookies imported from Italy. They are easily available in Italian markets or specialty food stores.

Apricot Cake

TORTA DI ALBICOCCHE

THIS IS A *simple, unassuming cake; my mother used to make a similar cake with apples. It can also be prepared with plums, peaches, or pears. If using apples or pears, there is no need to cook them beforehand. Simply peel and slice the fruit and fold it into the batter.*

SERVES 8 TO 10

4 ounces (1 stick) unsalted butter, at room temperature

1½ pounds ripe apricots or plums, halved, pitted, and cut into thin slices

1 cup granulated sugar

1 package active dry yeast

⅓ cup lukewarm water

4 extra-large eggs

2 cups unbleached all-purpose flour

2 tablespoons additional granulated sugar

Powdered sugar

PREHEAT the oven to 375°. Butter and flour a 10-inch springform cake pan.

HEAT 1 tablespoon of the butter in a large skillet over medium heat. When the butter foams, add the apricots and ½ cup of the sugar. Cook, stirring, until apricots begin to soften, 3 to 4 minutes. With a large slotted spoon scoop up the apricot slices and place them in a large bowl. Cook the juices in the skillet over high heat until only a few tablespoons of thick, glazy sauce are left. Pour over the apricots. Cool the apricots to room temperature or refrigerate until ready to use.

STIR the yeast into the water until dissolved and let it sit for 10 minutes until it foams up.

BEAT the eggs and the remaining sugar in a large bowl or in the bowl of a mixer until pale yellow and thick. Beat in the remaining butter and, when it is incorporated, beat in the flour and the yeast mixture. Add the apricots to the batter and fold in with a large spatula. Pour the batter into the buttered pan, level top with a spatula, and sprinkle with the 2 tablespoons of sugar.

BAKE 30 to 40 minutes, or until the top of the cake is golden brown. To test the cake for doneness, insert a toothpick in the center of the cake. If the toothpick comes out clean, the cake is done. If it is moist, bake cake a few minutes longer. Cool cake to room temperature. Serve sprinkled with powdered sugar.

Bolognese Jam Cake

LA PINZA BOLOGNESE

ONE OF THE *nicest treats my mother would bring us after her ritual early-morning shopping in Bologna's historic food market was a slice of freshly baked pinza. Pinza is a homey cake filled with jam, and it has a somewhat firm texture and a crumbly consistency. I remember this cake as "one of the most delicious things on earth."*

SERVES 8 TO 10

Butter and flour for the baking
    sheet
2 cups unbleached all-purpose flour
Grated zest of 2 lemons
½ cup plus 2 tablespoons
    granulated sugar
¼ pound unsalted butter, at room
    temperature

2 large eggs, lightly beaten in a
    small bowl
2 teaspoons active dry yeast,
    diluted in ⅓ cup
    lukewarm milk
1 cup plum jam, about 8 ounces

PREHEAT the oven to 350°. Butter and flour a large baking sheet.

IN a large bowl combine the flour with the grated lemon zest and ½ cup of the sugar, and mix well. Add the butter and rub it with your hands into the flour.

ADD the eggs and the milk with the diluted yeast, and mix well into the flour with a fork. Place the flour mixture on a work area, dust your hands with flour, and knead the mixture lightly into a soft dough. At this point the dough should be fairly rough in texture, soft, and a bit sticky.

FLATTEN the dough with your hands, and gently stretch it into a rectangle, approximately 9 × 11 inches. Spoon the jam lengthwise in the center of the dough and fold the long sides of the dough, slightly overlapping each other, over the jam. Lightly press the ends of the cake together with a fork to seal it and to make a pattern.

WITH two large metal spatulas, carefully transfer the pinza to the baking sheet. Sprinkle the cake with the remaining sugar and bake until golden brown, 45 to 50 minutes. Cool and serve.

Deep-Fried Sweet Pastry Balls

CASTAGNOLE FRITTE

FRITTERS! THE MERE *word brings back images of large platters piled with these light, golden balls made of rice, ricotta, or just flour, butter, sugar, and yeast. In my youth, every household in Bologna prepared fritters. They were delicious, simple to make, and inexpensive. Unfortunately, in Italy today this type of dessert is disappearing. It's too bad because even while trying to eat a healthier diet, we are also eliminating a most basic "comfort" food.*

MAKES 45 TO 50 FRITTERS

3 cups unbleached all-purpose flour
1 tablespoon active dry yeast,
    diluted in ½ cup plus 1
    tablespoon lukewarm water
Salt to taste
2 large eggs, lightly beaten

2 tablespoons unsalted butter, at
    room temperature
½ cup granulated sugar
Oil for frying
Additional granulated sugar,
    spread on a plate

You can fill the fritters with a dollop of thick jam, pastry cream, fruit puree, or zabaglione. Place the filling in a small pastry bag fitted with a small tip, press the tip into the fritters, and fill.

IN a large bowl combine 1 cup of the flour, the diluted yeast, and a pinch of salt into a soft batter. Cover the bowl with plastic wrap and let it rest for 20 to 30 minutes.

ADD the remaining flour, eggs, butter, and sugar to the batter, and mix well to incorporate. Knead the dough by hand, or with an electric mixer fitted with the dough hook, until it is smooth, soft, and pliable, and just a bit sticky, 5 to 6 minutes by hand or 2 to 3 minutes with the mixer. Place the dough in a lightly floured large bowl, cover with plastic wrap, and let rise in a warm, draft-free place until it has doubled in volume, 1 to 1½ hours.

TRANSFER the dough to a wooden board and flatten it down with your hands. Knead it lightly for a minute or two. Divide the dough into 2 or 3 pieces. Flour your hands lightly and roll out each piece of dough with a light back-and-forth motion into a roll about the thickness of a thin sausage. Cut each roll into 1-inch pieces and place them on a lightly floured platter or cookie sheet.

POUR 2 inches of oil in a medium-size saucepan. When the oil is very hot (375° on a thermometer), drop a few pieces of dough at a time into the hot oil. When the fritters are golden on both sides, remove them with a slotted spoon and drain on paper towels.

ROLL the fritters in the additional sugar, pile them on a serving platter, and serve hot.

St. Joseph's Day Rice Fritters

FRITTELLE DI SAN GIUSEPPE

RICE FRITTERS ARE *traditionally served throughout central Italy on March 19, St. Joseph's Day. The ingredients might change slightly, depending on the region and the cook.*

MY MOTHER WOULD *prepare them regularly for us, since they were inexpensive and simple to make. She would pile the golden, hot fritters on a large platter, dust them with powdered sugar, and in no time at all they would all disappear.*

MAKES 25 TO 30 FRITTERS

3 cups milk
1 cup imported Italian Arborio rice
Salt to taste
4 large eggs, separated and at room
    temperature
Grated zest of 1 lemon

½–¾ cup granulated sugar
½ cup unbleached all-purpose flour
¼ teaspoon ground cinnamon
¼ cup dark rum
Oil for frying
Powdered sugar

BRING the milk to a gentle boil in a medium-size saucepan over medium-low heat. Add the rice and a pinch of salt. Cook, uncovered, stirring occasionally until rice is quite tender and the milk is all evaporated, 30 to 40 minutes. Watch the rice carefully during the last minutes of cooking, since it might stick to the pot as the milk evaporates. Stir frequently. Spread the rice mixture on a flat platter and cool to room temperature.

continued

PUT the cooled rice in a large bowl and mix in all other ingredients except the egg whites. Taste and add a bit more sugar if needed. When all the ingredients are well incorporated, beat the egg whites with a pinch of sugar until stiff and fold them into the rice mixture.

POUR 2 inches of oil into a medium-size saucepan. When the oil is very hot (375° on a thermometer), drop the rice batter in small spoonsful at a time into the oil. When the fritters are golden on both sides, remove them with a slotted spoon and drain on paper towels. Repeat until all the batter has been used up.

PLACE the fritters on a serving platter, dust with powdered sugar, and serve hot.

Oven-Toasted Bread with Gorgonzola and Honey

CROSTONI AL GORGONZOLA E MIELE

YEARS AGO I *spent a delightful weekend at Le Tre Vasselle, an elegant hotel in Torgiano, in Umbria. The hotel restaurant is renowned for its traditional dishes as well as variations on classic themes, such as these crostoni. Great local bread, oven toasted, topped with creamy mild Gorgonzola and golden mellow honey, makes the perfect ending to a meal.*

SERVES 4

¼ pound Gorgonzola, cut into
    small pieces
2–3 tablespoons heavy cream

Eight ½-inch-thick slices bread
    cut from a baguette-style loaf,
    oven toasted or grilled
2–3 tablespoons honey

PREHEAT the oven to 400°.

PUT the Gorgonzola in a small bowl and break it down with a fork. Add the cream and beat with a wooden spoon until the cheese is smooth. Spoon or spread the cheese on the bread and drizzle some honey on top.

PLACE the bread slices on a baking sheet and bake for 1 to 2 minutes, or until the cheese begins to melt. Serve hot.

Sweet Flat Bread with Grapes

LA SCHIACCIATA CON L'UVA

SCHIACCIATA IS A *a sweet flat bread from Tuscany. Even though there are many variations, the most popular and certainly the most traditional is schiacciata with grapes. These are the types of wholesome yet unique dishes that capture the essence of Italy and delight the hearts, and appetites, of those who search them out. They are also absolutely delicious!*

SERVES 8

1 tablespoon active dry yeast
¾ cup lukewarm milk
2 cups unbleached all-purpose flour
½ cup plus 2 tablespoons
   granulated sugar

Oil for the baking pan
½ pound black seedless grapes
½ cup pine nuts, about 2½ ounces

DISSOLVE the yeast in the milk for 10 minutes.

IN a large bowl combine the flour with ½ cup of the sugar and mix well. Add the dissolved yeast and mix well into the flour with a fork. Place the mixture on a work surface, dust your hands lightly with flour, and knead the dough until it is smooth, pliable, and a bit sticky, 3 to 4 minutes. Shape the dough into a ball and place it in a lightly floured bowl. Cover with plastic wrap and let the dough rise in a warm, draft-free area for about 2 hours.

BRUSH a 10-inch springform pan lightly with oil.

PUT the risen dough on the work surface, and knead it again for 2 to 3 minutes. Spread the dough out into a thick circle, with your hands or with a rolling pin, then place it in the baking pan. Arrange the grapes snugly over the dough and add the pine nutes. Sprinkle with the remaining sugar. Cover the pan loosely with a kitchen towel and let the dough rise again until doubled in volume, about 1 hour.

WHILE the dough is rising, preheat the oven to 400°. Bake until the schiacciata has a nice golden-brown color, 30 to 40 minutes. Cool for 10 minutes, then remove from the pan and cool completely before serving.

Homemade Panettone

PANETTONE CASALINGO

PANETTONE IS A *tall, yeasty sweet bread, studded with raisins and sometimes citron, that is traditionally eaten at Christmas and New Year in Italy. Even though commercially made panettone can have a light, airy consistency, homemade panettone is in a class by itself. If you enjoy baking, I urge you to try this recipe. The results will please you.*

MAKES 2 PANETTONI

Two ¼-ounce packages active
    dry yeast
Pinch sugar
½ cup lukewarm water
4½ cups all-pupose flour
¾ cup granulated sugar
Pinch of salt
6 ounces unsalted butter, at room
    temperature, cut into small
    pieces

6 large eggs, at room temperature
2½ cups golden raisins, soaked
    in dry Marsala wine for
    30 minutes
1 large egg yolk, beaten with
    1 teaspoon cold water, for
    glazing

IN a small bowl combine the yeast, pinch of sugar, and water, and mix well to dissolve the yeast. Let stand for about 10 minutes to activate the yeast, or until small bubbles appear on the surface of the water.

PUT the flour, sugar, salt, butter, and eggs in the large bowl of an electric mixer and beat with the dough hook at low speed. Add the yeast mixture slowly. When all the ingredients are incorporated, beat at medium speed for 6 to 8 minutes, or until the dough is shiny, pliable, and gathers around the beater in a soft lump.

IF you are making the dough by hand, combine all the ingredients in a large bowl, then knead the dough on a lightly floured surface until it is smooth, soft, and pliable, about 10 minutes. Dust lightly with flour if the dough sticks to the work surface.

BRUSH a large bowl lightly with oil and add the dough. Cover with plastic wrap and place in a draft-free place to rise for 2 hours, or until it has doubled in volume. Take the risen dough and knead it energetically for a minute or two, then put it back into the bowl. Cover and let it rise again until doubled in bulk, about 2 more hours.

STRAIN the raisins and pat dry with paper towels. Lightly flour the work surface and your hands. Punch down the risen dough and flatten it out into a large circle with your hands. Sprinkle the raisins over the dough surface and fold the dough over the raisins. Knead the dough lightly until the raisins are well incorporated. Do not worry if some raisins fall out of the dough; simply knead them back in.

BUTTER two 1½-quart soufflé dishes. Divide the dough in half and shape each half into a round. Place the dough into the buttered dishes and with a sharp, thin knife cut a cross into the top of each ball of dough. Brush the dough with the beaten egg. Cover the dough loosely with foil and let it rise in a warm place for about 1 hour, or until it has doubled in volume.

PREHEAT the oven to 375°. When the oven is nice and hot, bake the panettoni for 35 to 45 minutes, or until they are golden brown. Unmold the panettoni and cool on a wire rack.

Mascarpone-Zabaglione Mousse

COPPA DI MASCARPONE ALLO ZABAGLIONE

IN THIS SIMPLE *yet luxurious dessert, fluffy, cognac-scented zabaglione sauce is folded into mascarpone, a soft, slightly tart Italian double cream cheese. A truly elegant dish for guests or family.*

SERVES 4

FOR THE ZABAGLIONE
8 large egg yolks
½ cup granulated sugar
⅓ cup cognac

1 pound mascarpone
Grated zest of 1 lemon
4 large egg whites, beaten with
    1 tablespoon sugar to a stiff
    consistency

PREPARE THE ZABAGLIONE: In a large bowl or the top part of a double boiler set over 2 inches of simmering water, beat the egg yolks with the sugar until thick and pale yellow. (Do not let the water boil or you will cook the eggs.) Add the cognac slowly, beating energetically with a large wire wisk to incorporate it. Keep cooking and beating the mixture until it doubles in volume and is soft, fluffy, and hot to the touch, 4 to 5 minutes. Place the bowl or the top part of the double boiler over a larger bowl containing ice, stir a few times, and let the zabaglione cool.

IN a large bowl or in the bowl of an electric mixer, beat the mascarpone with the lemon zest until soft and fluffy. Fold the cooled zabaglione into the mascarpone until thoroughly incorporated.

FOLD the egg whites thoroughly into the mascarpone mixture. Spoon the mousse into dessert glasses and refrigerate until ready to serve.

Strawberry-Lemon Gelato

GELATO DI FRAGOLE E LIMONE

ITALIAN GELATI ARE *light and fresh tasting. In a strawberry gelato, first and foremost, the strawberry flavor should come through. The amount of fat should be kept to a minimum, especially in fruit gelati. Here, the small amount of cream gives the gelato just enough creaminess and smoothness without making it heavy or too rich.*

SERVES 4

1 pound fresh strawberries, washed, hulled, and cut into halves (see Note)
½ cup granulated sugar

Juice of 1 lemon
½ cup cold whipping cream, beaten to a medium-thick consistency

Since it is impractical to make gelato at the very last moment, prepare it ahead and freeze it. Before you are ready to serve it, put the gelato in the refrigerator for 20 to 25 minutes to soften up somewhat first.

PUT the strawberries, sugar, and lemon juice into a food processor and process until smooth. Pour the mixture through a strainer and into the bowl of an ice cream machine. Run the machine for 10 to 15 minutes. Add the whipped cream and run the machine for 5 minutes longer, or until the ice cream has a smooth, fluffy consistency.

SERVE the gelato immediately or freeze it until you are ready to serve it.

Note: For different flavors and textures, use blackberries, blueberries, or boysenberries in the same proportions.

Black Cherry Granita

GRANITA DI AMARENE

FOR A SUMMER *treat that is low in fat as well as refreshing, make a granita. Choose your favorite fruit and puree it, then mix it with a sugar syrup and freeze it. When you're ready to serve the granita, just whisk it with a fork or in a food processor until it has a granular consistency. Serve the granita immediately, by itself or with a dollop of whipped cream.*

SERVES 4 TO 6

1 pound black cherries, stems removed, pitted
Juice of 1 lemon
2 cups cold water

1 cup cold whipping cream, beaten to a thick consistency with 2 tablespoons granulated sugar

In winter, when cherries are not available, I make a delicious granita by using amarene, cherries in heavy syrup imported from Italy. I drain the cherries, weigh the amount needed, and use them as directed in the recipe.

PUT the cherries, lemon juice, and water in a food processor or blender, and process until smooth. Pour mixture through a strainer and into a flat metal container or ice-cube tray and freeze it.

WHEN the cherry mixture is completely frozen, remove from the freezer and unmold the cubes. Put the cubes into a food processor fitted with the metal blade and turn the machine on and off until the cubes are coarsely ground. Spoon the granita into chilled glasses, top with whipped cream, and serve at once.

Espresso Granita

GRANITA DI CAFFÉ ESPRESSO

GRANITA IS AN *Italian ice dessert made of fruit juice that has been frozen into granular crystals. The most popular granita, however, is made with strong, hot, dark espresso coffee mixed with sugar. Serve this granita with a bit of whipped cream to complement the slightly bitter espresso.*

SERVES 4

2 cups freshly made espresso
   coffee
⅓ cup granulated sugar

½ cup cold whipping cream,
   beaten to a thick consistency
   with 2 tablespoons granulated
   sugar

Make sure that the coffee ice cubes are completely frozen before you put them in the food processor or the mixture will become too slushy. If the espresso mixture is not completely frozen, put it in a bowl and, with a wire wisk, beat it lightly until it has a granular texture.

IN a bowl combine the hot espresso with the sugar and mix well to dissolve the sugar. Cool the coffee to room temperature. Pour the cooled coffee into an ice-cube tray or a flat metal container and freeze it.

WHEN the coffee is completely frozen, remove it from the freezer and unmold the cubes. Put the cubes into a food processor fitted with the metal blade and turn the machine on and off until they are coarsely ground. Spoon the granita into chilled glasses, top with whipped cream, and serve at once.

Pear Sorbet

SORBETTO ALLE PERE

THE GREAT THING *about sorbets is that they are light, quick to prepare, and versatile, since they can be made with almost any kind of fruit. Here, juicy ripe pears are blended with grappa to make a quick but elegant dessert.*

SERVES 4

2 cups water
⅓ cup granulated sugar
4 medium-ripe pears, 1½ pounds, peeled, cored, and cut into pieces

Juice of 1 lemon
1 tablespoon grappa or pear brandy

PUT the water and sugar in a small saucepan and bring to a gentle boil over medium heat. Cook until sugar is all dissolved and syrup is medium thick, 6 to 7 minutes. Transfer syrup to a bowl and cool.

PUT the pears, lemon juice, grappa or pear brandy, and cooled syrup in a blender, and process until smooth. Pour the mixture through a strainer and into the bowl of an ice cream machine and freeze according to the manufacturer's instructions. Spoon into chilled glasses and serve.

Strawberries in Red Wine

FRAGOLE AL VINO ROSSO

IN ITALY SMALL, *fresh strawberries, fresh sliced peaches, or cherries are often served marinated in wine. If the fruit is ripe and sweet and the wine is of good quality, this makes the perfect hot weather dessert.*

SERVES 6

2 pints fresh strawberries, rinsed, hulled, and pat-dried with paper towels
Granulated sugar to taste

Juice of ½ lemon
2–3 cups good-quality fruity red wine

IF the strawberries are large, cut them in halves or into fourths. If they are small, leave them whole. Put the strawberries in a large bowl. Add the sugar, lemon juice, and wine. Mix well. Cover the bowl with plastic wrap and refrigerate for about 1 hour.

SPOON the strawberries and some of the wine into chilled glasses and serve.

VARIATION

Instead of red wine and lemon juice, substitute balsamic vinegar. A few drops of balsamic vinegar that is ten years or older will transform the strawberries into a sublime dessert treat. If the balsamic vinegar is not very old, start by adding 1 tablespoon of vinegar at a time into the strawberries. Mix and taste, and add more vinegar if needed. Keep in mind that the older the vinegar, the more concentrated and aromatic it is and the less you need to use. (See explanation of balsamic vinegar on page 197.)

Marinated Oranges

ARANCE MARINATE

A FEW ORANGES *and a little sugar and lemon juice add up to a sweet finale to a meal. I love to serve this dish at the end of a robust meal, since it cleanses and refreshes the palate and satisfies the desire for something sweet.*

SERVES 4

4 large oranges
Juice of 1 lemon
Juice of 1 large orange

¼ cup granulated sugar
¼ cup walnuts, coarsely chopped
  (optional)

WITH a sharp knife, cut off the ends of the oranges. Set each orange on a cutting board and slice off the peel, making sure to remove all the white spongy pith. Slice the oranges into thin rounds and remove all the seeds.

PUT the slices into a deep serving platter. Add the lemon and orange juices and sprinkle with the sugar and walnuts. Cover the platter with plastic wrap and refrigerate for about 1 hour. Serve with some of the juices poured over.

Baked Pears

PERE AL FORNO

BAKED PEARS AND *apples are common fare in Italian homes, and are a simple, delicious way to end a meal. In this preparation the pears are baked with Marsala wine, sugar, and lemon peel until they are soft, wrinkled, and meltingly delicious. The wine cooks down to a thick consistency so you can spoon it over the pears just before serving.*

SERVES 4

4 large unpeeled Bosc pears, stems on, washed

½ cup dry Marsala wine, such as Florio or Pellegrino

Grated zest of 1 lemon

½ cup granulated sugar

PREHEAT the oven to 350°.

STAND the pears in a baking dish and pour the wine over the pears. Add the lemon zest and sprinkle the sugar over the pears and into the wine. Bake until the pears are tender and their skin is wrinkled. Baste the pears a few times during cooking.

SERVE warm or at room temperature with a few tablespoons of the thickened wine sauce.

Index